HERITAGE HA.com
Auction Galleries

Dear Heritage Legacy client,

Please accept this copy of The Fantastic 1804 Dollar, Tribute Edition with the compliments of your friends at Heritage Auction Galleries. When we started collecting coins, we quickly learned about the 1804 dollar – you probably did as well. It maintains a status unrivalled by any other American coin, including some that are even rarer. Heritage holds the records for seven of the top ten numismatic auction prices, yet even for our numismatists, no other issue generates the special thrill that comes from holding this iconic item in your hand.

Over the years, Heritage has had the privilege of selling two different 1804 dollars –multiple times by private treaty, and twice at auction:

- The Class III Adams-Lyman-Carter-Flannagan PR58 PCGS;
  Private Treaty placement three times!;
- The Class I Original Mickley-Hawn-Queller PR62 NGC; realized $3,737,500;
  April 2008 Auction;
- The Class III Adams-Lyman-Carter-Flannagan PR58 PCGS; realized $2,300,000;
  May 2009 Auction.

We hope you will thoroughly enjoy spending time with this book, there is much to learn from it.

Heritage places – privately and quietly – millions of dollars of incredible numismatic material every year. If you wish to utilize our Private Treaty services, please contact Todd Imhof at ext. 1313. Naturally, when the time to sell comes, we hope that you will call Heritage first. Our reputation has been built on quality service to the most discerning clientele, whether buying or selling.

If you have any comments or questions we would like to hear from you. Our personal email addresses are Greg@HA.com and Todd @HA.com, or you can call us at 1-800-US COINS.

Sincerely,

Gregory J. Rohan
President

Todd Imhof
Executive Vice President

THE FANTASTIC
1804 DOLLAR

Photograph Courtesy Smithsonian Institution

THE FANTASTIC
1804 DOLLAR

By

ERIC P. NEWMAN

and

KENNETH E. BRESSETT

☆ ☆ ☆

Associates in Research,
Walter H. Breen and Lynn Glaser

WHITMAN PUBLISHING COMPANY
RACINE, WISCONSIN

No. 9376

© 1962 by WHITMAN PUBLISHING COMPANY
Printed in U.S.A. by
Western Printing and Lithographing Company
Library of Congress Catalog Card Number: 62-19453

QUOD VERUM EST, LATEAT QUAMVIS,

ALIQUANDO PATEBIT.

That which is the Truth, however well it may be concealed, will at some time come to light.

HORACE: *Epistles*, I.6.24

Preface

"THE KING OF AMERICAN COINS, THE UNITED STATES SILVER DOLLAR OF 1804.

"In all the history of numismatics of the entire world, there is not today and there never has been a single coin which was and is the subject of so much romance, interest, comment and upon which so much has been written and so much discussed as the U. S. dollar of 1804."

This comment was made in 1941 by B. Max Mehl in the catalogue for the sale of the Dunham collection which included an 1804 dollar. Despite all of the publicity and honor showered upon these coins, they still remain today as the world's most controversial coins. Many numismatists have been caught in the web of the intriguing research problems surrounding the 1804 dollar. To appease their curiosity, they have investigated the various aspects of the subject and have formed their opinions; yet no one has attempted to write up the subject as a whole.

"There is no authentic history of the 1804 dollar. Tradition, however is 'thousand tongued' in its regard." These comments published in 1883 in *Dye's Coin Encyclopaedia* have remained true through the years.

This book is a product of the research of a team. Walter Breen, Lynn Glaser, and both of the authors had been working independently on the subject for many years along with their other numismatic projects. In 1959, after learning of one another's activities, each of the group realized that he could be helpful to the others. There was a vigorous exchange of ideas and information, after which the authors began a fresh digest and analysis of the pertinent numismatic literature and a restudy of available facts. This suggested many additional research projects which the authors carried out together. New conclusions were derived from the findings brought to light by this work. This book is the result. The text has been written by Eric P. Newman. The pedigrees of the individual coins and the assembly of their illustrations was the work of Kenneth E. Bressett.

Many modern methods of numismatic investigation which have been used were not at the disposal of earlier authors and thus many of their conclusions have been corrected and modified with new findings. The opinions and aid of many numismatists have been sought and incorporated into this work.

7

A deep appreciation is due Raymond H. Williamson for the many suggestions, citations, and additions which he contributed to the refinement of the completed manuscript from his extensive fund of analyzed numismatic knowledge.

To Ann Barrett, Secretary of the Eric P. Newman Numismatic Education Society, and to Judith A. Mund for their sincere devotion to the tedious detail of typing and correspondence, the authors are particularly grateful. Andrew E. Newman, son of Eric P. Newman, enthusiastically performed the task of clarification of the original manuscript and proofreading.

For kind cooperation, thanks are also due to American Numismatic Society, Herbert M. Bergen, M. H. Bolender, Q. David Bowers, Elston Bradfield, Richard Breadon, British Museum, Dan Brown, Vernon L. Brown, Amon Carter, Jr., Chase Manhattan Bank, F. Newell Childs, Malcolm O. E. Chell-Frost, William Clark, *Coin World*, R. E. Cox, Jr., Mrs. Lammot DuPont, Willis H. DuPont, Aaron Feldman, Fiscal Branch of the General Records Division of the National Archives, John J. Ford, Jr., Sarah E. Freeman, George J. Fuld, Ruth Green, August Hausske, Ronald L. Heise, Lee Hewitt, Lyle J. Holverstott, Johns Hopkins University, Harold E. Hufford, Charles M. Johnson, D. Wayne Johnson, J. Hewitt Judd, Abe Kosoff, David S. Marvin, Massachusetts Historical Society, Geoffrey H. North, Mr. and Mrs. Alfred J. Ostheimer III, William A. Philpott, John Pittman, June Pond, Richard Picker, James B. Rhoads, James C. Risk, Gilroy Roberts, Margo Russell, Julian Ryer, M. Vernon Sheldon, Smithsonian Institution, David F. Spink, V. Clain-Stefanelli, Walter Thompson, Samuel W. Wolfson, and Randolph Zander.

Fred W. Eckfeldt was kind enough to furnish genealogical information about the Eckfeldt family.

Evelyn E. Newman combed through the diplomatic records of the United States with the Asian powers for the 1832–36 period.

TABLE OF CONTENTS

ILLUSTRATIONS

Individual 1804 Dollars

Introduction

The quantity of controversial material published regarding the U. S. silver dollar dated 1804 far surpasses in volume what has been written about any other American coin. For over a century the mysteries of its existence have been the basis of discussion, research, and writing. The numerous theories as to its background rival the many contradictions in data relating to its history. It would not be worthwhile to untangle the vast mass of material by writing new unsupported opinions. Facts have had to be assembled by new independent research so that the truths and fallacies could be separated in order to reconstruct the exciting background of the coin.

M. H. Bolender's book entitled *U. S. Early Silver Dollars from 1794 to 1803*, although a most valuable reference, did not encompass the subject of the 1804 dollar.

One of the most intriguing facets of the 1804 dollar is that throughout its history it has always been one of the most desired coins in the world. Whenever one of these coins has appeared at auction, it has almost always set records for the highest price paid for a single coin. Each new sale has always stirred the imagination of newspaper reporters, numismatic writers, and all collectors, whether or not they ever hoped to own such a coin.

Stories about the 1804 dollar were fabricated over one hundred years ago and have been repeated so often that they have become "truths." Official information concerning the coin is generally lacking, and most of the officers of the Mint who have commented on the subject have only helped to confuse the situation. The list of noted collectors who have had pride in the ownership of an 1804 dollar as part of their collections is paralleled by a list of equally famous collectors who could have owned one but refused to acquire it because of their convictions that the coin was not genuine.

This book, in addition to giving data and history of the 1804 dollars themselves, also touches on the related subject of the mass of forgeries and altered coins dated 1804 which have plagued collectors through the years.

Other related coins have also had to be examined and explained before the total story of the 1804 dollars could be told. These pieces include the 1801, 1802, and 1803 proof silver dollars, the proof 1804 Eagle, and the 1833, 1834, and 1835 proof half dollar "restrikes." The basic story, however, concerns the fantastic 1804 dollar. The large group of patterns, restrikes, and fabrications which may have been connected with the 1858 activities involving the 1804 dollar is not within the scope of this book.

As on most controversial numismatic subjects, opinions differ widely regarding the origin, date of coinage, history, and authenticity of this coin. To those who already have formed their opinions we hope that there may be found in this book reinforcement of their belief. To anyone who has an open mind about the 1804 dollar we invite him to begin reading and start studying the facts and problems just as the authors had the pleasure of doing.

The ultimate goal of the authors was, naturally, to try to write "the last word on the subject." Although this goal may be just an idle dream, it is hoped that readers will find that a sincere attempt has been made to be accurate, unambiguous, and thorough.

The Official Records

The published official U. S. Mint records show that 19,570 silver dollars were coined in 1804 and 321 silver dollars in 1805. To interpret, correct, or confirm these statistics requires a study of the original records and reports.

The Act of April 2, 1792, establishing the United States Mint, required that the receipts and disbursements arising in the course of Mint operations be furnished to the Treasury Department quarter-annually and that the Treasury Department once each year summarize this data for the Congress (Sec. 7). In addition, the Director of the Mint felt that it was his duty to report directly to the President each year. During the first years of the nineteenth century, the Director furnished his report to the President immediately on the close of each calendar year, which would be several months prior to the more detailed summary by the Comptroller of the Treasury. A schedule of the denominations and the number of pieces coined was included in both reports. The dates were entered on the records of the Mint Treasurer when the Coiner intermittently transferred the coins to the Mint Treasurer and not actually when the coins were struck.

The April 2, 1792, legislation (Sec. 10) in providing the design and legend requirements for coins, specified that the pieces contain "the year of the coinage." The coins reported as minted during any year should therefore bear the date of that year if the law were complied with. Reverse dies might be reused lawfully from year to year as in the case of dollars,[1] but the law implied that obverse dies were not to be used without having the proper date. Due to the time and difficulty required to make dies, a general practice of overdating took place on all denominations. Some dollar dies were overdated for the years 1799 and 1802. Overdating did, however, mar the appearance of the coins.

When the coinage records are compared with known coins, it becomes clear that these coins did not always bear the date of their supposed coinage. The following coins, excluding dollars minted in the year 1804, do not exist even though the records show that coins were struck in these years in the amounts shown:

---

[1] The following groups have common reverses:
1795 (B-14), 1796 (B-1, 2 and 3), 1797 (B-2) and 1798 (B-2);
1797 (B-1) and 1798 (B-1); 1801 (B-2), 1802 (B-1, 4 and 6), and 1803 (B-4 and 6);
1801 (B-4), 1802 (B-2, 3, 5 and 9) and 1803 (B-1 and 5).

DENOMINATION	YEAR	COINS STRUCK[2]
Half Cent	1799	12,167
Dime	1810	6,355
Quarter	1797	252
Half Dollar	1804	156,519
Half Dollar	1816	47,150
Quarter Eagle	1799	480
Quarter Eagle	1803	423
Half Eagle	1801	26,006
Eagle	1802	15,090

Cents dated 1803 (S-243) are known with a perfect reverse die, and yet this identical reverse die is found with several die breaks used in combination with an 1802 (S-241) obverse, proving that 1802 cents were struck during the year 1803 or thereafter.[3]

The conclusion is therefore inescapable that for practical considerations the Mint during its early period used obverse dies for coinage in years subsequent to their dating. It was not expedient to overdate the dies in every case, particularly if a die had been used for coining in the year of its dating. An unused die might be more safely annealed, overdated and rehardened without as severe a risk of breakage as a die which had been used. The only American obverse dies which were used in the year of their dating and then overdated are the 1805 quarter (Browning 4) which became 1806 over 1805 (Browning 1) and the 1805 quarter eagle which became the 1806 over 1805. From the rarity of the 1805 pieces it would appear that the dies were used sparingly for 1805 coinage, and were almost new when overdated.

There is no inconsistency in the records of coinage of dollars in 1804. The January 1, 1805, report of Elias Boudinot, the Director of the Mint, was prepared by Benjamin Rush, Mint Treasurer, on December 31, 1804, and shows 19,570 silver dollars coined in the first quarter of 1804. This is confirmed by the Treasury Department's report dated February 26, 1805, except that the period within 1804 in which dollars were coined is not stated.[4] In the Bullion Ledger 1802–10, page 57, the detail of the delivery by the Chief Coiner during the entire year 1804 is as follows:[5]

1804		DOLLARS
Jany 7	By the Bank of the United States a/c S/C[6]	2500
19	Ditto	8000
Feby 1	Sundry Accounts	5500
March 27	The Bank of the United States a/c S/Coins	2840
31	Ditto	730
		19570

[2] Reports of the Director of the Mint; Lynn Glaser, "Some Undiscovered Coins," *Numismatic Scrap book Magazine*, Vol. 26, No. 9 (Sept., 1960), p. 2513.

[3] George W. Rice, "The Copper Cent of the United States," *The Numismatist*, Vol. 14, No. 5 (May 1901), p. 65; Frank G. Duffield, "Coins Not Always Struck in the Year They Are Dated," *The Numismatist*, Vol. 40, No. 4 (Apr., 1927), p. 214; Sheldon, Paschal & Breen, *Penny Whimsy* (New York, 1958).

[4] *American State Papers—Finance* (Washington, 1832), pp. 119 and 136.

[5] All Mint Records hereafter referred to are in Record Group 104, Bureau of the Mint, National Archives, Washington, D. C.

[6] S/C is the abbreviation for Silver Coin.

These figures are confirmed and further explained by entries in the Bullion Waste Book 1794–1806. The weight of the coins is set out. The delivery to Sundry Accounts was divided between the Bank of the United States ($5283.19½) and the Bank of Pennsylvania ($216.80½), change for one dollar having been made. The group of 730 dollars was shown to have been delivered to the Mint Treasurer on February 11, 1804, and therefore was delayed in delivery to the Bank until March 31, 1804. The coinage of dollars in 1804 was therefore completed by March 27, 1804, or earlier. The Bullion Ledger B 1802–10, page 25, indicates that by February 13, 1804, six dollars were reserved for assaying out of a total of seven so withdrawn.[7]

The dates which these dollars bore is in no way indicated in the records. Whether they are dated 1804 or struck with dies from prior years must be determined from other facts.

With respect to the 321 dollars stated to have been coined in 1805, there is an inconsistency between the report of Robert Patterson, the Director of the Mint, dated January 3, 1806, and the report of the Treasury Department dated March 28, 1806. In schedule No. 1 of the Director's Report prepared by Benjamin Rush, there is "An Abstract of the Coins struck at the Mint of the United States, from the 1st of January to 31st of December, 1805," which lists silver coinage of 211,722 half dollars, 121,394 quarters, 120,780 dimes, and 15,600 half dimes (469,496 pieces having a face value of $149,067.50) and makes no mention of dollars being struck. The Treasury Department report covers "the different species of coins made and paid on account of deposits" and lists as "Silver coins made at the Mint from the 1st January to the 31st December, 1805, viz.: Dollars, 321, half dollars 211,722, quarter dollars 121,394, dimes 120,780 and half dimes 15,600" having a face value of $149,388.50.[8] The only difference between these reports is the 321 dollars. To determine which is correct, the relevant bookkeeping entries have been examined.

There are many entries in the Mint records relative to the 321 dollar item. Bullion Journal A contains four crediting entries dated June 28, 1805, as follows:

Silver Bullion. Dr. to Melter & Refiner his account of Silver Received from him in pursuance of a warrant of the Director No. 309
278 Ounces 4 dwts Standard Silver Bullion — 321

Chief Coiner his account of Silver Dr. to Silver Bullion delivered him in pursuance of a Warrant of the Director No. 192
278 Ounces 4 dwts Standard Silver Bullion — 321

Silver Coinage   Dr to Chief Coiner his account of Silver Received from him in pursuance of a Warrant of the Director No. 349
    34,000 Quarter dollars
    321 Dollars, being found amongst Spanish Dollars brought to the mint.
    7644 Ounces 17 dwt 8 Grains Standard Silver — 8821

[7] See Frank H. Stewart, *History of the First United States Mint* (Camden, 1924), p. 109.
[8] *American State Papers—Finance* (Washington, 1832), Vol. II, pp. 165, 166 and 199.

The Bank of the United States account of Silver Coins
Dr. to Silver Coinage   Deposited in said Bank to the credit of
the Treasurer of the Mint, the amount of Silver Coins received
this day from the Chief Coiner   8821

The warrants referred to are no longer in existence, but by analyzing these entries made pursuant to early American bookkeeping methods, it is clear that the 321 dollars theoretically passed from Melter and Refiner to the Coiner to the Mint Treasurer to the Bank of the United States in one circuitous bookkeeping journey on June 28, 1805. The 321 coined United States dollars were found by the Melter and Refiner in a deposit of silver otherwise consisting of Spanish dollars. The United States dollars weighing 416 grains each or a total of 278 ounces 4 pennyweights were delivered directly to the Mint Treasurer by the Melter and Refiner, but the Coiner was charged with the standard silver and credited with coins delivered to the Mint Treasurer in order to fit in to the normal routing of silver through the Mint. The Coiner obviously had no contact whatever with the 321 coined dollars in this transaction.

All of these entries are confirmed by entries on June 28, 1805, in the Bullion Waste Book 1794–1806, page 341, with identically the same meaning, although the critical wording is not as detailed and reads "321 Dollars being found among Spanish Dollars." All of the above entries are in black ink.

In Bullion Ledger B, page 58, containing a schedule by date and denomination of the delivery of coinage to the Mint Treasurer, the 321 dollar transaction is recorded in red ink[9] as is the 321 total of dollars for the year 1805. Every other entry on the page is in black ink. The red ink was used as a warning to flag this 321 coined dollars as being a bookkeeping entry which was not to be entered as actual 1805 coinage.

In 1860 there was a dispute among numismatists about this dollar coinage in 1805, and Mint Director James Ross Snowden in his book pointed out the entry in Bullion Journal A.[10] This satisfied Mint officials that no dollars dated 1805 existed and that no coinage of dollars took place in 1805. Snowden, however, was completely silent as to dollars dated 1804, in view of the "scandal" which had taken place in 1858 at the Mint. (See Chapter XI.)

It has been suggested that 321 United States dollars were part of a deposit of silver bullion aggregating $30,000 in value made June 3, 1805, by the Bank of the United States,[11] and this seems highly probable. No charge was made for converting the bullion into silver coinage because immediate delivery was not demanded and no substandard silver was deposited.

---

[9] First noted by Walter Thompson, "What the Archives Reveal About 1804 Dollars," *Numismatic Scrapbook Magazine*, Vol. 27, No. 8 (Aug., 1961), p. 1986.
[10] *A Description of the Ancient and Modern Coins in the Cabinet of the Mint of the United States* (Philadelphia, 1860), p. 109; see John F. Jones, "The 1804 United States Dollar," *The Numismatist*, Vol. 51, No. 1 (Jan., 1938), p. 20; Walter Breen, "Research in the Archives," *Coin Collector's Journal*, Vol. 18, No. 4 (July, 1951), p. 87; Lynn Glaser, "Some Undiscovered Coins," *Numismatic Scrapbook Magazine*, Vol. 26, No. 9 (Sept., 1960), p. 2514.
[11] *Bullion Waste Book 1794–1806*, Record Group 104, National Archives; Frank H. Stewart, *History of the First United States Mint* (Camden, 1924), p. 111; *The Numismatist*, Vol. 50, No. 8 (Aug., 1937), p. 705; Walter Thompson, "The Archivist," *Numismatic Scrapbook Magazine*, Vol. 24, No. 7 (July, 1958), p. 1559.

The 321 dollars removed from the deposit were from circulation and no doubt included a mixture of prior dates.

Therefore, the discrepancy between the Director's report of January 3, 1806, and the Treasury Department report of March 28, 1806, is explained. The Mint Director was correct in showing that no dollars were coined in 1805. The Treasury Department was interested in an audit more than in numismatic statistics and thus perpetuated a misunderstanding which has been followed in published official summaries to date—even by the Mint which accepted bookkeeping summaries as fact rather than its own Director's accurate report to the President. The dollars coined in 1804 were, therefore, the last of the bust type silver dollars.

The knowledge of an United States dollar dated 1804 is first evidenced on its illustration as Item No. 3 on Plate II of *A Manual of Gold and Silver Coins of All Nations*, published in 1842. At that time, the authors of that book, Jacob R. Eckfeldt and William E. DuBois, were respectively assayer and assistant assayer of the Philadelphia Mint. The first notation referring to the illustration stated, "Dollar, 1797–1805." After a few descriptive words, a most significant statement follows: "No dollars were coined from 1806 to 1835." The combined meaning of these two comments is that the authors intended to convey the idea that dollars were struck in 1804 and in 1805 and could be dated 1804 and 1805. This assumption and speculation could have had no other source than the Mint records relating to the production of dollars. If 19,570 dollars were believed to have been coined in 1804, those authors might logically assume that dollars dated 1804 did exist, even though they had never seen any. Their assumption about dollars being dated 1804 was substantially strengthened by their apparent erroneous assumption that dollar production continued into the year 1805, when according to Mint statistics 321 were supposedly coined.

The officers of the Mint were well aware that the Mint records were based upon the delivery of coin by the Coiner to the Mint Treasurer, rather than the actual date of coinage or the date of the coins. On August 15, 1838, Robert M. Patterson, Mint Director, wrote to W. G. Stearns of Boston:

> Cents were certainly coined with the date 1823, for I have now a specimen before me; but no delivery of cents was made, in that year, from the Coiner to the Treasurer and hence the omission in our table. The quarter dollar of 1824 must, I presume, be explained in the same way, but we have no specimen of this coinage in our collection.

The Mint records show no coinage of cents in 1823 or quarters in 1824, but denominations with those dates exist in quantity.

CHAPTER

II | *Discontinuance of Dollar Coinage*

The coinage of silver dollars at the United States Mint was discontinued in 1804 as an economic necessity. Beginning in 1800, the number of coined dollars was drastically reduced, as evidenced by the following reports:

YEAR	NUMBER MINTED
1798	327,536
1799	423,515
1800	220,920
1801	54,454
1802	41,650
1803	66,064
1804	19,570
1805–35	0 (Corrected)

The Act of April 2, 1792, provided that United States dollar or unit was "to be the value of a Spanish milled dollar as the same is now current." Theoretically the Spanish milled dollar was required by Spanish law to contain 377 grains of silver (less one grain for tolerance) and to be 902 fine, thereby having a total weight of about 417 grains. American officials believed that the weight of silver in the two issues of circulating Spanish milled dollars minted just prior to 1791 had dropped from 374 to 368 grains according to London and Amsterdam analyses. These were minted primarily in the Central and South American Spanish colonies. The House of Representatives of the United States ordered an assay of foreign coin on November 29, 1792, and the tests made on Spanish milled dollars at the Mint, admittedly containing "a small source of error," showed 1782 mintage to be 892.1 fine, 1790 mintage to be 891.7 fine and 1791 mintage to be 895.4 fine. Based primarily upon Hamilton's recommendation in his January 28, 1791, report that the quantity of silver in the United States dollar be the mean between the two previous issues of Spanish milled dollars, the standard for the United States dollar or unit was set at a gross weight of 416 grains with a fineness of 892.4 and a net weight of 371¼ grains of pure silver.[12] The minimum weight required of Spanish milled dollars to be acceptable for circulation in the

---

[12] Alexander Hamilton, "On the Establishment of a Mint" (Jan. 28, 1791), *American State Papers— Finance*—(Washington, 1832), Vol. 1, p. 92, 185.

United States was then set by the Act of February 9, 1793, as 415 grains. Most normal Spanish milled dollars had averaged about 373 grains of pure silver and therefore had one-half per cent more silver than the United States dollar. The worn or clipped Spanish milled dollars of the lowest weight acceptable for United States circulation had about one-half per cent less silver than the coined dollars of the United States.

These conditions and laws placed the United States dollar in a disadvantageous position. Those Spanish milled dollars which were light in silver weight through coinage or through wear or clipping were brought to the United States for circulation if they weighed about 415 grains. The normal Spanish milled dollars which were circulating in the United States or came into circulation were consistently either withdrawn for export or turned into the United States Mint for recoinage into United States coin so as to take advantage of the one-half per cent differential. Since a United States dollar was acceptable in the West Indies in place of a Spanish milled dollar, there was a flow of United States dollars in that direction. All of these conditions resulted in the bad money driving the good money out of circulation in accordance with Gresham's economic law.[13]

There was, however, a much more important reason why United States dollars would not stay in circulation within the country. There was a worldwide practice of making exchanges and payments in foreign trade by the shipment of coined dollars. This was particularly true of the China trade. Spanish dollars were treated as "more an article of commerce than a standard by which to ascertain the value of other articles."[14] In the years before 1804 it was realized that United States dollars were also being sent throughout the world as a commodity rather than being used primarily as a circulating medium by the people of the country for which they were minted. Dollars were, peculiarly enough, acceptable in world trade, whereas fractional portions of dollars usually were not. Thus, 2 half dollars or 10 dimes having exactly the same amount of metal and intrinsic value as a dollar would not be as apt to be exported as a coined dollar, because of commercial habits. If the general purpose in trade was to acquire silver coin to melt for recoinage, then fractional silver money might be exported as well as dollars, but the primary desire for silver coin was only for foreign trade. Transaction with other countries would continually move coined dollars into and out of the United States. Traders had little interest as to which dollars they dealt with so long as the intrinsic value was properly calculated. U. S. dollars might be shipped away in one transaction, and Spanish milled dollars might be returned in the next transaction, leaving the American public with the same amount of specie, but not in United States specie. For that reason, emphasis

---

[13] Neil Carothers, *Fractional Money* (New York, 1930), p. 74; John M. Willem, Jr., *The United States Trade Dollar* (New York, 1959), p. 12, 30; Charles H. Schmall, "The Breach in the American Silver Dollar Series from 1804 to 1836," *The Numismatist*, Vol. 45, No. 11 (Nov., 1932), p. 691; Walter Breen, "Research in the Archives," *Coin Collector's Journal*, Vol. 18, No. 4 (July, 1951), p. 88; *American State Papers—Finance* (Washington, 1832), Vol. 1, p. 98.
[14] *American State Papers—Finance*, Vol. III (Washington, 1834), p. 395.

at the United States Mint was turned from dollars to fractional silver as Mint production increased.

The report of the Director of the Mint for 1804 stated:[15]

> The issues of silver coins, notwithstanding the mercantile embarrassments attending the importation of bullion, having greatly exceeded that of the year 1803, and the advantage of a public mint has been sensibly experienced, by the greatest part of deposites being issued in small coin, which has been found very beneficial to the citizens, at large, under the late scarcity of Spanish dollars, occasioned by the great exportation of them for mercantile purposes.

The report of the Director of the Mint for 1805 stated:[16]

> The striking of small coins is a measure which has been adopted to accommodate the banks and other depositors, and at their particular request, both with a view of furnishing a supply of small change and to prevent the exportation of the specie of the United States to foreign countries.

In order to obtain an official ruling on the practice which was established, the following directive on behalf of President Jefferson from the Secretary of State to the Director of the Mint was issued:[17]

> Department of State,
> 1 May 1806
>
> Sir: In consequence of a representation from the Director of the Bank of the United States, that considerable purchases have been made of dollars coined at the mint for the purpose of exporting them, and as it is probable further purchases and exportations will be made, the President directs that all the silver to be coined at the mint shall be of small denominations, so that the value of the largest pieces shall not exceed half a dollar.
>
> I have the honor to be Sir,
> With Great respect
> Your most obed. servt.
> JAMES MADISON
>
> Robert Patterson, Esq.
> Director of the Mint.

Compliance with the directive was shown in Mint reports but was reported by a separate letter to Jefferson as follows:[18]

> Philadelphia, April 2, 1807.
>
> Sir: With respect, Sir, to small coins, the practice of the Mint has been, and still continues to be in strict conformity with your wishes and instructions. No Eagles nor Dollars have been struck during the last two years.
>
> I am, your most humble and obedient servant,
> Robert Patterson,
> Director of the Mint.
>
> To His Excellency,
> Thomas Jefferson,
> President of the United States

---

[15] *American State Papers—Finance*, Vol. II (Washington, 1832), p. 118.
[16] *American State Papers—Finance*, Vol. II (Washington, 1832), p. 165.
[17] Archives of the United States of America, Department of State, *Domestic Letters*, Vol. 15, p. 112; *Coinage Laws of the United States* (Washington, 1894), p. 84; *The Numismatist*, Vol. 46, No. 12 (Dec., 1933), p. 762, and Vol. 27, No. 3 (Mar., 1914), p. 145.
[18] Record Group 104, National Archives; *The Numismatist*, Vol. 46, No. 12 (Dec., 1933), p. 762; *American Journal of Numismatics*, Vol. 13, No. 1 (July, 1878), p. 15.

The report of the Director of the Mint for 1826 stated:[19]

The coinage of half dollars, in preference, generally to that of the dollar was adopted in the year 1805, on a suggestion, it is understood, from a source entitled to the highest respect, that this form of silver coin would impose a beneficial restraint on its exit from the country.

Dr. J. L. Riddell, the melter and refiner of the New Orleans Mint, summarized the situation in 1845 as follows:[20]

The coinage of Dollars in the United States, virtually commencing in 1795, has never been large. The policy of our government has been to issue a great preponderance of halves, and the smaller denominations of coins, under the impression that they would be less likely to be exported from the country.

The aforementioned documents justify and explain the action of the Mint but do not give any indication of the date on the dollars coined in 1804.

It is interesting to note that the eagle, as the largest gold coin, was discontinued in 1804 until 1838, just as the dollar was discontinued in 1804 until the patterns of 1836. In the case of the eagle, however, business strikes dated 1804 are identical in all respects to those struck in prior years.

The foregoing facts show that the Mint did strike silver dollars in the year 1804. Information in the following pages will show that the 1804 date was not used on these coins.

---

[19] *American State Papers—Finance*, Vol. V (Washington, 1859), p. 620; Frank H. Stewart, *History of the First United States Mint* (Camden, 1924), p. 111.
[20] A Monograph of the Silver Dollar (New Orleans, 1845), p. 9.

Disappearance Stories

During the last century many numismatists as well as the Mint officials believed that the official production records of the Mint meant that 19,570 dollars dated 1804 were actually coined during 1804. Some story was necessary to explain their disappearance. The most important historical activity during the year 1804 was the war between the United States and the Barbary Pirates. One story indicates that all of the "1804" dollars were aboard the United States frigate *Philadelphia*, which ran aground in Tripoli Harbor, and was captured by the Barbary Pirates. Except for a few of such dollars which were supposedly paid out to sailors or for supplies prior to the capture of the ship, the balance were assumed to have been melted. Stephen Decatur, then a lieutenant, led a boat crew into the harbor and blew up the *Philadelphia*.[21] This "1804" dollar story collapses when we realize that the *Philadelphia* ran aground in October, 1803, and that the "1804" dollars would not even have been coined by that time.

Other versions of the story indicate that a boat containing the entire issue of "1804" dollars was on its way to Tripoli to pay ransom for an American prisoner or to pay our armed forces, but that the boat sunk en route.[22] A variant indicates that after the ship arrived, the "1804" dollars were scattered in Europe and few found their way back.[23]

Still another tale is as follows:[24]

> In 1804, an expedition was started from the United States against Tripoli, headed by Captain Eaton and Hamet Carmanly, exile and elder brother of the bashaw of Tripoli. Their march lay across a thousand miles of desert; yet it was accomplished, with indescribable fatigue and suffering, in fifty days. To pay the seamen, these 1804 dollars were shipped to the coast of Africa, and only very few of them, if any, were brought back by the returned victors.

There was another belief that all of the "1804" dollars were shipped to Central America and that only a few of them drifted back to the United States.[25]

---

[21] "The 1804 Dollar Again," *The Numismatist*, Vol. 12, No. 3 (Mar., 1899), p. 56; L. A. D. Montague, *Mehl's Numismatic Monthly*, Vol. 8, No. 10 (Oct., 1917), p. 132.
[22] A. H. Brooke, "Counterfeits and Forgeries," *The Numismatist*, Vol. 50, No. 7 (July, 1937), p. 617; *The Numismatist*, Vol. 22, No. 9 (Sept. 1904), p. 273.
[23] *The Numismatist*, Vol. 22, No. 9 (Sept., 1904), p. 271.
[24] Ivan C. Michels, *The Current Gold and Silver Coins of All Nations* (Philadelphia, 1880, and subsequent editions), p. 10.
[25] "The 1804 Dollar Again," *The Numismatist*, Vol. 12, No. 3 (Mar. 1899), p. 56; Vol. 45, No. 12 (Dec., 1932), p. 774.

In an entertaining piece of fiction entitled "The 1804 Dollar" and subtitled "A True Story"[26] a perfectly struck, brilliant, nearly proof, almost high relief, sharp, strong dollar of 1804 was in an oval morocco case. The gold lettering inscribed on the outside of the case was

Presented to
FRANK S. HOUGHTON, ESQ'RE
on the occasion of his visit at the
NATIONAL MINT IN PHILADELPHIA
JULY 4th, 1804,
his fortieth birthday
Elias Boudinot, Director.

It is disillusioning that the Mint has not kept up such a pleasant custom of giving birthday presents on a national holiday when it was closed.

Another yarn indicated that all of the "1804" dollars were put on a merchant ship bound for China to be given to a captain of a United States frigate for necessary expenses, and that the ship containing the dollars sank in a typhoon. Walter Winchell even repeated this myth.[27]

A weird variation of this rumor asserts that a Huguenot employee at the Mint in 1804 noticed a resemblance between the portrait on the "1804" dollar and Martha Washington, causing the Huguenots in United States to cry out against the use of the wife of a president for such a purpose. As a result the "1804" dollars were not distributed but were shipped to Hong Kong and lost at sea.[28] The fact that dollars dated between 1795 and 1803 contained the identical portrait was apparently unknown to this storyteller.

Frank H. Stewart, who did extensive research on the first U. S. Mint, gave his opinion that "1804" dollars were exported or turned into bullion because their metal value exceeded their face value.[29] This was amplified by claims in a Washington, D.C., newspaper based upon an interview with a Mint employee that in 1804 a silver dollar contained $1.26 in silver.[30]

Another myth relates that one 1804 dollar was found in Liverpool under the mainmast of a Yankee schooner which was built in 1804, there being a custom to put under the mast a coin bearing the date the ship was constructed.[31] This story was based upon the fact that a Liverpool collector, C. A. Watters, owned an 1804 dollar (Class I).

Finally, it has been suggested that the dollars of 1804 were thrown back into the melting pot at the Mint itself.[32] In further amplification of that thought, it was urged that the then known 1804 dollars (Class I) were the seven specimens which the 1804 records show were reserved for assay, and

[26] Edouard Frossard, *Numisma*, Vol. 8, No. 3 (May, 1884).
[27] George G. Evans, *Illustrated History of the United States Mint* (Philadelphia, 1885), p. 64; *American Journal of Numismatics*, Vol. 36, No. 4 (Apr., 1902), p. 123; *Mehl's Numismatic Monthly*, Vol. 8, No. 10 (Oct., 1917), p. 132; *The Numismatist*, Vol. 17, No. 9 (Sept., 1904), p. 271; John S. Dye, *Dye's Coin Encyclopaedia* (Philadelphia, 1883), p. 4; *The Numismatist*, Vol. 50, No. 9 (Sept., 1937), p. 833.
[28] "Will Remain Forever in Chicago," *The Numismatist*, Vol. 18, No. 2 (Feb., 1905), p. 52.
[29] *The Numismatist*, Vol. 45, No. 12 (Dec., 1932), p. 774.
[30] "The Bullion Value of 1804 Silver Dollars," *The Numismatist*, Vol. 50, No. 10 (Oct., 1937), p. 962.
[31] "Where the 1804 Dollars Went," *The Numismatist*, Vol. 22, No. 4 (Apr., 1909), p. 119.
[32] "The Latest 1804 Dollar," *The Coin Collector's Journal*, Vol. 10 (July, 1885), p. 111; *Numismatic Scrapbook Magazine*, Vol. 15, No. 8 (Aug., 1949), p. 732.

all of the regularly coined 1804 dollars (as well as the 1804 half dollars) were melted.[33] In other words, this illogical assumption was that those coins intended to be melted were not melted and that those not intended to be melted were melted.

No facts have come to light which give any support to any of the foregoing stories.[34] They are contradictory of one another and entirely speculatory. When the United States Government was making every effort to keep its coined silver dollars in the United States and prevent their export, it would be completely contrary to policy to have the government ship its own coins out of the United States for use elsewhere. Melting newly minted 1804 dollars at the Mint would be unauthorized, unreasonable, and without purpose. It has been shown that the economic factors tending to cause the exportation of United States dollars would operate on all such dollars regardless of date. Even if exported, dollars dated "1804" would probably have been circulated or hoarded as coined dollars rather than melted for recoinage or other bullion use. The melting of virtually an entire issue of one date while all other dates survived in quantity is most unlikely, particularly when deliveries of dollars in 1804 were made to the Bank of the United States on five different occasions and to the Bank of Pennsylvania on one occasion.

The proof of disappearance of objects requires that they must first have been in existence. The existence of dollars dated 1804 is based upon those specimens now known, which for the purpose of argument must be assumed to have existed in 1804. If there are or were no dollars dated 1804 coined in 1804, it is pointless to discuss their disappearance. It is better to determine whether or not dollars dated 1804 were actually coined in 1804.

[33] *The Numismatist*, Vol. 50, No. 8 (Aug., 1937), p. 706.
[34] Arthur D. McIlvaine, *The Silver Dollars of the United States of America*, Numismatic Notes and Monographs No. 95 (New York, 1941), p. 26.

<table>
<tr><td>CHAPTER
IV</td><td>*Changes in Coin Production*
Methods After 1804</td></tr>
</table>

CHAPTER | *Changes in Coin Production*
IV | *Methods After 1804*

Before reviewing the characteristics of existing examples of dollars dated 1804, it is essential to outline certain details in the manufacture of coins at the United States Mint during the 1804 period, particularly the application of the edge decoration.

The planchet, or blank, after being punched out of a drawn sheet of metal, was first taken to a milling machine either to letter the edge, in the case of dollars and half dollars, or to produce a reeded edge, in the case of smaller silver coins and all of the gold pieces. The edge lettering device produced incuse or intaglio lettering around the edge. There were two straight and parallel die holders, one fixed and one movable. The movable die holder was mounted on a sliding bar having a rack of teeth facing upward. The bar could be activated by a large hand-cranked vertical gear. An edging die with raised letters for half of the text of the edge was attached to the fixed holder, and another edging die, with the other half of the text, was attached to the holder on the movable bar.[35] The schematic drawing of this machine accompanying this text will more clearly show its operation. In the case of the dollar, one die read:

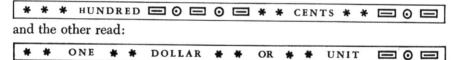

* * * HUNDRED ▭ ⊙ ▭ ⊙ ▭ * * CENTS * * ▭ ⊙ ▭

and the other read:

* * ONE * * DOLLAR * * OR * * UNIT ▭ ⊙ ▭

The distance between these edging dies was slightly less than the diameter of the planchet so that the letters would sink into the planchet and the edge would be squeezed. As the movable die was cranked past the fixed die, the planchet was caught between them and rolled 180 degrees whereupon it became free. To eliminate the possibility of a gap, the two parallel dies were each just slightly longer than half of the circumference of the planchet; this often caused a slight overlap of the edge decoration on opposite sides of the coins so lettered. The pressure of the edge lettering machine also raised a

[35] George E. Sellers, "Early Engineering Reminiscences," *American Machinist*, Vol. 16, Nos. 18, 20 and 23 (May and June, 1893); Raymond H. Williamson, "A Visit to the U. S. Mint in 1812," *The Numismatist*, Vol. 64, No. 1 (Jan., 1951), p. 8; S. H. Chapman, "The Edges of the 1793 Cents," *The Numismatist*, Vol. 41, No. 4 (Apr., 1928), p. 242. For a similar machine at Tower Mint, see H. G. Stride, "The Royal Mint" (Chap. XIX), *Seaby's Coin and Medal Bulletin*, No. 485 (Oct., 1958), p. 398.

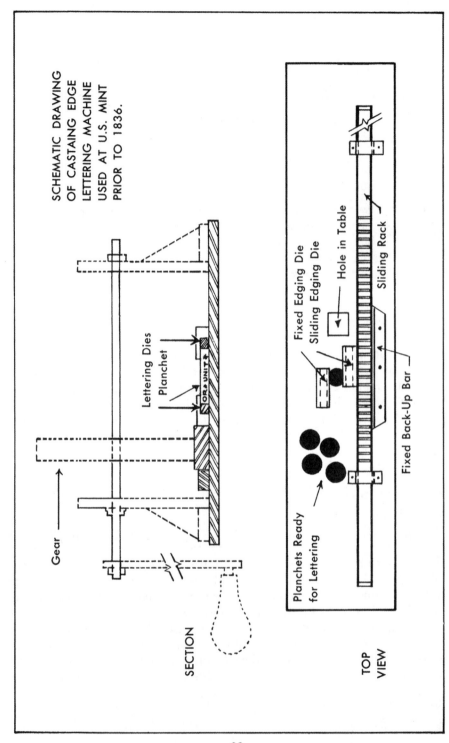

SCHEMATIC DRAWING OF CASTAING EDGE LETTERING MACHINE USED AT U.S. MINT PRIOR TO 1836.

Gear

Lettering Dies

Planchet

FOR A UNIT ★

SECTION

Planchets Ready for Lettering

Fixed Edging Die

Sliding Edging Die

Hole in Table

Sliding Rack

Fixed Back-Up Bar

TOP VIEW

marginal ridge, performing the function of upsetting the border. After edge lettering, the planchets dropped through a hole in the table into a container. Since the planchets were handled in bulk before coinage, the edge lettering is found both facing up and facing down relative to the obverse.

This edge lettering procedure was perfected by the French engineer Castaing in 1685. As used in the Royal Mint in England it was crudely illustrated in 1750 in the *Universal Magazine*. The operation as used in the French Mint was shown in an engraving published in 1771.[36] (See illustration.)

1771 French illustration of the Castaing edge decorating machine in use.

Reeding of the edge was done in a similar fashion. Since the reeding was a repetitive design, the edging dies could be made longer so that the two planchets could be inserted one behind the other and each rolled a full turn or more with one operation of the crank. Since lettering was not repetitive, the same part of the circumference could not be rolled along both dies.

It would not have been practical to do any edge work on a struck coin because the metal was hardened in striking and the finished circumferential radials would be disturbed.

The dies for the obverse and the reverse were made from soft steel in a cylindrical form. The flat end, after smoothing, was cut with a punch or hub

---

[36] Denis Diderot and Jean D'Alembert, "Monnoyage (Art de fabriquer les monnoies)," *Encyclopedie* (Geneva, Switzerland, 1751–1765 and subsequent early editions, the illustrations relating to coinage having been published in Volume VIII of the plates in 1771 at Paris); Sir John Craig, *The Mint* (Cambridge, England, 1953), Plate IX; John Pinkerton, *An Essay on Medals* (London, 1784), Vol. I, p. 201 and Vol. II, p. 129; Montroville W. Dickeson, *The American Numismatical Manual* (Philadelphia, 1859), p. 35; C. Wilson Peck, *English Copper Tin and Bronze Coins in the British Museum* (London, 1960), p. 142.

containing a bust for an obverse, or an eagle for a reverse. Dentilation extending radially to the circumferential edge was then rolled onto the border of the die by rotating it in a lathe, no specific number of dentils being standard. The lettering was then stamped in, letter by letter. Each star on both obverse and reverse and each figure of the date was punched sep-

Enlarged date of 1804 half eagle showing use of individual figure punches. The 1 is double cut and the properly sized 8 is recut with an 8 from a smaller set of punches.

arately. The die was then hardened by heating and immersion in liquid. Each finished die was made slightly larger in diameter than the planchet to be used. Since the planchet was expanded by the striking force developed by the weighted levers of the hand-operated screw press, the dies also had to be larger than the finished coin. In striking, the edge was free to expand outward, and therefore the shape of the lettering or reeding was not noticeably disturbed. Since the dentilation on the border of the die extended beyond the expanding planchet, the dentilation on the coin extended all the way to its circumference.

In order to assist the operator who placed the planchet on the lower die, a centering device was used. It consisted of a thin resilient plate with an opening slightly larger than the finished coin. A section was cut out facing the operator so that he could quickly slide a new planchet into a proper position over the lower die while removing the coin struck by the previous blow. The plate would not interfere with the radial expansion of the coin during striking. It would neither decorate, shape nor mar the edge of the coin; nor would there be any pinching of the struck coin interfering with its removal. This plate has been referred to as an "open collar" or "loose plain collar." The circular steel collar applied in 1836 to steam coinage (see infra) was originally referred to as the "close collar" to distinguish it from the "open collar" of prior years.[37] For the sake of clarity, the close collar in this text will be called a collar die.

Although a steam engine had been substituted for horses at the Mint in 1816 for rolling ingots, it was not until Franklin Peale (1795–1870) was sent to Europe by the Mint in May, 1833, to study metallurgical and coining procedures principally in the English and French mints, that other steam powered machinery was finally developed. The Royal Mint in London operated steam powered vacuum actuated coining presses and Adam Eckfeldt urged the adoption of this procedure. Peale's recommendation, however, was a

[37] Letter dated November 8, 1836, from R. M. Patterson, Director of the United States Mint to Levi Woodbury, Secretary of the Treasury; Walter Breen, "The Secret History of the Gobrecht Coinage," Coin Collectors Journal, Vol. 21, No. 5 (Sept., 1954), p. 14, 23; S. Hudson Chapman, "The Edges of the 1793 Cents," The Numismatist, Vol. 41, No. 4 (Apr., 1928), p. 242; Walter Breen, "Research in the Archives," Coin Collectors Journal, Vol. 18, No. 4 (July, 1951), p. 86.

coining press with the upper die operated by a knuckle or toggle driven by a reciprocating linkage connected to a steam powered flywheel. This type of coinage press had just been developed by Nicolas Thonnelier, at the French Mint in 1834.[38] It had the advantage of speed, with uniform squeezing pressure in coining instead of impact, along with ample force to shape the edge in a collar die. Intermittent sketches, ideas, and reports were mailed back to the Mint by Peale during his two year study, following which he returned to participate in the completion of machinery for the new Philadelphia Mint on Juniper and Chestnut Streets, the cornerstone of which had been laid July 4, 1829. The new steam-operated lever presses, which were put in operation on March 23, 1836, had sufficient pressure to produce either a smooth or reeded edge by confining the planchet in a collar die when striking occurred and by letting the face dies squeeze the metal against the collar die. This method eliminated the possibility of lettered edges because the coin had to slide out of the collar die vertically and a coin with either raised or incuse edge letters could not have been extricated from the collar die. The idea of a jointed collar for edge lettering had been used in Europe before the invention of the Castaing machine in 1685, but was impractical because the application to the planchet was by hand hammering. Edge lettering by the use of a retractable collar of separate segments was developed in the French Mint by H. P. Droz and in 1786 was shown to both Boulton and Watt on their visit. They found it impractical.[39] It was tried out at the U. S. Mint in making the 1885 pattern dollar (Judd 1747-9; A-W 1714-6) and was first used for U. S. Mint business strikes in the coining of the 1907 double eagle.

Matthew Boulton in the installation of his newly invented coining machinery at the Soho Mint near Birmingham in 1788 had made use of a one-piece plain collar die of steel. When the Royal Mint installed new steam-operated screw presses in the 1810–12 period one-piece collar dies were adopted for all coinage. Collar dies were either plain or reeded depending on the type of edge desired. The collar die was actuated upwardly to surround the planchet after it was fed into position over the lower die and, after striking occurred, the collar die retracted. Adam Eckfeldt in connection with the development of new machinery for the Philadelphia Mint conceived the idea of having the collar remain stationary and was working on such collar die mechanisms while Peale was in Europe.

Another change in the 1836 machinery was the introduction of a steam driven circular milling machine to upset the edges of the planchets by raising a marginal ridge. The planchets were fed by gravity from a tube to the space between a fixed outside circular groove and an inner rotating circular groove and squeezed between them as they rolled along. This process thickened the circumferential border and reduced the diameter of the planchet. The

[38] Thonnelier, *Notice Historique Sur Le Balancier et Sur La Presse Monétaire* (Paris, 1834), p. 7 and plate.
[39] Montroville W. Dickeson, *The American Numismatical Manual* (Philadelphia, 1859), p. 35; John Pinkerton, *An Essay on Medals* (London, 1784), Vol. II, p. 129; H. W. Dickinson, *Matthew Boulton* (Cambridge, England, 1937), p. 206.

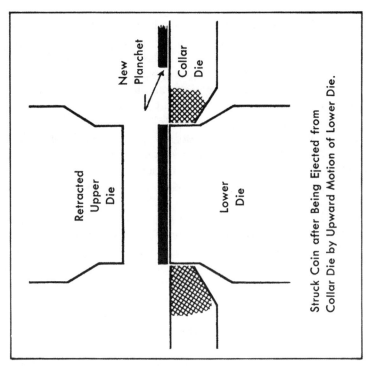

Struck Coin after Being Ejected from Collar Die by Upward Motion of Lower Die.

Retracted Upper Die

Lower Die

New Planchet

Collar Die

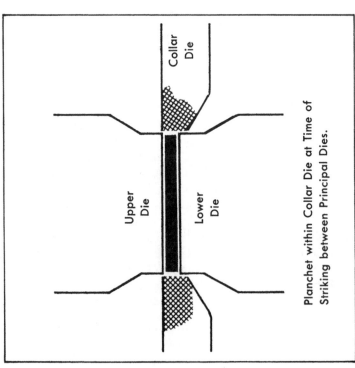

Planchet within Collar Die at Time of Striking between Principal Dies.

Upper Die

Lower Die

Collar Die

DIAGRAMS SHOWING RELATIONSHIP OF PLANCHET, PRINCIPAL DIES, COLLAR DIE AND STRUCK COIN IN STEAM OPERATED LEVER PRESS IN USE AT U. S. MINT AFTER 1836.

edge remained smooth. The device is illustrated and explained in numismatic literature in 1861 and thereafter.[40] The Mint Report for 1836 stated "the milling of the pieces, heretofore done exclusively by hand, is now by means of an instrument contrived and made here for that purpose also executed by the power of a steam engine."

The principal dies were adapted to the new coining presses by being reduced in diameter to a size which would fit inside the fixed collar die. While prior to the final adoption of collar dies in 1836, the obverse and reverse dies were larger than the struck coin, and the use of the collar die required the principal dies to be slightly smaller than the struck coin. The upper die, forced downward by the flywheel and its linkage, traveled inside the collar die to a small extent when the coin was struck. The lower die, however, after the striking had occurred, was actuated upwardly into the collar die by a cam, forcing the struck coin out of the fixed collar die so that the coin could be automatically pushed aside before the new planchet was moved into position (see diagram). The lower die retracted in time for the new planchet to be carried forward by mechanical fingers and dropped into the collar die to await the next stroke of the upper die.[41] With this mechanism, the obverse and reverse dies and the collar die would have to fit one another minutely. A wire rim on a coin would result if the planchet had too much metal in it or if the principal dies were set too close, for excess metal would then be squeezed between the sides of the principal dies and the collar die. The use of the collar die also permitted easier application of a smooth raised border in the design of the coin. Such a border as used previously on screw press coinage had the advantage of protecting the center design from wear, but principally improved the stacking quality of coins. The planchet having been upset by the milling machine had a rough border on each side, and by machining a slight offset into the obverse and reverse dies at their circumference, a smooth border could be formed in the course of striking.

The same relative size of principal dies, planchets and collar die exist today at the United States Mint with the following measurements for current half dollars:

Cut planchet—1.195 inches

Upset planchet—1.182 inches

Obverse die neck—1.186 inches

Reverse die neck—1.184 inches

Collar die opening—1.205 inches

Coin size—1.205 inches

As is evident from the foregoing measurements, the planchet broadens to fill the collar die, and the obverse and reverse dies are smaller than the finished coin or the collar die opening.

---

[40] Waldo Abbott, "Making Money," *Harper's Monthly*, Vol. 24 (Dec. 1861), p. 22; George G. Evans, *Illustrated History of the United States Mint* (Philadelphia, 1885), p. 36; A. M. Smith, *Coins and Coinage* (Philadelphia, 1881), p. 23–4.

[41] *Mason's Coin and Stamp Collectors' Magazine*, Vol. 4, No. 2 (Dec., 1870), p. 181; George G. Evans, *Illustrated History of the United States Mint* (Philadelphia, 1885), p. 39; Andrew M. Smith, *Visitor's Guide and History of the United States Mint* (Philadelphia, 1885), p. 21.

The steam-operated lever press for half dollars began production at the U. S. Mint on November 8, 1836, and initially was engaged in striking 1836 half dollars with plain flat borders and with edges reeded by the use of a collar die. These coins weighed 206¼ grains and were 900 fine (instead of 208 grains, 892.4 fine) to conform with the then pending legislation which received final approval on January 18, 1837. In order to be struck in a collar die it was found practical to make the diameter of these pieces about one-tenth of an inch smaller than the lettered edge 1836 half dollars. Temporarily the steam operated lever press was then used to strike old style 1836 half dollars by eliminating the use of the collar die because lettered edge planchets were used.

The 1836 Gobrecht pattern dollars were also smaller in diameter than the early U. S. dollars. The large screw press at the Mint was used to coin the 1836 pattern dollars because the lever press for dollars was not yet completed. Instructions from Director Patterson to Adam Eckfeldt in a letter dated September 22, 1836, requested that these pieces be struck in a "close reeded or grooved collar," but this was not practical. Instead a smooth collar was used for the one thousand specimens which were struck and in order to extricate the coins they were withdrawn from the collar die by sliding it over the lower die.

In numismatic literature and parlance the ridged or fluted edges on coins are referred to as "milled" or "reeded" edges. The terms, "milled edge" and "milling," developed because the process by which the edge design was originally applied was by milling. Reeding is descriptive of the edge itself. When the same type of reeded edge design was subsequently produced by the use of a collar die instead of a milling process, the term "milling" was no longer technically correct in describing the edge and only was correct in describing the upsetting of the circumferential border. Lettered or otherwise decorated edges should also be referred to as milled edges only if their means of application is by milling.

Distinctive Characteristics of 1804 Dollars

Classification

The 1804 dollars are known in two die combinations. There is only one obverse die. The reverse of the first known 1804 dollar at the U. S. Mint will be designated as Reverse X. This reverse has the first S of STATES straddling the first two clouds on the left side and the O of OF entirely over the second cloud from the right. This combination is referred to herein as Class I and has been termed by others as the "original." There are eight known examples of Class I dollars. (See Chapter XIX.)

The same 1804 obverse is mated with another reverse, which will be designated as Reverse Y. This reverse has the first S of STATES entirely over the first cloud on the left side and the O of OF straddling the first two clouds on the right. Reverse Y leaves a much larger space between STATES and OF than the first reverse. This combination is referred to herein as Class II and Class III dollars and has been termed by others as the "restrike."

The only distinction between Class II and Class III dollars is that Class II has a plain smooth edge and Class III has a lettered edge. The only existing specimen of Class II is in the U. S. Mint collection. There are six known examples of Class III dollars. (See Chapter XIX.)

Other Matings of the Dies

The die for Reverse X of the Class I 1804 dollars is also found used as the reverse of proof dollars dated 1801, 1802, and 1803 and classified by M. H. Bolender as 1801 (B-5), 1802 (B-8), and 1803 (B-7), respectively. These three coins have always been known as "restrikes." Their individual characteristics are discussed in Chapter VI.

The die for Reverse Y of the Class II and Class III 1804 dollars is not found as a reverse on any other coin. These matings are shown on an accompanying plate.

Other Observations

The most important characteristics of the 1804 dollar, such as the raised flat border, the low short border dentils, the crushed or defective edge lettering, the missing curl tip, the size of the dies, etc., are discussed in Chapter

The U. S. Mint (Smithsonian Institution) specimen of the Class I 1804 dollar.
Photograph courtesy Smithsonian Institution

The U. S. Mint (Smithsonian Institution) specimen of the Class II 1804 dollar.
Photograph courtesy Smithsonian Institution

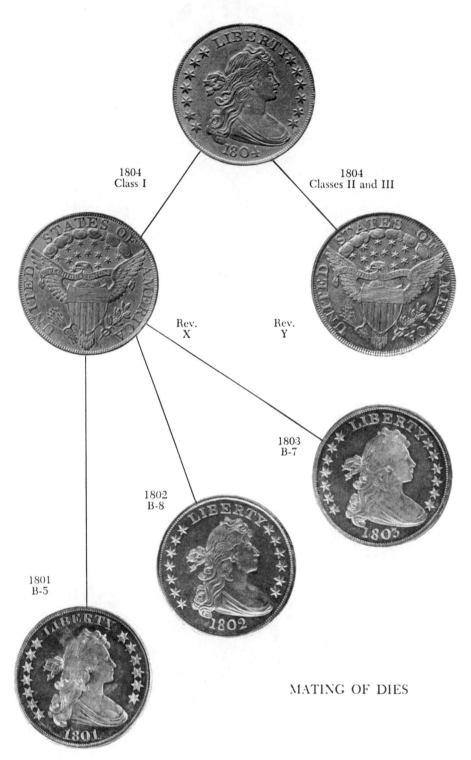

1804
Class I

1804
Classes II and III

Rev.
X

Rev.
Y

1803
B-7

1802
B-8

1801
B-5

MATING OF DIES

VII, in which items common to the 1804 dollar as well as to the 1801, 1802, and 1803 proof dollars are described and considered. The following characteristics are applicable to the 1804 dollars alone.

The 4 in the Date

The figure 4 in the date of the 1804 dollars (see illustration) is unusual in that it is lacking a crosslet or vertical serif at the right end of the horizontal

Enlargement of date of 1804 dollar showing lack of crosslet on 4 and showing 90 degree intersection of sides of upright of 4 with top of base. Raised flat border and shape of dentils are also evident .

Regular 1804 U. S. Eagle
Showing Crosslet on 4

Regular 1804 U. S. Half Eagle
Showing Crosslet on 4

stroke, but does have a base on the upright. All genuine eagle[42] and half eagle dies of 1804, being for the larger gold coins, have both a crosslet and a base on the 4, whereas the 1804 quarter eagle, being small, has neither. Sim-

---

[42] The 1804 eagle fabrication without a crosslet is described in Chapter VII hereof.

ilarly, all half dollars and quarter dollar dies of 1804, being for the larger silver coins,[43] have both a crosslet and base on the 4, whereas the 1804 dime, being small, has neither. The 1804 half dollar dies are known only through two obverses used on 1805 over 1804 half dollar coinage[44] (see illustration).

Beistle 1-A

Beistle 2-C

The two varieties of obverses on 1805 over 1804 half dollars each have a crosslet on the 4.

Enlargement of date of 1805 over 1804 half dollar (Beistle 2) showing crosslet on 4 and curving intersection between right side of upright and base of 4.

The cent and five obverses of half cents of 1804 have both a crosslet and a base on the 4, whereas one half cent obverse (Gilbert No. 1) has a base but no crosslet. Excluding the silver dollar, all silver and gold 1804 coinage, therefore, shows that each large figure 4 punch used to make the large 1804 coins consistently has a crosslet and a base, whereas each small figure 4 punch for the small 1804 coins has neither. From these facts one could assume that the 1804 silver dollar was cut with an improperly made punch, because there is

[43] The 1804 dollar is excluded because it is under study. There is no 1804 half dime.
[44] Beistle obverse varieties 1 and 2.

40

no reason why the largest silver piece should not match the style and design detail of the other large pieces. Except as to size, the bust punch, the eagle punch, the letter, star and other figure punches are uniform on all 1804 silver and gold coins. In the copper coinage of 1804 the half cent obverse without a crosslet has a base, and its die also seems to have been cut with an improperly made figure 4 punch. The problem, therefore, is to determine, if possible, whether or not these facts point to the die for the 1804 dollar being made other than at the time of its dating.

The proof 1804 eagle has a base on the 4 but no crosslet, and the 1804 altered date restrike cent does not have either. Even though both of them

Proof Eagle Antedated 1804 and Having No Crosslet on 4

are products of a much later period than their dating, they show that in making antedated dies little care was taken to conform tiny details of this nature to the original coinage.

The few coins dated 1794 show a similar relationship between the figure 4 on large and small coins. All 1794 half dimes and half cents, being small coins, have no crosslet and no base on the 4. All 1794 cents, half dollars and dollars, being the larger coins of that year, have a crosslet and base on the 4.

In 1814, cents are with and without a crosslet, but all have a base. The other 1814 coins—the dime, the half dollar, and the half eagle—have both a crosslet and a base.

The 4 on all 1824 coins has a base but no crosslet. The 4 in coinage for 1834 has a base but is found with and without a crosslet, there being no apparent size basis for the distinction.

Based upon the lack of a crosslet on the 4 of the 1804 dollar, the only conclusion which can be drawn is that the wrong style 4 punch was used. Although this error could have occurred in 1804, it seems more likely to have taken place at a time when crosslets on a 4 were not considered essential.

It is amusing to note that *Dye's Coin Encyclopaedia* (Philadelphia, 1883) adds to the confusion by erroneously having a crosslet on the 4 in its illustration of the 1804 dollar.

Another feature of the 4 of the 1804 dollar is that the intersection of both sides of the upright with the top of the base is at right angles, whereas on the 1 of the date there is a fillet or curve at the corresponding connection. This difference in styling was pointed out by Lyman H. Low in his Catalogue of the Sale on October 11, 1904, of the H. G. Brown collection and, according to Low, showed "evidence of partnership in the finishing of dies" and was diagnostic in identifying a genuine 1804 dollar. Low did not realize that this stylistic difference between the 1 and 4 is also found on every other 1804 denomination where the 4 has a base. It was therefore erroneous for Low to infer that "in the finishing of the dies" either more than one man participated in the cutting or that the final figure 4 was added at a later date to an earlier die with an incompleted date. Before the sale, however, it was pointed out that the difference in the style of the connections between the uprights and the bases was customary in preparing figures.[45]

Die Breaks

All Class I coins evidence an obverse die break extending from the outside point of the top left star across the top of the letters LIBERT to the Y. On Class II and Class III coins the same die break has extended slightly to the left so as to have a terminus over the top of the second star from the top on the left side.

All Class I coins evidence two die breaks on Reverse X, one across the top portion of letters NITED to the wing tip on the left side and the other across the top of the space between ES in STATES.

Reverse Y, found on Class II and Class III coins, does not show any die break.

Concavity and Convexity

The Class III 1804 dollars are slightly concave on the reverse and slightly convex on the obverse.[46] This phenomenon is unusually freakish. The dies would straighten out a slightly deformed planchet in the course of striking, and thus the shape of the planchet was not the cause. Neither of the dies could have been made in a cupped shape, since all Class I and Class II dollars are perfectly flat. If the steel used for dies is not properly carbonized and hardened the dies can become slightly concave in the center portion from use. This is seen in the reverses of the 1793 Liberty Cap cents, the reverses of many 1794 cents, the reverse of the 1804 half cent (Gilbert 1), etc., where a weak impression in the center portion of the coin results. But no flat hardened steel die can become convex from use. The 1804 dollar obverse die produced sharp flat impressions when used to strike Class I and Class II coins and could not become convex in the coining of Class III pieces. Reverse Y on the Class III 1804 dollars is struck sharply and shows no weakness in the center or otherwise. The buckling of the Class III 1804 dollars could not have resulted, therefore, from changes in the dies themselves. The only logical explanation of the buckling or cupping is that the struck coins were rolled along under uniform but excessive side pressure in the Castaing edge

[45] *American Journal of Numismatics*, Vol. 39, No. 1, (July, 1904), p. 28.
[46] As to the Idler 1804 dollar, see: *The Numismatist*, Vol. 22, No. 4 (Apr., 1909), p. 105. As to the Berg specimen, see: *Mason's Coin Collectors' Magazine*, Vol. 1, No. 12 (May, 1885), p. 121.

lettering machine. Thus, the slight buckling is evidence that the striking took place before the edge lettering on the Class III dollars. This order is the opposite of what would have occurred if the Class III coins had been struck in a screw press in 1804 or at any other time. It points to the fact that the edge lettering could not be applied first because the coins were to be struck in a collar die which would crush the edge.

Juxtaposition of Dies

The relative position of the obverses and reverses on the Class I 1804 dollars is normal, being 180 degrees offset so that the top of one side is directly opposite the bottom of the other. The relative position of the dies on the Class II and Class III 1804 dollars is abnormal by over five degrees, the 0 in 1804 being opposite the second T in STATES, and the center of the tail of the eagle being opposite the space between IB of LIBERTY. To find the juxtaposition of the obverse and reverse, abnormally and identically offset with respect to all Class II and Class III coins, leads to the query of whether or not they were struck at the same time. The odds that the obverse and reverse dies were accidentally set in the press at the same improper angle on two separate occasions are almost nil. Thus, it is sound to recognize that all Class II and Class III coins were struck at the same time.

Sharpness of Impressions

The Class II and Class III 1804 dollars are much more sharply struck up than those of Class I. This was observed by the Chapmans who attributed this characteristic to the recutting of the lettering, stars, and date on the obverse.[47] Actually the obverse die was not recut in any way and the difference in sharpness is explained by the difference of force in striking. A screw press would result in different force for each piece whereas a lever press would produce uniform force. Since the Class II and Class III specimens are of uniform sharpness it would seem that they were struck on a lever press. Since the Class I specimens vary in sharpness it would seem that they were struck in a screw press which applies varying pressure as to each coin struck and therefore were coined before the use in 1836 of the lever press.

Partial Double Impression

When a die is slightly loose in its holder at the time of striking, its movement will often cause coins to be double struck. Each Class II and Class III 1804 dollar is partially double struck on the reverse, indicating that the reverse die was not firmly secured. This chattering is clearly noticeable on the border dentils on the right side (see illustration). On the Berg (Class III) specimen the rotation of the position of the ribbon on the coin in a clock-

---

[47] Catalogue of the Sale of the Chapman Collection, May 14, 1885, p. 24; George G. Evans, *Illustrated History of the United States Mint* (Philadelphia, 1885, et seq.), p. 65; *The Numismatist*, Vol. 50, No. 7 (July, 1937), p. 614; *Selections from The Numismatist* (Racine, 1960), Vol. I, p. 128.

Class III 1804 dollar showing double impression on reverse along ribbon and at dentils on right side, and indicating movement of reverse die during striking.

wise direction is evident. Coupled with the evidence of the abnormal juxtaposition of the dies, the chattering is further proof of the fact that the Class II and Class III coins were struck at the same time.

Rust Spots

Reverse Y as used on all of the Class II and Class III dollars shows that the die had rusted slightly when used. This rusting had pitted the upper part of the left upright of U in UNITED and the adjacent field on its left. Little lumps on the coins evidence this condition of the die (see illustration).

The existence of rust lumps on all coins on which the second reverse die was used indicates that the die was cut long prior to its use. Dies were originally well cared for while in use, and rusting would take place only in the course of storage for substantial periods. This is evidence that if the dies were cut in the year 1834, which will be shown, the second reverse could have acquired slight rust spots by the time the obverse and the second reverse were used in 1858. (See Chapter XI.)

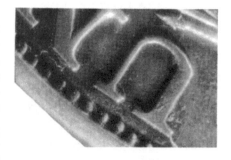

Rust spots on and around U on reverse of 1804 Class II and Class III dollars.

S. H. Chapman in the Catalogue of the Lyman sale held November 7, 1913, used the rust spots inaccurately to prove that the Adams specimen (Class III) which he was then selling was made in a batch prior to the Mint's Class II specimen and long prior to the other Class III dollars. He therefore pronounced it unique.[48]

---

[48] Reprinted in *Numismatic Scrapbook Magazine,* Vol. 6, No. 5 (May, 1940), p. 284.

Distinctive Characteristics of Proof 1801, 1802, and 1803 Dollars

The dollars dated 1804, as heretofore indicated, have two separate reverse dies, X and Y. Only Reverse X, the first known reverse, was used in striking dollars of other dates, namely proofs of 1801 (B-5), 1802 (B-8), and 1803 (B-7). These three die varieties are also known as the "restrike" dollars of 1801, 1802, and 1803, but will be referred to herein as "proofs," as there are no other known proof dollars having those dates. It is fundamental to note that not one of the obverse dies used in striking these proofs is found mated with any other reverse. Only about a dozen specimens each of these proof 1801, 1802, and 1803 dollars are known, and no business strike or normal production from any of these dies exists. A hoard of about twenty or more of each of such proof dollars is rumored to be in the hands of a member of the Linderman family.

The extent to which these proof dollars have unusual characteristics in common with the 1804 dollar will be covered in the next chapter. The other distinctive features of the 1801, 1802, and 1803 proof dollars are as follows:

1. Each figure "1" in the date of the 1801 (B-5) obverse is cut with a figure punch which has an upper serif with a curved top sloping down to the left, whereas all other dollars dated 1803 and prior thereto, including 1802 (B-8) and 1803 (B-7), and also the dollars dated 1804, have a flat topped serif on the figure "1." Stylistically, the curved top "1" was not used on United States coinage until 1813 on the half eagle, 1815 on the quarter dollar, 1819 on the one cent and fifty cents, 1820 on the dime, 1821 on the quarter eagle, 1825 on the half cent, 1829 on the half dime, 1838 on the eagle, and 1847 on the silver dollar. The curved topped "1" was therefore not in use in the 1801 period (see comparative illustrations).

2. In the 1801 (B-5) the sides of the inner outline of the figure "0" in the date are straight, whereas on all other dollars dated 1803 and prior thereto, including the 1802 (B-8) and 1803 (B-7), and also on the dollars dated 1804, the inner outline of the figure "0" is curved. Stylistically, the "0" with straight internal sides was not introduced into United States coinage until 1820 on the cent, dime, quarter dollar, and half dollar, and until 1830 on the half dime, quarter eagle, and half eagle. The "0" with the straight sides on its inner outline was therefore not in use in the 1801 period.

Proof 1801 Dollar (B-5)

Regular 1801 Dollar (B-2)

Major style differences between numerals on 1801 proof dollar and numerals on regular 1801 dollar. Differences in border detail are also evident.

Proof 1802 Dollar (B-8)

Regular 1802 Dollar (B-6)

Style difference in the numeral 2 on 1802 proof dollar and on regular 1802 dollar. Differences in border detail are also evident.

3. The figure "2" in the date of the 1802 (B-8) is cut with a figure punch in which the top end points directly upward after curling inside the rounded top, whereas the upper end of the figure "2" on all other 1802 dies ends in a horizontal position. Stylistically, the figure "2" with its top end pointing upward was not used on United States coinage until 1820 when it was used on the one cent, quarter dollar, half dollar, and half eagle. Stylistically, the type of curved base on the figure "2" in the date of the 1802 (B-8) is also not found on United States coinage until 1820. The "2" with its top end pointing directly upward and with a curved base was therefore not in use in the 1802 period (see comparative illustrations).

4. On the reverse of the 1801 and 1803 proof dollars, there is a depression in the open area between UM of UNUM on the ribbon and the right upper corner of the shield (see illustration). This depression is a horizontal straight

Dent below ribbon found on reverses of 1801 and 1803 proof dollars and caused by sliver of metal adhering to die during striking.

line but has an end rising upward to the right. This defect does not appear on the 1802 proof dollars or on the Class I 1804 dollars which have the same reverse. It is not a defect in the coins occurring after striking because there is an identical depression on the 1801 and 1803 pieces. It could only occur by something projecting from or adhering to the surface of the die. Its sharpness shows that it is not from rust. It must have been caused by a sliver of metal falling on and adhering to the reverse die. It proves conclusively that the 1801 (B-5) and the 1803 (B-7) were struck at the same time.

5. The 1803 proof is struck from a die which was heavily rusted on the inside point and the area surrounding the fourth star on the left, and has

1801
B-5

1802
B-8

1803
B-7

Proof dollars dated 1801, 1802, and 1803—formerly referred to as restrikes.

slight rust marks between the 1 and 8 of the date. This shows that the coin was struck a substantial time after the die was cut (see illustration).

Rust spots on and around fourth star on left side of 1803 proof dollar.

6. The 1801 proof die has horizontal and vertical line scratches on the bust; these lines were used in locating the center point for finishing the die. It also has a heavy die break along the outside of the stars on the left and continuing across the bottom of the date. The "0" in the date is double cut.

7. The letters in LIBERTY on the 1801 (B-5) dollar have serifs which have right angle corners at their intersection with the strokes of the letters, whereas all other dollars dated 1803 and prior thereto, including the 1802 (B-8) and the 1803 (B-7), and in addition the dollars dated 1804, have serifs which have sweeping curves at their intersection with the strokes of the letters.

8. The weights of the 1801, 1802, and 1803 proofs examined are greater than the 416 grain standard, the lightest one noted being 419½ grains and the heaviest 423 grains, whereas the weights of normal dollars are at or slightly below the standard.

9. There would have been no reason in the Mint procedures existing during the first years of the nineteenth century to keep any obverse or reverse dies and never use them for normal production, for dies required too much tedious labor to prepare. Obverse dies were used until they failed, and good dies were not withdrawn when the year of their dating had passed. The same reverse dies were used from year to year on dollars until they failed. Five normal 1801 obverse dies were even overdated, by repunching, to produce dies dated 1802 (B-1, B-2, B-3, B-4, and B-9), and there would be no justification for one virtually unused 1801 obverse die not being used or overdated, and yet two new 1802 dies were prepared, such as B-5 and B-6 not including the B-8 under inquiry. Likewise, there would be no reason for three 1803 dies, including the 1803 (B-7) under inquiry, to be cut when an 1802 (B-8) die had never been used for production and could be overdated or used as it existed. The reverse die used on each of these proofs was likewise never used for production. This situation shows that the 1801 (B-5), 1802 (B-8), and 1803 (B-7) could not have existed at the time of their dating, and likewise that the reverse could not have been available during any of those dates.

CHAPTER VII	*Characteristics Common to 1804 and to Proof 1801, 1802, and 1803 Dollars*

The two combinations of the dollar dated 1804 and the 1801, 1802, and 1803 proof dollars have been shown to be an isolated group, unconnected by die combination with any other dollars. The distinctive individual characteristics of the 1804 dollars have been noted. The distinctive individual characteristics of the 1801, 1802, and 1803 proof dollars have been listed. The special characteristics common to both groups can now be added; they are by far the most provocative of conclusions.

Borders

A raised flat circumferential border with a ring of dentils extending from the inside of the border is found on the 1804 dollar obverse, reverses X and Y, with which it is mated, and on the obverses of the proof 1801, 1802, and 1803 dollars with which reverse X is mated. The border work is identical on these dies and cut with the same tools. There are 188 dentils on those four obverses and 184 on the two reverses. Most of these dentils are semi-circular in outline with their straight side blending into the flat border, but a few of them have a small neck of equal width indicating that they are not cut in with a punch with a round cross section. Their top surfaces are spherical rather than flat. On the coins they do not rise as high as the flat border, since the border is machined deeper into the die than the dentils are punched.[49] This type of low dentil and raised flat border combination is unknown on any other U. S. coins prior to 1828,[50] and a description of the borders on coins struck at the U. S. Mint will be effective to show when the dies with this style of border were cut.

Only a plain raised lip was used as a border on the 1793 chain type cents. This was eliminated on the balance of cents for 1793, and a ring of dots was substituted as a border. The 1793 half cents also had a ring of dots as a border. On all other dies for U. S. gold, silver, and copper coinage up to 1828, the border consisted of flat finger-like radials and no other circumferential border. These radials would extend to the circumferential edge of the coin unless a planchet was struck substantially off center. Their curved blunt ends pointed to the center of the coin. They served their purpose to protect

---

[49] The dentils are sometimes called beading, but because this border work on many U. S. coins is bullet shaped, scalloped, or semicircular, this term is not used in this text.
[50] The so-called eagle restrike of 1804 is excluded from consideration. (Judd 33, 34; A-W 23.)

the center design from wear and to add to stacking convenience.

Beginning in 1828, William Kneass, as Mint Engraver, introduced on the dime the raised flat border with an adjoining inside ring of lower dentils.[51] His new design for the half dime in 1829 and his dies for the quarter eagle and half eagle of the same year adopted the new border, as did his new design for the quarter in 1831 and his half cent of 1831. The new border was used on some 1834 cent dies and in 1836 on the new type of half dollar.[52] Once the new style border was adopted with respect to a denomination, it was continued in use into the twentieth century with minor exceptions.

There are some coins of the period prior to 1828 which may appear to have a raised flat border and dentils instead of elongated radials. This is caused by wear or by an off-center strike. In every case, well struck specimens of the same variety in choice condition show the radials. S. H. Chapman was doing wishful thinking in the sale of the Adams specimen of the 1804 dollar in the Lyman collection sale on November 7, 1913, when he stated that the 1804 dime had a raised flat border with dentilation like the 1804 dollar border.[53]

As further evidence of the fact that the raised flat border was an entirely new feature introduced in 1828 on United States coinage and in no way used in the 1804 period, the written comments of Mint Director Samuel Moore to Samuel D. Ingham, Secretary of the Treasury, are conclusive.[54] With respect to the 1829 half dimes he expressed the opinion that they were "superior to any coins heretofore issued;—the higher edge given by the milling, with the blank margin round the bead are valuable improvements." When the small size quarters were introduced in 1831 he wrote:

> The changes from the former coins of this denomination consist partly in the reduction of the diameter of the dies, the employment of milling to form an elevated margin and leaving a portion of this margin blank, corresponding in these particulars with the improvements made in the Half and quarter eagles, dismes and half dismes. A similar improvement will as soon as practicable be introduced into the larger coins.

In analyzing the borders on the 1804 obverse die, the reverses used with it, and the dies mated with them, it appears that all of them are cut with borders of a technique and style introduced in 1828 and in extensive use during the year 1834. The borders, therefore, are positive evidence that the dies were cut and that the coins were struck from them after 1828, and that this group is an antedated coinage created in other than normal Mint operations.

Even nonexistent coinage corroborates the foregoing conclusions. The two obverse dies of half dollars dated 1805 which are cut over 1804 dies (Beistle 1 and 2) have radials for borders, showing specifically that radials

---

[51] Walter H. Breen, "How Our Coinage Became Mechanized," *The Numismatist*, Vol. 64, No. 3 (Mar., 1951), p. 286.
[52] Some proof 1833, 1834 and 1835 half dollars have raised flat borders, but not the business strikes.
[53] Walter Breen, "Silver Coinages of the Philadelphia Mint, 1794–1916," *Coin Collector's Journal*, 1958, p. 17.
[54] Letters dated August 8, 1829, and January 29, 1831, *Mint Letter Book No. 2* (1824–1831), p. 80 and 108, Record Group 104, National Archives.

Pattern 1838 dollar designed by Gobrecht showing raised flat border and lower dentils.

rather than raised flat borders with dentils would have resulted if 1804 half dollar coinage had taken place from the dies before overdating.

The foregoing conclusions are reached without the need of pointing out any similarity between the dentils on the antedated coinage and the dentils on the Gobrecht pattern dollars dated 1836, 1838, and 1839 (see illustration).

An examination of illustrations which are to be found on pages 39, 46, 47, and 49 enables a clear and revealing comparison to be made between the border of a normal silver dollar dated 1803 or prior thereto, on the one hand, and that of the 1804 dollar and the proof 1801, 1802 and 1803 dollars on the other hand. The long radials extending to the circumference on the former group contrast with the raised flat border and low semicircular dentils of the latter group. In addition, the former group under magnification clearly shows the radial expansion of the planchet during striking on a screw press. Since the portions nearer the circumference move the greatest distance, the radials slide outward in the die, leaving only a trace of an impression on their inner ends. The latter group shows a clear sharp impression on the inner outline of the dentils, indicating that outward radial movement was imperceptible and that the planchets were confined in a collar die when struck.

The Missing Curl Tip

It is well known that the 1804 obverse die was made with a defective bust punch. The left tip of the curl is missing on the wave of hair on the top of

Missing curl tip on 1804 dollar.

the head and below the right side of the letter B. The curl ends in a 60 degree jagged diagonal, sloping down to the right. This shows that this curl tip had broken off the bust punch before the 1804 obverse die was cut. All other

54

Missing curl tip on 1801 proof dollar (above) compared with pointed curl tip on 1802 proof dollar (below).

dollars of the same design dated 1803 or prior thereto have a tip on the curl pointing upward, except the 1801 (B-5) proof dollar, on which it was first noticed, in 1961, that the curl tip is broken off in identically the same way as that of the 1804 dollar (see comparative illustrations). The 1804 obverse and the 1801 (B-5) obverse are therefore conclusively proven to have been cut with the same broken bust punch. Not counting the missing curl tip, the busts on the 1801, 1802, and 1803 proofs, the 1804 dollars, and all other draped bust dollars are identical except for hand finishing. A tiny unnatural dent in the back of the hair above the bow links them all together. This would lead to the incontrovertible conclusion that all obverse production dies, as well as the 1802 (B-8) and 1803 (B-7) dies, were prepared before the 1801 (B-5) and 1804 dies. The tip of the curl broke off the punch either in cutting the 1801 (B-5) or the 1804 die (whichever was first cut) or by being carelessly bumped or dropped prior to making the first one of them.

It could be argued that there was more than one working bust punch made from the same matrix and that the one used for all other draped bust dollar dies was different from the one used on the 1801 (B-5) and the 1804 dies. Forgetting for the moment that hand punching and hand finishing of large complex punches makes those punches distinguishable in the dies made from them and in the coins struck from those dies, let us review that possibility.

Extra working punches were not prepared at the Mint without a need for them. If a bust punch were not noticeably broken, there would be no reason to prepare another. If this minute defect were noticed and was important enough to cause a new punch to be made, the old bust punch would have been thrown away. If the bust punch had lost the tip of its curl in 1801 and the defect either went unnoticed or was considered inconsequential, then the missing curl tip should have subsequently shown up in the normal 1801, 1802, and 1803 obverses used for production. It did not show up on any of them. The fact that it appeared on only two dies, 1801 (B-5) and the 1804, and not on any other dollars shows that these two dies were the last cut with the punch. Because an 1802 (B-8) with a 2 of the 1820 period must have been cut prior to both the 1801 (B-5) and the 1804, we have another independent line of evidence from the missing curl tip that the 1801 (B-5) and the 1804 dollar were cut after 1820 and not during the period of their dating.

Size of Dies

It has been shown that the diameter of dies used in the 1804 period was larger than the finished coin and that the size of dies used in conjunction with collar die coinage was smaller than the finished coin because the obverse and reverse dies had to pass inside the collar die. At least one specimen of the Class I 1804 dollars (Watters) and at least one specimen of the Class III 1804 dollars (Adams) has a wire rim both on the obverse and on the reverse. The only Class II specimen also has such wire rims. Most of the 1801, 1802, and

1803 proof dollars which have been examined have wire rims on the obverse and on the reverse extending far above the raised flat border and creating a bevel. The existence of wire rims on some specimens of the 1804 Class I, Class II, and Class III pieces as well as on the 1801, 1802, and 1803 proofs shows not only that they were struck in a collar die but also that the principal dies from which they were struck must have fitted inside the wire rim. Therefore, the principal dies were smaller in diameter than the finished coin and were prepared for use in conjunction with a collar die. It has been shown in Chapter IV that wire rims may or may not be produced depending upon the size of the planchets used or upon the variable impact of a manually powered screw press. In a lever press the force of striking is uniform and planchets of the same size should all have wire rims if any do, but if planchet sizes vary slightly, wire rims may appear on some coins but not others. Therefore, even if some specimens of 1804 dollars have no wire rims, the conclusion that all 1804 dollars of every class are struck with dies prepared for coinage in a collar die is nevertheless valid.

The United States ten dollar gold coinage was discontinued in 1804 just as was the silver dollar coinage. The eagles coined in 1804 included $10 pieces dated 1804. The 1804 eagles have radials as a border, a crosslet on the 4, and in every respect have the characteristics of the eagles of prior years.

There is a second type of 1804 eagle known as a "restrike." It is a proof struck both in gold (Judd 33) and in silver (Judd 34; AW-23). The dies are not used on other coinage. The 4 is without a crosslet. The upper left star almost touches the cap instead of being distant from it.[55] The edge is reeded. The punches for the letters, stars, and date differ from those used on the 1804 dollar dies. The coins struck from the eagle dies have wire rims, indicating that the dies were sunk for use with a reeded collar die. It therefore appears that the 1804 eagle proofs and their dies were made in the same manner as the Class I 1804 dollars and their dies were made (see comparative illustrations on pages 39 and 41).

Edge Lettering Defects

All 1804 dollars have edge lettering except the one specimen of Class II. All Class I and Class III dollars have major defects in that edge lettering. All Class I dollars have most letters on their edges crushed so as to close up in various degrees the indented strokes of the letters. Some letters are unreadable, others completely sealed up. This condition is not found on any other United States coinage except one variety each of proof half dollars dated 1833, 1834, and 1835. Even the Class III 1804 dollars and the 1801 (B-5), 1802 (B-8), and 1803 (B-7) dollars, which all have edge lettering defects, do not have smoothly crushed edges. It has been shown in Chapter IV that the edge lettering and reeding from the opening of the U. S. Mint

---

[55] A restrike illustrated as genuine, No. 8 on Plate opp. p. 25, *American Journal of Numismatics*, Vol. 4, No. 4 (Aug., 1869), p. 25.

until 1836 was applied to the planchets in the Castaing machine before striking occurred. In 1836 the collar die was used when the coin was struck to apply reeding to the edge or to form a smooth circumference. If Class I 1804 dollars had been normally coined on a screw press of the type discontinued in 1836, the edges would not have been crushed. Obsolete machinery was sold at auction from the old Mint after the steam operated lever presses were put in operation in 1836 in the new Mint building.[56]

If a lettered edge planchet were struck while held in a smooth collar die, the striking pressure expanding the coin laterally would squeeze the edges against the collar die and tend to close any openings such as indented edge lettering. The crushed edge lettering on Class I 1804 dollars could have taken place only if the coins were being struck in a collar die during or after 1833 when collar die experimentation began for use in new presses.

The same conclusion is sound with respect to the above mentioned 1833, 1834, and 1835 proof half dollars with crushed edge lettering. The obverses of these coins are found mated only with a single common reverse which is distinguishable by a thorn-like projection from the end of the stem and an extension to the right of the serif on the right base of the A in STATES. This reverse is also used on 1836 lettered edge proofs and business strikes[57] (see illustrations).

The 1833, 1834, and 1835 proof half dollars with crushed edge lettering also show that a smooth collar was used in the striking of a lettered edge planchet. It was undertaken during or prior to 1836 because the reverse die was also used for regular lettered edge business strikes in 1836. The collar die had to be cut a special size to fit over the ends of the existing screw press dies. This must have been done in 1835 or 1836 prior to the preparation of the reeded collar die for the new style 1836 half dollar with the smaller diameter. The smooth collar die in which the 1804 Class I dollars were struck must also have been cut in a special size, since it was larger than any collar die needed for the Gobrecht pattern dollar coinage or for any other normal minting purpose.

The edging die used to letter the edges on all 1804 dollars (Class I and Class III) and the 1801, 1802, and 1803 proof dollars was the same as the one used for all standard U. S. dollars dated 1803 and prior thereto. The H in HUNDRED is much smaller in size than the other letters. (See illustration on page 27). A master die with incuse letters must have been used to make one or more production edging dies with projecting letters. A worn production edge lettering die for dollars was no doubt retained after production of dollars ceased at the U. S. Mint in 1804 in case of resumption of coinage. Such an edging die was still available in 1834 to insert into the Castaing machine to letter the edges of dollar planchets.

[56] George E. Sellers, "Early Engineering Reminiscences," *American Machinist,* Vol. 16, No. 20 (May 18, 1893), p. 4.
[57] Walter Breen, "Proof Coins Struck by the United States Mint, 1817–1921," *Coin Collector's Journal,* Vol. 20, No. 2 (Mar., 1953), p. 27; Walter Breen, "Silver Coinages of the Philadelphia Mint 1794– 1916," *Coin Collector's Journal,* 1958, p. 15; *Standard Catalogue of United States Coins* (New York, 16th and subsequent editions), p. 171.

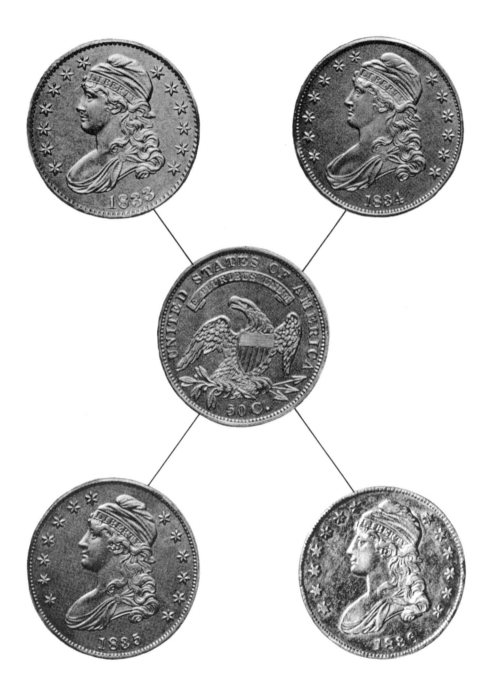

1833, 1834, and 1835 proof half dollars with crushed edge lettering and 1836 regular half dollar with normal edge lettering, all having a common reverse.

The Class II 1804 dollars, of which only one specimen remains, were made with a plain smooth edge in order to use the steam operated lever press and yet avoid the bungled appearance of the edge lettering which resulted on the Class I group. When this discrepancy was discovered (see Chapter XI), the problem of properly lettering the edges had to be given further thought.

The Class III 1804 dollars and the 1801, 1802, and 1803 proof dollars have irregularly lettered edges on most of which the word CENTS is impressed twice (see illustration), the second impression beginning over the underlying

Double impression of CENTS on edge of 1801, 1802, and 1803 proof dollars and on some 1804 Class III dollars.

ENTS, so that C is over E, E over N, N over T, and T over S.[58] The depth and clarity of the edge lettering is much more irregular than that on normal dollars dated 1803 and prior thereto. If the Class III 1804 dollars and the 1801, 1802, and 1803 proof dollars had edge lettering put on before striking in a collar die, their edges would be crushed. If they were struck without a collar die, they could not have wire rims, which they have. Therefore, the edges must have been lettered after the coins were struck in a smooth collar die.

It has been asserted that both Class I and Class III 1804 dollars were produced by normal dollars dated 1803 or prior thereto, being "smoothed down, used as planchets, in consequence of having the lettered edges."[59] Assuming that no trace of the under type remained and that no weight was lost by smoothing, such a method could not be employed in a steam operated lever press because it would spread the sides of a coin unless a collar die were used. A collar die would crush the edge lettering just as it did in the Class I 1804 dollars.

Many problems exist in using a Castaing machine to letter the edge after a coin is struck. The metal has become hardened in striking. The pressure of the Castaing machine increases the thickness at the margin, and either the letters or the pressure may disturb the surface of the coin at the circumferential border. The distance between edging dies is set for the planchet size and not for the struck coin size. If the distance were slightly too great, the coin could readily slip while rolling along worn edging dies under pressure; the result would be rerolling over a few of the same letters. The guide plate overlapping each edging die to keep the planchet from climbing out would scratch the finished coin unless removed or set higher. If the coin is annealed before lettering, it will have to be cleaned and will lose its finish

[58] As to the Linderman 1804 dollar, see: *American Journal of Numismatics*, Vol. 22, No. 4 (Apr., 1888), p. 100; as to the Berg 1804 dollar, see: *The Numismatist*, Vol. 22, No. 4 (Apr., 1909), p. 105.
[59] *Mason's Coin Collectors' Magazine*, Vol. 1, No. 12 (May, 1885), p. 121; Walter Breen, "Research in the Archives," *Coin Collector's Journal*, Vol. 18, No. 4 (July, 1951), p. 86.

and hardness. If it is fed into the Castaing machine and the letters do not sink easily into the metal, or if the edging dies are too close, the coin may buckle, as the Class III 1804 dollars did.

The wire rims on some of the 1801, 1802, and 1803 proofs are folded inward against the coin. This could have happened only if the Castaing machine was used after the coins were struck and the guides to hold the coins in line pressed back the wire rims remaining from striking.

Thus, it appears that by using the Castaing machine for purposes for which it was not intended, and in addition, by using worn or rusted lettering dies in it, the edge lettering was poorly applied. The 1804 Class III dollars and the 1801, 1802, and 1803 proofs, therefore, yield their own evidence that their edge lettering was applied after they were struck in a smooth collar.

Proof Condition

Some of each class of 1804 dollars are in proof condition. Others show evidence of wear, and some have been cleaned. The two first known of Class I, being the Mint specimen and the Stickney specimen, are proofs. The one specimen of Class II may not technically be a proof, for it is struck over another coin, but it appears to be a proof. The condition of each 1804 dollar is included with its pedigree in Chapter XIX.

All of the 1801 (B-5), 1802 (B-8), and 1803 (B-7) dollars which were examined or described by others in the past are brilliant proofs.

To produce true proofs, the dies as well as the rolled sheets from which the planchets were cut had to be polished. The first use of the polished dies in this manner produced the brilliant proof as distinguished from a master coin or a first strike on planchets made for normal production.

Proofs were first produced at the United States Mint in 1817.[60] No dollars dated 1803 or prior thereto are known in proof condition except the 1801 (B-5), 1802 (B-8) and 1803 (B-7), and, therefore, it is evident that no dies for normal production of dollars in that period were polished. This, is therefore, further "proof" that the 1804 dollars and the 1801, 1802, and 1803 proofs were struck from dies prepared after 1817 and were actually struck after 1817.

---

[60] Walter H. Breen, "Proof Coins Struck at the United States Mint 1817–1916," *Coin Collector's Journal*, Vol. 20, No. 2 (Mar., 1953), p. 1.

| *The Diplomatic Gift Background*

For those who believed that the 1804 dollars were not struck in the period of their dating, it was sound to look for some justifiable reason why the 1804 dollars were actually made at the Mint at a later date.

The story as written by W. Elliot Woodward for the Boston *Transcript* in May, 1867, was as follows:[61]

> Some time during the Administration of President Jackson a present was received from the Imaum of Muscat, and our Government, wishing to make a proper return to that magnate, caused, amongst other things, a set of coins to be made for him, and the only dollar dies existing being those of 1804, a few pieces were struck from them, one of which was used as intended, one retained in the mint and one found its way into a private cabinet.
>
> It may interest numismatists to know that the one sent to Muscat is no longer to be found. The enthusiasm with which coin collecting is pursued may be illustrated by stating the fact that a gentleman of New York City caused an investigation to be made in the palace of the Imaum in 1865, and learned that the dollar was not there, and had not been for a long time.

Charles E. Anthon and Joseph N. T. Levick, editors of the *American Journal of Numismatics*, stated as to the 1804 dollars that "Those restruck, during President Jackson's administration, to furnish specimens for the Imaum of Muscat, were properly inscribed on the edge, and in all respects, therefore like the original issue."[62] Subsequent editors claimed the story was mythical.[63]

In another version of the story it is stated:[64]

> The Silver Dollar of 1804 is very rare, not more than ten are known to be in existence, and it is alleged that the dies were not made in the year for which they were dated, but long after that time, and for the purpose of striking coins for presentation.

Beginning in 1832 the United States Department of State sent Edmund Roberts as its special agent to negotiate trade treaties with Muscat, Burma, Siam, Cochin-China, Sumatra, Malaya, Borneo and Japan. A special agent was a diplomatic representative selected for a specific project and his ap-

---

[61] *American Journal of Numismatics*, Vol. 2, No. 2 (June, 1867), p. 24; see also Vol. 34, No. 1 (July, 1899), p. 32.
[62] *American Journal of Numismatics*, Vol. 3, No. 1 (May, 1868), p. 7.
[63] *American Journal of Numismatics*, Vol. 34, No. 1 (July, 1899), p. 32.
[64] Andrew M. Smith, *Visitor's Guide and History of the United States Mint* (Philadelphia, 1885), p. 49; Andrew M. Smith, *Coins and Coinage* (Philadelphia, 1881), p. 61.

pointment was not submitted to the Senate for approval. Roberts was given blank passports to fill in as he thought best and the Asiatic powers to be visited were in his discretion. He was to conceal his mission because of the trade competition from other nations and was to pretend he was the captain's clerk on the U. S. Sloop of War, Peacock, which was assigned to transport him to his Asiatic destinations. He carried a supply of gifts, the usefulness of which he described in a letter dated June 20, 1833, from Batavia, as follows:

> "I must not omit to mention that *presents* are *widespread* in these countries, & are considered as a mark of respect. They render the donor of more or less consequence according to their *magnitude*. Both in C. China & Siam, among the first questions asked was 'What presents have you for the king?', considering it as a matter of course that you have not come empty handed."

On his first voyage he successfully reached an understanding as to a trade treaty with Siam through the P'hra Klang (the Prime Minister). Roberts also worked out a trade treaty with Muscat which attained its zenith under its great Moslem ruler, Said Said bin Sultan (1804–1856), as Imaum of Muscat. After long negotiations with subordinates in Cochin-China Roberts left without even seeing the Emperor. The list of gifts taken on the voyage did not include coins for presentation. The two tentative treaties with Siam and Muscat had to be ratified by the United States Senate which was done on June 30, 1834, and each signed treaty was to be taken back for the final approval of the other power.

In planning his second journey, the State Department on September 26, 1834, asked Roberts to suggest presents for Muscat "without requiring any large expenditure of money." His reply dated October 8, 1834, pointed out that United States' presents are cheap, inadequate, and insulting from an Asiatic point of view and that such actions make America appear provincial instead of important. The letter continued as follows:

> I am rather at a loss to know what articles will be most acceptable to the Sultan, but I suppose a complete set of new gold & silver & copper coins of the U. S. neatly arranged in a morrocco case & then to have an outward covering would be proper to send not only to the sultan, but to other Asiatics.

He also recommended maps, firearms, clocks, cut glass, ship models, etc. John Forsyth complied with the suggestion on November 11, 1834, by writing Samuel Moore, Director of the Mint, as follows:

Dept. of State
Washington   Nov. 11, 1834

Sir:

> The President has directed that a complete set of the coins of the United States be sent to the King of Siam, and another to the Sultan of Muscat. You are requested, therefore, to forward to the Department for that purpose, duplicate specimens of each kind now in use, whether of gold, silver, or copper. As boxes, in which they are to be contained, may

be more neatly and appropriately made at Philadelphia, under your direction, than they could be here, you are desired to procure them, if it will
not be too much trouble, and have the coins suitably arranged in them
before they are sent on. They should be of as small a size as is consistent
with the purpose in which they are intended; and should be of wood, covered with plain morocco. The color of one should be yellow, and the
other crimson.

You are authorized to draw upon the Department for the value of the
coins, and the expense of the boxes.

I have the honor to be, Sir,

Very respectfully
Your obed. serv.
John Forsyth

To
Dr. Samuel Moore
Director of Mint

Naturally new and attractive coins were desired for the gifts. The use of
the expression "a complete set" and "specimens of each kind now in use" is
not specific numismatically. All denominations struck by the United States
Mint were in current production at the time of the request except the dollar
and the eagle, both of which were last struck in 1804. The dollar had for all
practical purposes dropped out of circulation, as confirmed by the Report
of the Director of the Mint for 1836 where it is stated that "the unit of our
monetary system was rarely to be met with in circulation." The eagle had
ceased circulation as a $10 denomination because its bullion value exceeded
its nominal value by over five per cent. This premium was recognized in the
Act of June 28, 1834, when the amount of pure gold provided for with respect to coinage of eagles was lowered from 247½ grains to 232 grains and all
eagles minted prior to July 31, 1834, were made receivable for $10.66½ each.
If dollars or eagles dated 1834 or dies to strike them dated 1834 had been on
hand, these denominations would naturally have been included in the set. If
dollars or eagles of the early period were available in beautiful condition
that would have sufficed. The problem therefore arose at the Mint as to how
to interpret and comply with the order. Should the authorized coins not in
current production be included?

No directive or instruction from the President or the Secretary of State
could override Section 10 of the Act of Congress passed April 2, 1792, which
provided that "the year of the coinage" be placed on each coin or change the
reduced weight of the eagle in Section 1 of the Act of June 28, 1834. If the
Secretary of State or the President had been asked to clarify the matter after
being told that no dollar or eagle dies or beautiful old specimens were on
hand, the exclusion of these denominations would have been the obvious
answer. No written inquiries were made by the Mint about this problem and
the President and the Secretary of State apparently remained unaware of it.
However, the Secretary of State in a letter dated December 2, 1834, requested national emblems to be placed on the exterior of the case in which the

coins were to be sent and set a deadline of December 20, 1834, for completion (see Appendix F).

The set of coins for Siam and Muscat were completed and delivered to Roberts. Prior to the scheduled sailing of the Peacock on April 10, 1835, a list of presents was suggested for Cochin-China and another list for Japan. Both lists included a "Set of Coins from the Mint of the U. States." John Forsyth wrote Roberts on March 31, 1835, "A letter has been written from the Department to the Director of the Mint requesting that the coins mentioned in the lists may be put up in a proper manner, and be forwarded to you at New York, under cover to the Collector of the Port." The text of the letter referred to is in Appendix G. These presentation sets should have consisted of coins dated 1835, all of which were in normal production except for the dollar and the eagle.

The sailing of the Peacock was delayed until April 27, 1835, and on April 21, 1835, Roberts wrote Forsyth from New York:

> I rec'd the small package containing the two sets of coins from the Director of the Mint by S. Swartwout Esq.—as it was sent per mail, it was taxed with a heavy postage of Twelve Dollars & 75 cents which I paid to Mr. S.

Roberts' memorandum book shows that he delivered "one box Coins (American)" to the Sultan of Muscat on October 1, 1835, and to the King of Siam "1 case U.S. Coins 1 package" on April 5, 1836.

Roberts contracted dysentery in Siam while celebrating the completion of the treaty and died at Macao on June 12, 1836, without contacting any other powers.[65] Captain Edmund P. Kennedy of the Peacock wrote to the State Department from Canton on June 30, 1836, that the expedition to Japan had to be given up and "I have directed that the presents be forwarded to the United States by the first vessel directed to the State Department." The two sets of U. S. coins for the Emperors of Cochin-China and Japan were no doubt returned in the manner indicated.

The exchange of presents between the Imaum of Muscat and the United States of America finally reached a climax when on September 3, 1839, the Imaum forcibly delivered a full grown lion and a lioness to the United States Consul in Tangier, who had to keep the animals in his house until he received permission by sea mail from the United States Department of State to send them to the zoo in Washington, D. C.[66] No inference is to be drawn from the foregoing that 1804 dollars are "Lyon" dollars[67] although there has been considerable lyin' concerning their status.

---

[65] Archives of the United States, Department of State, Record Group 59, Communications of Special Agents, Vol. 10 (Feb. 1, 1832, to Mar. 4, 1837); Domestic Letters, Vol. 27, p. 108 and 284.

[66] *Executive Documents*, 26th Congress, 1st Session, Vol. 360, Senate Doc. 488 (May 21, 1840).

[67] Dutch Crowns. The November 12, 1709, currency issue of the Colony of New York was payable in Lyon dollars.

The Origin of 1804 "Originals"

At the 1962 American Numismatic Association Annual Convention, David B. Spink spoke on "New Facts about an Old American Coin."[68] Spink, with James C. Risk participating, not only disclosed the existence of a previously unknown 1804 dollar but also revealed the fact that it was in a presentation case with other United States coins.

The case was covered in yellow morocco embossed with an American eagle and had depressions in blue velvet for eleven coins. Only nine coins were in the case.[69] These consisted of proofs of the 1834 half cent, one cent, dime, quarter, half dollar, quarter eagle without motto, and half eagle, as well as proofs of an 1804 dollar and an 1804 eagle. The unfilled openings were the size of an 1834 half dime and an 1834 quarter eagle with motto. The case, therefore, was designed for a complete set of 1834 coinage plus a dollar and an eagle. The case conforms in design and color to the case ordered for the King of Siam on November 11, 1834, and delivered to him on April 5, 1836. (See Chapter VIII and illustration on page 70.)

This 1804 dollar (Class I) has a raised flat border, crushed edge lettering, obverse die break, and all other characteristics of other known Class I specimens. The 1804 eagle is identical to the pattern described as Judd 33 (see illustration on page 41) and has no crosslet on the 4.

For the first time in numismatic history specific evidence has now come to light concerning the origin of the 1804 dollar. This discovery constitutes definite proof that the sets of United States coins given to the King of Siam and the Imaum of Muscat contained a dollar and an eagle, both dated 1804.

There is substantial evidence that the set for Muscat also contained the same coins. In the catalog of the sale of the American collection of C. A. Watters on June 14, 1917, in addition to the 1804 dollar there were an 1834 half dollar, quarter dollar, and half dime, all in proof condition,[70] and the 1834 dime, cent, and half cent, the condition of which were not specifically described but which probably were proofs.[71] Watters did not collect U. S. gold coins, accounting for the absence of the proof 1804 eagle. There were

---

[68] *Coin World,* Vol. 3, No. 124 (Aug. 31, 1962); *Numismatic News,* Vol. 10, No. 17 (Sept. 3, 1962).
[69] An uncirculated 1834 half dime has recently been placed in the hole provided for the missing proof 1834 half dime.
[70] Glendining & Co., Ltd., in London, included respectively in Lots 240, 246, and 254.
[71] Lots 250, 278, and 283 respectively contained groups of coins of one denomination graded in bulk.

no proofs of any other regular U. S. coinage dated prior to 1860. From the rarity of the 1834 proofs it is probable that the Watters 1804 dollar was from the set given to the Imaum of Muscat.

The sets to be given to the Emperors of Cochin-China and Japan were prepared in April, 1835, and apparently contained proofs dated 1835 with the exception of the dollar and the eagle. It has been shown that the dies for the proof 1801, 1802, and 1803 dollars were prepared at the same time as the 1804 dies, making it possible that the date of the dollar in the undelivered sets could be one of those dates. However, since no specimens of the proof 1801, 1802, or 1803 dollars are known whose striking can be attributed to the 1835 period, it must be assumed that the undelivered sets contained a proof 1804 dollar and a proof 1804 eagle.

The foregoing accounts for four specimens of the Class I 1804 dollars and the additional four known pieces must have been extra pieces prepared at the same time.

Although most early production dies were broken in coining operations,[72] some few in worn condition were retained. Punches, by their limited use, usually stayed in good condition, although the T punch used in cutting the die for the 1802 (B-6) dollar and the missing curl tip on the bust punch used on the 1801 (B-5) and the 1804 dollar dies are examples of damage to a punch. New letter and figure punches were sometimes bought outside the Mint.[73] Franklin Peale had carefully assembled, marked, and retained punches, tools, and dies dating from as far back as 1800, and on his discharge from the Mint in 1854, these were in the Coiner's possession. By 1869, there were over 700 such items on hand.[74] In the year 1834, certain punches for cutting early dollar dies still remained, such as the draped bust punch, the heraldic eagle punch, the large and small star punches, the letter punches, and some figure punches. Figure punches 1, 8, 0, and 3 remained even though the early figure 2 punch was broken, rusted, or lost. The edge lettering dies for dollars were also on hand. An early type figure 4 punch of the size for dollar dies was not apparently available.

Cutting new dies for early coins was easy, if the temptation or opportunity arose. Most of the die making tools prepared by former mint engravers and artists were available. The stage was set for the reincarnation of real or imaginary coinage as the employees of the Mint had substantial idle time on the job prior to the influx of gold after its discovery in California.[75]

The production during the winter of 1834 of dies for coins dated 1801, 1802, 1803, and 1804 cannot in any sense be construed to be experimental and thereby justified. The preparation of pattern dies and trial specimens was normal when carried out in connection with then current plans for Mint

[72] Reminiscences of Chas. K. Warner, *The Numismatist*, Vol. 23, No. 12 (Dec., 1910), p. 258.
[73] Frank H. Stewart, *History of the First United States Mint* (Camden, 1924), pp. 180, 185, 187–188.
[74] Interview of A. L. Snowden by S. K. Harzfeldt, October 12, 1880, *Numisma* (Nov., 1880), reprinted in *The Numismatist*, Vol. 50, No. 5 (May, 1937), p. 401, and in *Numismatic Scrapbook Magazine*, Vol. 22, No. 3 (Mar., 1956), p. 389; Letter of A. L. Snowden to E. Mason, Jr., dated December 14, 1871, in *Mason's Coin Collectors' Magazine*, Vol. 6, No. 1 (Jan., 1872), p. 15.
[75] "Report of an Investigation into the Official Conduct of the Chief Coiner," July 15, 1852, Letters from the U. S. Mint and Branches, Vol. 9 (V Series), National Archives.

production. The cutting of dies dated back thirty years or more is not a forward-looking experiment.

It is perfectly clear that if the Mint employees participating in the production of dies for and coinage of the 1804 dollar had felt that they were authorized or justified in making dies for an 1804 dollar in 1834 they would not have hesitated to say so. They actually did everything in their power to conceal that fact. It has been shown that the dies for the 1802 and 1803 proof dollars, because of hair curl evidence, were prepared just prior to the proof 1801 and 1804 dollar dies (see Chapter VII). This shows that the Mint employees did not intend to prepare only one dollar die for the sole purpose of filling in the presentation case. It shows that they were interested in producing a dollar dated 1804. They could have used the 1802 or 1803 dollar dies they prepared at the same time, but they knew that they had no legal right to make antedated dies or coins from them. Their authorization to make presentation sets did not call for any such improper action. They obviously thought that there would be no harm in cutting antedated dies with respect to a few pieces, but subsequently they must have learned the error of their ways.

No Mint official has ever disclosed when, why, or by whom the dies were made or the Class I 1804 dollars struck. If there had been any proper authorization or defensible justification for the 1804 dollar, it would have been pointed out at some time thereafter, instead of being whitewashed and avoided. Many of the employees must have known all the facts.

One of the reasons for a lack of any comment and a thorough concealment of what took place is that the principal Mint employees were one big happy family. During most of the nineteenth century the Mint was actually overflowing in nepotism. John Jacob Eckfeldt, a machinist and blacksmith, moved from Nuremberg, Bavaria, to Philadelphia before the American Revolution, and in 1783 made dies for the Mint of North America project sponsored by Robert Morris, for which Eckfeldt was paid $5^{18}\!/_{90}$ dollars by the government.[76] His son, Adam Eckfeldt (1769–1852), did blacksmith work for the Mint in 1792, became a full time employee in 1795, and was Chief Coiner from 1814 until 1839. His son, Jacob Reese Eckfeldt (1802–1872), co-author of *A Manual of Gold and Silver Coins of All Nations* and its supplements, began at the Mint in the assaying department in 1832 and continued for forty years.[77] The latter's son, Jacob Bausch Eckfeldt (1846–1938) began at the Mint in 1865, worked his way up to Assayer in 1881, and was in Mint service over sixty-four years.[78] George J. Eckfeldt, nephew of Adam Eckfeldt, was in the employ of the Mint as foreman of the Engraving Department beginning in 1830 and continuing for over thirty years. John M. Eckfeldt, son of George J. Eckfeldt, became the first Chief Coiner of the San Francisco Mint, serving

[76] Sylvester S. Crosby, *Early Coins of America* (Boston, 1875), p. 310; Frank H. Stewart, *History of the First United States Mint* (Camden, 1924), p. 81; *The Numismatist,* Vol. 39, No. 4 (Apr., 1926), p. 191.
[77] "The Passing of the Eckfeldts," *The Numismatist,* Vol. 43, No. 1 (Jan., 1930), p. 28; George G. Evans, *Illustrated History of the United States Mint* (Philadelphia, 1885 et seq.), p. 125 or 118.
[78] *The Numismatist,* Vol. 51, No. 10 (Oct., 1938), p. 886.

from 1854 until 1862 and returning in 1874 to that mint in the capacity of Melter and Refiner for a few months. William E. DuBois (1810–1881) began at the Mint in 1833, married Susanna Eckfeldt (sister of Jacob Reese Eckfeldt) in 1840, and eventually became Assayer on the death of his brother-in-law in 1872. The mother of William E. DuBois was Martha Patterson, the daughter of Robert Patterson (Mint Director 1806–1824) and the sister of Dr. Robert Maskell Patterson (Mint Director 1835–1851). Patterson DuBois, the son of William E. DuBois and Susanna Eckfeldt, began at the Mint in 1867 and became Assistant Assayer in 1882. It can be seen that the interrelated Eckfeldt-DuBois-Patterson clan contributed many principal officers in Mint operations for 100 years. James Ross Snowden (Mint Director 1853–1861) was the uncle of A. Loudon Snowden, who began his Mint service in 1857, becoming Coiner in 1866 and Superintendent in 1879. In addition, many other employees were close personal friends of those named.

This group consisted of efficient and loyal government employees with long records of devoted service. A mistake or over-enthusiastic numismatic impulse by one or more of this large group could readily be buried by the power of the other relatives, and actually was.

The Mint officials did not feel it necessary to justify their actions. They only pretended that the 1804 dollars were from genuine dies, and they kept discreetly quiet. They had no feeling that they had done anything really wrong. They put one specimen in the Mint Cabinet in 1838 and slowly began distributing the others at substantial intervals.

The Class I dollars dated 1804 have been distinguished by being called "originals," and in view of their true status, a change in that appellation would seem advisable. The word "original" implies an origin at the time of the 1804 date which appears on the coin, and because it can be misleading, should be abandoned when referring to the 1804 Class I dollars. They could be called "mint struck copies" if they were copies of a genuine 1804 dollar, but since no genuine 1804 dollar die or coin has ever existed, they are imaginary and might well be called "antedated fantasies." Some might even wish to call all of the 1804 dollars "Pieces de Caprice" or fabrications.

Although "the year of the coinage" was required to be on all coins by virtue of Section 10 of the Act of April 2, 1792, there was no penalty for violating this requirement. However, it could be claimed that antedated coins are in violation of the counterfeiting law of March 3, 1825, Chapter LXV, Section 20, which makes it a felony to falsely make, forge, or counterfeit or cause or procure to be made, forged or counterfeited any coin in the resemblance or similitude of the gold or silver coin which has been and may be coined at the Mint of the United States. The addition of the words "resemblance or similitude" made the 1825 Act much more effective than the Act of April 21, 1806, Chapter XLIX, Section 1, where those words were not included. It, therefore, could not be argued that because no genuine 1804 dollar existed the change in the date of the coin would make the coin completely different from a silver coin made at the United States Mint. The fact that the preparation of the dies and the coining of dollars dated 1804 took place at the Mint by Mint employees might not affect their illegality. Numismatic technicalities were not in the minds of the lawmakers when those statutes were written.

It is strange that no counterfeiting of the early dollars of the United States ever took place during the period of their circulation. Dr. J. D. Riddell, melter and refiner at the New Orleans Mint and professor of chemistry at the Medical College of Louisiana, was highly skilled in the detection of counterfeit coins circulating in the United States and said in 1845, "No counterfeits of the United States Dollar, have come under my observation."[79] If he had only known what had happened at the parent Mint!

The proof set of U. S. coins in its original presentation case as given to the King of Siam. The half dime and the half eagle with motto were missing from their openings in the case when it was found.

If Mint officials felt that each presentation set ordered late in 1834 should have included a dollar and an eagle there was a simple and proper solution. They should have obtained from banks in Philadelphia beautiful examples of dollars and eagles coined during the 1794–1804 period (but these would not have been proofs) or they should have prepared new dies with an 1834 date for dollars and eagles in order to strike proofs which complied with the 1834 standard of weight and fineness.

[79] J. D. Riddell, *A Monograph of the Silver Dollar* (New Orleans, 1845), p. 13.

The Exchange Between Stickney and the U. S. Mint

Matthew A. Stickney (1805–94) of Salem, Massachusetts, who acquired an 1804 dollar from the U. S. Mint on May 9, 1843, was the first private collector to obtain one. The transaction, as described in his own words in a letter to Edward Cogan, a New York coin dealer, dated Salem, Mass., July 2, 1867, was as follows:

✻ ✻ ✻

I was applied to by letter, July 4, 1866, by Mr. T. A. Andrews of Charlestown, Mass., for the Dollar of 1804, which he understood I had in my possession, and wished to obtain by purchase, for a friend in California, or information where he could get another. In reply I stated: 'I have a genuine Proof Dollar of the United States Coinage of 1804; I do not dispose of any coins not duplicates, at any price. It is not likely that if I parted with this dollar, I could ever obtain another, as I have been told by a gentleman (W. Elliot Woodward, Esq.), largely engaged in selling Coins at Auction, that he thought that it might bring one thousand dollars.' On the 18th of November, 1866, Mr. Andrews wrote me again, offering in the name of his friend '$1,000 in currency or the value in gold coin,' saying: 'I merely make the offer as requested to do, being aware that you stated that you did not dispose of coins except duplicates.' I declined the offer on the 23rd of the same month.

✻ ✻ ✻ Of the genuineness of my U. S. Dollar of 1804, I think there cannot be entertained a doubt, as it was handed me directly from the Cabinet of the U. S. Mint in Philadelphia, on the 9th of May, 1843, by one of its officers (Mr. W. E. DuBois), who still holds the same situation there, and can testify to it. It was not then considered any more valuable than any other of the series, and I only desired it to help make up the Chronological Series, which I perhaps was the first to attempt to make, of U. S. Coins.

✻ ✻ ✻

This dollar has never been out of my house since, or even handled by those who called to see it; and I was very careful that Monsieur Vattemare, when at my house, should not by some sleight of hand exchange it.

It is a perfect specimen; and I was not aware that there was any other original one existing, save the one left in the Cabinet of the Mint. It was obtained with other coins, by an honorable exchange of Pine-Tree money, and rarities not in their collection, one piece of which has since proved to be of exceeding rarity: the 'Immune Columbia' in gold, 1785—which Mr. Du Bois notices as a guinea re-struck and bearing the date of 1783, p. 129

of his work on the Collection of Coins belonging to the U. S. Mint, 1846—
and which I had obtained, the day before, of Beebee & Parshells in New
York.

As regards the authenticity of other specimens of the U. S. Dollar of
1804, I have no knowledge. Those having dollars of that date (Cohen and
Mickley) were not then known at the Mint as collectors, as appears by the
list of which I send you a copy, then obtained, 1843, from Mr. DuBois,
which remains, in his hand-writing, in my possession, with the addition
of the names of Philip Hone of New York and Robert Gilmore of Baltimore, which were added in the hand-writing of the late John Allan of
New York, who was also a distinguished collector.

Amateurs of Coins:—Dr. Roper, J. G. Morris, Esq.; Mr. David (nephew
of Mr. Morris); Mr. W. G. Mason; C. C. Ashmead; John Reeve; Mr.
Cooper, Camden; H. A. Muhlenberg, Reading; Rev. Dr. Robbins of Hartford (my uncle); Edward B. Wynn, Hamilton.

I have been for nearly fifty years a systematic collector of coins; and
for a very long period, almost without a competitor; and very many of
the rare coins which now enrich other cabinets were, by great solicitation,
obtained from me. My facilities for collecting coins were remarkably
good, through the friendship of Beebee & Parshell's Bullion Exchange,
22½ Wall Street, New York. I received from them, quarterly, from 1843,
rare coins I was in search of, at par; and under all the changes of the firm,
they continued to favor me till 1854, when in consequence of ill health, I
gave up my business, and ceased to make active efforts for additions to
my cabinet, only obtaining the regular series of proof coins from the
Mint which I have received from them for twenty-five years.[80]

There are many statements in the foregoing letter which give rise to
further inquiry. Stickney had been a systematic collector of American coins
for almost 26 years at the time of the transaction and probably was the most
experienced person in American numismatics at the time.

1. If we assume that he owned his Brasher doubloon by 1843, why did he
dispose of the only other American gold coin he had ever seen from the
period prior to the establishment of the United States Mint? The two Mark
Newby farthings in gold and the unique 1792 Washington President in gold
were not then known, and the 1787 Fugio (Newman 103-EE) had not yet
been struck.

2. If he did "not part with any coins not duplicates at any price" why did
he violate his policy in this case as to the gold Immune Columbia?

3. Why did he trade a theretofore unknown Immune Columbia gold piece
along with Pine Tree coinages for an 1804 dollar "which was not considered
any more valuable than other of the series" in 1843?

4. Since he was visiting New York when he acquired the Immune Columbia, why did he part with what he knew was a rarity without even bringing
it home to Salem, Massachusetts, to compare to his similar copper pieces?

5. Since he must have known that the Mint had a duplicate 1804 dollar

---

[80] Matthew A. Stickney, "More About the 1804 Dollar," *American Journal of Numismatics*, Vol. 2. No. 4
(Aug., 1867), p. 1; Henry Chapman, *Catalogue of the Stickney Sale held June 25, 1907*, p. 81; Wayte
Raymond, *The History of the Stickney 1804 Dollar* (New York, 1931); B. Max Mehl, *Catalogue of the
William C. Atwater collection sold June 11, 1946*, Item 213; Arthur D. McIlvaine, "The Silver Dollars of
the United States of America," *Numismatic Notes and Monographs No. 95* (New York, 1941), p. 33.

available before he went to Philadelphia, why didn't he use some of the many other duplicates he had for the exchange?

6. Since Stickney was trying to prove that his trade with the Mint was "honorable," why does he say that the Immune Columbia piece "has since proved to be of extreme rarity," indicating that neither he nor Wm. DuBois recognized it as such at the time?

7. Why did he accept a proof coin dated 1804 as "original" when he knew such a type of brilliant proof was not made in that period?

8. Since Pine Tree shillings were quoted at 16 cents in current money exchange lists,[81] why does he mention the Pine Tree money as the principal part of the trade with the Mint and indicate that the Immune Columbia gold piece was just an incidental part?

9. How panicky can a man be in finding an unknown gold rarity in New York on one day and immediately taking a horse drawn stage coach to Philadelphia to trade it by the next day?

The Immune Columbia—Nova Constellatio gold piece (Crosby VII-30) which the United States Mint received in the exchange and which today is a part of the collection of the Smithsonian Institution is unique.[82] It is struck over an English guinea dated 1775 and not 1783 as the letter stated. The design of the English guinea shows clearly on both sides. This indicates that the gold piece was not made as a pattern for submission for coinage or as a presentation piece. It shows only that a smooth gold planchet was not available, and, therefore, it was not made by a properly equipped minting enterprise as were the copper Immune Columbia pieces.

Much unpublished data has been assembled about the Immune Columbia pieces since Crosby. The Edwards copies of the Immune Columbia pieces which Crosby and others described as fabrications[83] are struck from genuine dies, as evidenced by the identical hub, letter, and figure punches found both on the genuine pieces and on the "Edwards" pieces. In addition, another Immune Columbia gold piece struck over an English guinea has appeared struck with a combination of the admittedly genuine 1785 Immune Columbia die and the "Edwards" Nova Constellatio die, tying the genuine dies and the "Edwards" dies together. It is well known that the genuine Immune Columbia obverse die was used in combination with both a Vermont obverse and an imitation English halfpence obverse in the 1787–9 period at the Machin's Mills mint near Newburgh, New York. It is also noticeable that one specimen of the "Edwards" silver piece is struck with rusted dies over a reeded edge foreign coin of the type produced by a collar. It is identical in circumference and reeding to a florin of Victoria which was minted first in 1849. If a florin

[81] J. Thompson, *Coin Chart Manual* (New York, 1849); "Gold and Silver Coins Most Generally Found in Circulation," *Lord's Supplement to the Cincinnati Detector* (Cincinnati, 1850), p. 24; *Taylor's United States Money Reporter* (New York, 1851), p. 37.
[82] Sylvester S. Crosby, *Early Coins of America* (Boston, 1875), pp. 313, 314; T. L. Comparette, *Catalogue of the Coins, Tokens and Metals of the Mint of the United States of America at Philadelphia* (Washington, D. C., 1912), p. 10, p. 20, Plate 1; V. Clain-Stefanelli, *The Numismatist*, Vol. 71, No. 1 (Jan., 1958), p. 43.
[83] Sylvester S. Crosby, *Early Coins of America* (Boston, 1875), Plate X-26; Richard D. Kenney, "Struck Copies of Early American Coins," *Coin Collector's Journal*, Vol. 19, No. 1 (Jan., 1952), p. 11; E. J. Attinelli, *Numisgraphics* (New York, 1876), p. 42.

of Queen Victoria was the base of the "Edwards" piece, as it seems to be, the existence of some of the Immune Columbia dies is extended until years after 1843 when the gold Immune Columbia made its dramatic appearance.

John A. Nexsen was the first challenger of Stickney's sincerity, based upon the fact that the two 1804 dollars Stickney saw when he visited the Mint were both brilliant proofs. Nexsen questions Stickney's use of the word "original" by noting, "It does seem very strange that Mr. Stickney, who had been collecting coins since 1817 and had not come across an 1804 dollar, when confronted with two 'proof specimens' at the Mint in 1843, should have accepted them as 'originals' without questioning the source from which they came."[84] Owners of questionable rarities are often reluctant to state facts or opinions contrary to what they want to believe, and Stickney may have been influenced by this common human trait. He was proud of his 1804 dollar and did not hesitate to defend it.

Armed with the foregoing facts, we can subject the inconsistencies of Stickney's actions and statements to a new hypothesis. If Stickney knew that the Immune Columbia gold piece which was obtained from a bullion exchange was a restrike prepared by someone by using the existing dies, he would have no respect for the coin and would not hesitate to part with it. Wm. DuBois naturally knew that the 1804 dollar was struck from dies which the Mint had recently cut, and he had no respect for his dollar. Whether each knew what the other knew is unimportant. The important fact is that the trade was in a warped sense quite "honorable," that is, as honorable for one party to the transaction as for the other. Each apparently knowingly traded a fabrication to the other in one of the "fastest" transactions in numismatic history, and both were delighted with the outcome.

B. Max Mehl had his own interpretation of Stickney's letter. In describing the Cohen 1804 dollar, Mehl, in the catalogue of the Manning collection sold May 17, 1921, stated that the Stickney letter was "important in establishing beyond a doubt not only that the dollar of 1804 is contemporaneous, but what is most important in the case, he mentions the fact that Messrs. Eckfeldt and DuBois did not know of Col. Cohen and his 1804 dollar at the time they published their book in 1842."[85] To refute Mehl's erroneous assertion, it is sufficient to mention that (a) Eckfeldt's name is not even mentioned in Stickney's letter; (b) likewise, the 1842 book is not mentioned; (c) the 1842 book makes no comment on the subject; and (d) Stickney did not mention whether DuBois knew or did not know of any other 1804 dollars. All Stickney said was that he (Stickney) was not aware of any other 1804 dollar than the Mint piece and that DuBois knew ten coin collectors in 1843 other than Stickney. Stickney even mentioned other collectors who were not known to DuBois.

As to why Stickney wrote the July 2, 1867, letter, see Chapter XIII.

[84] "Dollar of 1804," *American Journal of Numismatics,* Vol. 32, No. 1 (July, 1897), p. 11.
[85] *The Numismatist,* Vol. 50, No. 7 (July, 1937), p. 612; *Selections from The Numismatist,* Vol. I, p. 126.

The Scandal of 1858

A few years prior to the "scandal" of 1858, there had been unwholesome practices in the Mint which had encouraged the use of the facilities for personal gain. The officers of the Mint had been cutting dies for medals and striking them not only for governmental purposes but also for private persons or corporations. The compensation for private work was received by the officials personally, even though the work was done at the Mint during business hours and by Mint employees.[86] The New York *Evening Express* of November 14, 1850, called the Mint "a workshop for their private gain," even though the intrinsic value of the bullion used was paid to the Mint. Adam Eckfeldt, in addition, had struck copies of national medals from Mint dies, and Franklin Peale had followed that custom. Charges were made against Franklin Peale in 1851 that Peale had used the Mint for his personal benefit "to carry on an extensive lucrative and improper business of manufacturing medals" and further that he required the Mint workmen to labor for him "without just distribution of the profits of said business to the workmen." By 1854 there had been removed from the Mint sixty-eight sets of dies for national medals, and the report of their recovery by Eckfeldt and Peale was transmitted to Congress with a request for legislation to authorize copies to be struck.[87] Peale's discharge from the Mint followed this "recovery" so quickly that one wonders whether or not they were recovered from Peale himself.

The only 1804 dollar known with a plain unlettered edge is the U. S. Mint specimen now in the Smithsonian Institution. It is a combination of the 1804 obverse with reverse Y and is designated as the Class II 1804 dollar. It weighs only 381½ grains, about 8 per cent less than the 416 grain standard for early silver dollars. The obverse and reverse are about 175 degrees offset rather than 180 degrees. It is struck over a 5 franc Bern Shooting Thaler dated 1857, which ordinarily weighs 385 grains as minted (see illustration). From the date of the coin over which this 1804 dollar was struck there is no question that the overstrike was made after 1857, and therefore at least 15

---

[86] Letters of the U. S. Mint and Branches, 7/1/51–12/31/52, Vol. 9 (V Series), National Archives.
[87] Letter dated April 5, 1854, from James R. Snowden to James Guthrie and letter dated March 21, 1854, from Franklin Peale to James R. Snowden in *Executive Documents,* 725-106 (33rd Congress, 1st Session).

The obverse of the 1804 Class II dollar (top) struck over the reverse of an 1857 Bern Shooting Thaler (bottom). The dollar shows traces of the rays projecting from the lower and right arms of the cross, the right gun stock, the wreath knot and the border dentils of the Thaler.

The reverse of the 1804 Class II dollar (top) placed into a position to be compared to the obverse of an 1857 Bern Shooting Thaler (bottom). The dollar shows traces of the gun barrel, the sword hilt and handle, the lower legs and the border dentils of the Thaler.

77

years after the illustration of the Class I dollar appeared in the Eckfeldt and DuBois 1842 publication. The overstrike is the first appearance of the reverse Y.

The earliest clue to the appearance of other than Class I 1804 dollars is found in the first numismatic book on American coinage, published in 1858. In Supplement No. 1, entitled "Recent Prices of American Coins,"[88] there is innocently stated, "Flying eagle, dollars and halves, 1836, '38 and '39, $5 and $10 each and even more. Dollars of 1804, 1851, 1852 each $5."

The very publication of the book showed the spreading interest in American coinage, but the particular mention of the rare dates in dollars of 1804, 1851, and 1852 was significant. The flying eagle patterns were each alleged to have an equal or greater value than an 1804 dollar. Hickcox must have had a clue that more of each of these coins were available, although he may not have known that specimens of each had currently been produced (see Chapter XII).

James Ross Snowden, Director of the United States Mint (1853–61), admitted early in 1859 that collectors had sought and were seeking rare types of United States coins (and patterns) and that a few of such coins were issued. His letter asking the Secretary of the Treasury for permission to continue to do so is as follows:

Mint of the United States,
Philadelphia, Jan. 22, 1859

Sir,

    We are daily pressed upon, by Collectors of Coins from all parts of the country either by letter or in person, for specimens of pattern pieces of coin, and rare types. A few of these having been in every case issued,— some of them got into the hands of dealers and are sold at excessive prices. I propose, with your approbation, to check this traffic, and at the same time to gratify a taste which has lately greatly increased in this country, and seems to be increasing every day, namely, by striking some of each kind and affixing a price to them, so that the profits may enure to the benefit of the Mint Cabinet of Coins and ores which is the property of the U. States; an exact account of which will be kept and rendered to the Department.

I have the honor to be
with great respect,
Your faithful servant
James Ross Snowden
Director of the Mint

Hon.—Howell Cobb
   Sec.—of the Treasury
    Washington City

Since no reply to this letter has been located in the Archives and no account book of the suggested profits has been found, it is proper to conclude that no permission was granted.[89] The letter also indicates that the previous disposition of "rare types" of coins was done with Director Snowden's knowl-

---

[88] John J. Hickcox, *An Historical Account of American Coinage* (Albany, 1858), p. 149.
[89] National Archives, Record Group 104, Letters Mint & Branches, General Correspondence. File Box 78; Walter Breen, "Semiofficial Restrikes of the Philadelphia Mint," *The Numismatist*, Vol. 66, No. 10 (Oct., 1953), p. 1038.

edge. His complaint that the dealers charged excessive prices for the coins does not consider the right or wrong of accommodating the individuals seeking the coins. It is perfectly clear that Snowden thought the action of his department was questionable and wished a favorable Treasury Department ruling based upon the theory that the profits would help the Mint Cabinet. The serious question was whether or not the individual employees of the Mint had been profiting personally from the disposition of rare coins. The subsequent action relative to the dollars dated 1804 gives us the answer.

Apparently, the earliest written inquiry concerning the Class II group of dollars dated 1804 was an unanswered letter dated July 18, 1860, from Jeremiah Colburn of Boston to Snowden in Philadelphia, as follows:[90]

> I have just received from your city a dollar of 1804, the price of which is $75.00, the person who sends it says—I feel perfectly satisfied that if not an original that it is from the original die. I shall be greatly obliged if you will inform me if the die is in the Mint and if specimens have been struck from it.

A. J. K. Curtis, a New York City antiquarian dealer, wrote to Director James R. Snowden on July 19, 1860, "Will you please inform me if the 1804 Dollar has been restruck at the Mint as I have heard that several have been seen and offered for sale." To this Director Snowden replied, "In response to your inquiry I have to state that no specimen of the dollar of 1804 has been struck at the Mint; and I am informed by the foreman of the dies that there are no means of doing so."

Apparently, Colburn and other respected members of the Boston Numismatic Society investigated the matter further. After the appointment of a new Director of the Mint, they then wrote the following:

Boston, Mass; Nov. 12, 1861.

Hon. James Pollock,
    Director of the Mint of the United States.

The undersigned, a committee of the Boston Numismatic Society, were instructed to call your attention to the abuses which have of late years been practiced at the Mint of the United States, whereby numbers of Pattern pieces, and coins from dies of former years, have been freely struck, and disposed of by Employes of the Mint to dealers who have in turn disposed of them at great prices. Two years since Members of this Society were offered specimens of the dollar of 1804, of which, previously only three or four examples were known; on applying to the Director of the Mint he peremptorily replied that none had been struck; further investigation resulted in the fact being proven that three specimens had been struck, two of which had been sold for $75.00 each; various pattern pieces, in large numbers, have also been issued without the sanction of the proper officers. Under these circumstances we respectfully urge the expediency of destroying the dies of the current coin, and also of pattern pieces at the close of each year.

Very Respectfully Yours,
    George W. Pratt, Winslow Lewis, Henry Davenport, Jere'h Colburn

[90] Record Group 104, National Archives; Walter Thompson, "What the Archives Reveal About the 1804 Dollars," *The Numismatist*, Vol. 27, No. 8 (Aug., 1961), p. 1993.

This letter confirms the fact that 1859 was the date when dealers offered 1804 dollars for sale to collectors, that at least three had been struck, and that two had been sold for $75.00 each. It also alleged that the previous Director of the Mint, James Ross Snowden, had denied the fact that any additional dollars had been struck during his administration (1853–1860). The letter charges that Mint employees struck and sold coins for personal gain.

The reply is as follows:[91]

Nov. 21 (1861)

Gentlemen

Yours of the 12 inst. has been rec'd.

The abuses to which you refer, if they have ever had an existence, can no longer be practiced in this Institution. The practice of striking pattern pieces and coins from dies of former years cannot be too strongly condemned, and great care is now taken to prevent the re-currence of any such abuse. All the dies of former years are secured in such manner that it is impossible for any one to obtain possession of them without the knowledge of the director. The dies of the current coins and of pattern pieces will be destroyed at the close of the year. The dies of the past few years have also been destroyed.

J. A. Pollock
Director

The fact that this answer does not deny any of the charges is important. Granted, it carefully intends to avoid admitting anything, but the author makes a slip by confessing that "care is now taken to prevent the re-currence of any such abuse." It also admits that certain early dies were being retained in safekeeping and that the Director would have knowledge if they were removed.

It took many years to smoke out the facts. In 1868 it was pointed out that the 1804 dollars which got out of the Mint in 1858 had plain smooth edges instead of lettered edges; that C. P. Nichols of Springfield, Massachusetts, bought one from William Idler, the Philadelphia coin dealer, for $75.00; that Edward Cogan, the New York coin dealer, had received one; and that both were returned to the United States Mint on request.[92]

Because it was reported to the Numismatic and Antiquarian Society of Philadelphia in 1878 that 1804 dollars struck from "genuine dies" were then being offered for sale, an inquiry was directed to William E. DuBois, Curator of Numismatics of the Mint Cabinet. His written response denied the fact, but added other comments. As to the 1858–60 episode (which DuBois inadvertently dated 1868), he stated that five 1804 dollars (Class II) were then coined; that four were recovered, three being destroyed in his presence, and one being placed in the Mint Cabinet. He pointed out that "the fifth is lying around loose somewhere unknown, like a raging lion ready to prey on the unwary." He confesses that "in these latter days of virtue no such practices

[91] Record Group 104, National Archives; Walter Thompson, "What the Archives Reveal About 1804 Dollars," *The Numismatist*, Vol. 27, No. 8 (Aug., 1961), p. 1993.
[92] *American Journal of Numismatics*, Vol. 3, No. 1 (May, 1868), p. 7; Vol. 36, No. 4 (Apr., 1902), p. 122; see Vol. 39, No. 4 (Apr., 1905), p. 103.

are indulged in." The excerpts from this correspondence are reported in the *American Journal of Numismatics*, Vol. 12, No. 4 (April, 1878), p. 102.

The fifth specimen referred to has never appeared unless its edge was lettered so as to convert it into a Class III specimen. The statement however is an official admission of the 1858–60 reuse of the dies and of the fact that the moral standards at the Mint had previously been much less virtuous. DuBois apparently did not know that in 1878 Class III 1804 dollars were being offered for sale.

Finally, in 1880 S. K. Harzfeld, a Philadelphia coin dealer, became disturbed over unfair distribution of patterns and coins by the Mint and had an interview with the Director, A. Loudon Snowden, nephew of James R. Snowden, who had, according to the Boston Numismatic Society committee, denied the production of 1804 dollars. The younger Snowden stated that coins were restruck at the Mint during his uncle's administration for exchange of specimens to improve the Mint Cabinet, but that his uncle did not personally benefit.[93] The report of the interview continued as follows:

> About this period an old employe of the mint, a relative of one of the first and most valuable officers of the mint, who had charge of the dies in the engraver's department, was discovered by the sales made by an erring son to have taken impressions from 1804 and some other dies. On this discovery vigorous efforts were put forth to recover the coins, and it is believed that most, if not all, were returned and destroyed, and precautions were taken to prevent a re-occurrence of a like error. Several of these dies were destroyed, and the balance—four or five in number—were boxed and sealed up and placed in the director's vault, . . .

Ebenezer Locke Mason, in describing personal numismatic reminiscences when he operated a store in Philadelphia on the east side of North Second St. near Buttonwood St. (which building, curiously enough, was owned by numismatist Montroville W. Dickeson) during the year 1860, said:[94]

"Here was offered by young Eckfeldt three genuine U. S. 1804 dollars at $70 each and nearly all the rare ½ cents in dozens of duplicates were purchased."

Whereas A. Loudon Snowden gives facts from which the reader should infer that a young Eckfeldt was the person who offered the 1804 dollars for sale, Mason specifically names Eckfeldt. A young Eckfeldt, accompanied by a friend, was also accused by W. Elliot Woodward of selling rare patterns during the same period.[95] According to the A. Loudon Snowden interview quoted above, George J. Eckfeldt who had been in the employ of the Mint since 1830 and who was foreman in the Engraving Department in 1858 is the man behind the 1858 restriking. The "erring son" (assuming the scorekeeper should not charge the father with the error) must have been Theodore Eckfeldt (1837–1893) because the other son, John M. Eckfeldt (1831–1874), had been in California since 1854 as Chief Coiner of the San Francisco Mint.

[93] Edouard Frossard, *Numisma*, Nov., 1880; *The Numismatist*, Vol. 50, No. 5 (May, 1937), p. 401; *Numismatic Scrapbook Magazine*, Vol. 22, No. 3 (Mar., 1956), p. 389.
[94] *Mason's Coin Collectors' Magazine*, Vol. 4 (June, 1882), p. 10.
[95] W. Elliot Woodward's Catalogue of the Sale of the Heman Ely collection on January 8, 1884, Lot 561, and of the Sale of the Ferguson Haines collection on October 13, 1880, Lot 921.

Although in 1885 the Chapmans, whose comments are included in the official history of the U. S. Mint,[96] confirmed the 1858 restriking of 1804 dollars, the most thorough report came from Mason in answer to an inquiry sent in to his magazine.[97] Mason repeats much of what he previously said and states that the plain edge restrikes were "surreptitiously struck." They were proof-like, and one was bought by Wm. Idler, Philadelphia coin dealer, sold to a collector (C. P. Nichols), recovered with two others through the efforts of R. C. Davis, and returned to the U. S. Mint for destruction. The Mint retained one and melted the two others. The dies were then sealed up.

It has been asserted that R. L. Stuart, a sugar refiner, caused the 1858 restriking through political influence,[98] but this does not seem likely.

The flurry of comment made it appear as though a heinous crime had been committed. It was alleged that there was "Connivance of some of the employees at the Mint" and that the coins "were struck surreptitiously, in the dead of night."[99] In these same articles it is stated that the coins were struck without a collar. This erroneous conclusion was reached because the edge was plain.

Actually, there was almost no control over the restriking and disposition of patterns of every type, including the Gobrecht dollars and regular issues of the 1851 and 1852 dollars, 1827 quarter, and a long series of rare half cents. This was being done to add to the Mint Cabinet Collection, to have trading material to exchange for coins the Mint Cabinet did not have,[100] to develop Director James R. Snowden's personal collection of Washington coins and medals by exchanges,[101] and to add to the personal collection of Mint Coiner Linderman and many others. One of the clearest pieces of evidence of what was then going on is the existence of an 1838 Gobrecht pattern dollar in proof condition struck over an 1859 United States Dollar.[102] Mint employees, dealers, and collectors were "raiding the ice box" to satisfy their appetites. There was no chaperone, for Director James R. Snowden was hungry, too.

The real cause for the commotion was the irritation and wrath of collectors who already had dollars dated 1804 in their collections. They were startled by the new group of 1804 dollars and saw their "rarities" becoming more common by chicanery. It was W. Elliot Woodward, a Boston coin dealer,

[96] S. H. and H. Chapman, *The Chapman Collection Sale* on May 14, 1885, No. 354; George G. Evans, *Illustrated History of the United States Mint* (Philadelphia, 1885, *et seq.*), p. 64; *The Numismatist*, Vol. 50, No. 7 (July, 1937), p. 614.

[97] *Mason's Monthly Illustrated Coin Collectors' Magazine*, Vol. 1, No. 12 (May, 1885), p. 121.

[98] Geoffrey C. Adams, "The 1804 Dollar?," *The Numismatist*, Vol. 17, No. 9 (Sept., 1904), p. 274.

[99] *American Journal of Numismatics*, Vol. 36, No. 4 (Apr., 1902), p. 122; *Mason's Coin Collectors' Magazine*, Vol. 13, No. 1 (June, 1890), p. 5; *American Journal of Numismatics*, Vol. 39, No. 4 (Apr., 1905), p. 103.

[100] *Numisma* (Nov., 1880), reprinted in *The Numismatist*, Vol. 50, No. 5 (May, 1937), p. 401, and in *The Numismatic Scrapbook Magazine*, Vol. 22, No. 3 (Mar., 1956), p. 389; See comment by W. Elliot Woodward in sale catalog of Ferguson Haines collection on Oct. 13, 1880, Lot 921.

[101] Walter Thompson, "What the Archives Reveal About 1804 Dollars," *The Numismatic Scrapbook Magazine*, Vol. 27, No. 8 (Aug., 1961), p. 1991; W. C. Prime, "Coin in America," *Harper's New Monthly Magazine*, Vol. 20 (Mar., 1860), p. 475.

[102] Discovered by Louis Werner. See: Walter Breen, "Some Unpublished Rarities," *The Numismatist*, Vol. 70, No. 5 (May, 1957), p. 531; A. M. Kagin and Paul Kagin, "The Most Notorious U. S. Coin," *The Numismatic Scrapbook Magazine*, Vol. 27, No. 10 (Oct., 1961), p. 2587.

who noticed that the edges were not lettered.[103] Thus, there was no denial that inadvertently a clue remained clearly differentiating the new dollars from the Class I lettered edge pieces.

Although the different reverse die was probably not noticed on the new supply of 1804 dollars before their recall, the failure to letter the edge was sufficient evidence to condemn the enterprise. Fortunately, the Mint Cabinet kept a specimen of this coinage.

By 1887, a novel excuse had been developed for the 1858 connivance. E. L. Royal, Assistant Curator of the Mint Cabinet, described the plain edged 1804 dollar as a restrike which was "struck from the original die, but is much lighter in weight and intended merely to exhibit the reverse side of the coin."[104] This "whitewash" is not thick enough to keep its fallacies from showing through. He obviously did not check the reverse die to ascertain that it was different from the Mint's lettered edge piece. He should have known that any heraldic reverse dollar from 1798 to 1803 was adequate to show a similar reverse and also that the Mint collection did not keep two specimens of each United States coin to show the reverse.

By 1913, S. H. Chapman had forgotten what he wrote in 1885 and made many careless comments.[105] When he increased the number of plain edge restrikes from 3 to 10, changed the date of their striking from 1858 to 1870, and stated that one was still in England, he contradicted what he had said in 1885. He further confused the matter by writing that a subsequent group of restrikes were made in 1876, which was 7 years after the date at which he previously said the dies had been destroyed. He named as the guilty Mint official, the nephew of a Director of the Mint; he should have said uncle if he intended to involve Director James R. Snowden as a participant in the restriking project. Chapman also inflated the prices which had been paid for the plain edge 1804 dollars from $75 to $200 each. His 1913 comments must therefore be considered of no reliability.

It is important to point out that in all of the comment involving the discovery and recall of the plain edge 1804 dollars during the 1858–60 period, there was no indication that any collector or dealer felt that the Class I 1804 dollars were not actually coined in 1804.

---

[103] *American Journal of Numismatics*, Vol. 36, No. 4 (Apr., 1902), p. 122.
[104] *American Journal of Numismatics*, Vol. 22, No. 2 (Oct., 1887), p. 48.
[105] S. H. Chapman, *Sale of the Lyman Collection on November 7, 1913*, Lot 16; *The Numismatist*, Vol. 50, No. 7 (July, 1937), p. 610; *Selections from The Numismatist* (Racine, 1960), Vol. I, p. 124; *Numismatic Scrapbook Magazine*, Vol. 6, No. 5 (May, 1940), p. 284.

Aftermath of the Scandal

Public knowledge of the use of dies at the Mint for striking coins for the personal financial benefit of its employees initiated many changes to prevent a recurrence of such a situation. Discussions were formalized by James B. Longacre, Mint Engraver, in letters dated August 17, 1860, and August 22, 1860, to John R. Snowden, Mint Director, suggesting "for the better security of the dies, etc.—a more precise control of the striking presses, etc.—necessary process connected with the use of them" that the responsibility be placed on the engraver. Any use of the dies without the engraver's knowledge "offers a temptation if not a pretext for indirect proceedings whenever there may be sufficient inducement" and "is now demonstrably unsafe." A written order for every use of the dies should be required stating the nature of the pieces to be struck, the number to be struck, and to whom to be delivered. A register of all dies should be prepared. All dies not in use should be sealed up and identified. Any employee should be suspended for a violation of the rules.

On July 30, 1860, the 1804 dollar obverse die, with about thirty other dies, was sealed up and put in a box for safekeeping in the Mint Director's vault. It was due to the loss of the list of these dies that a recheck of the contents of the box was undertaken in 1867, and the following important document, located in 1961 by Walter Thompson,[106] was prepared:

> May 18, 1867
>
> On the 8th of July 1859 several experimental Dies were boxed, sealed, and placed in the Vault in the Cabinet by the then Director of the Mint and a list thereof was filed in the Director's Office. Another sealed box of experimental Dies was placed in said vault July 30, 1860, and a list filed in the same office. Neither of these papers can now be found, and the Director deems it proper to have the boxes opened and again sealed up. It is ordered that the boxes referred to shall be opened this day in the presence of the Director, Chief Coiner & Engraver. A list of the Dies shall then be made. Immediately after which the dies shall be replaced in the boxes and sealed up under the official seals of the Director & Engraver.
>
> H. R. Linderman
> Director

---

[106] Record Group 104, National Archives; Walter Thompson, "The 1804 Dollar Die and Others Found at the Mint in 1867," *Numismatic Scrapbook Magazine*, Vol. 27, No. 12 (Dec., 1961), p. 3185.

List of Dies Sealed up in Box by Director of the Mint July 30th 1860
& resealed May 18th 1867

Dollar Die 1804
Silver Dollar Dies 1838
Silver Dollar Dies 1836
Silver Dollar Dies 1839
Experiment Dies half dollars 1 head & 4 Rev. 1859
Paquet Half Dollar Dies 1859
Paquet Quarter Dollar Die 1859
Half Dollar Die 1858
Half Dollar Die 1859
Dollar Dies (Silver) ....1851 & 1852
Half Cent Die 1836
Half Cent Die 1851
Half Cent Die 1852
Half Cent Die 1844
Half Cent Die 1846
Half Cent Die 1847
Half Cent Die 1848
Half Cent Die 1842
Half Cent Die 1840
Half Cent Die 1852
Quarter Dollar Die 1827
Experimental Gold Dollar Die 1852
Experimental Gold Dollar Die 1836

May 18, 1867

List of Dies Sealed up in Box by Director of the Mint July 8th 1859 &
resealed May 18th 1867

3 Flying Eagles 1 Cent obverses ....2–1854 & 1–1855
1 Liberty Head 1 Cent obverse 1854
1 Reverse 1 Cent obverse
1 Ring Cent obverse & Reverse 1850
1 Cent (Liberty Seated) obverse & Reverse 1851
1 Tenth Silver Cent obverse & Reverse
1 Cent blank obverse & wreath Reverse
1 2 Cent Eagle obverse & Reverse
1 3 Cent Liberty Cap obverse & Reverse Silver
1 3 Cent Figure 3 obverse & Reverse Silver

The significance of the foregoing record is enormous.

The document refers to all the dies as "experimental dies." If any of the dies had been regular production dies, then Linderman should not have called them experimental dies in each case. This includes the 1804 dollar, the 1827 quarter, the group of half cent dies, and the 1851 and 1852 dollar dies. All of the others are recognized as patterns. This can properly be construed as Director Linderman's admission that the die for the 1804 dollar (first on the list) should be classed as experimental rather than an old remaining production die. As heretofore shown, it cannot even be classified as experimental because it is antedated and does not relate to future Mint production. Referring to the 1804 dollar die as experimental appears to be more of an excuse for its existence.

The document lists "Dollar Die 1804," in the singular, and not Dollar Dies 1804, in the plural. It lists "Quarter Dollar Die 1827," and not Quarter Dollar Dies 1827, etc. In other instances, such as the Gobrecht pattern dollars of 1836, 1838, and 1839, the plural "Dies" is used. In still other instances, obverse or reverse or both are mentioned. It is therefore obvious that both of the reverses of the 1804 dollar, the reverse of the 1827 quarter, the reverse of the half cents, etc., were not included. The dies for the 1801, 1802, and 1803 proof dollars were also missing. Although it is possible that some of these missing dies could have been secreted by Mint employees, it is highly improbable. It would be purposeless for anyone to hold out a group of reverses when the corresponding obverses were under special safekeeping. The only sound conclusion is that the reverse dies of the 1804 dollar, the 1827 quarter, etc., were destroyed in 1860, shortly after the misuse of the 1804 dollar dies was disclosed in the Mint scandal. The conclusion was confirmed on October 12, 1880, when S. K. Harzfeld interviewed A. Loudon Snowden, then Mint Superintendent, and Snowden pointed out that "precautions were taken to prevent a re-occurrence of a like error. Several of these dies were destroyed, and the balance—four or five in number—were boxed and sealed up and placed in the Director's vault."[107] It can be noted that "several," not all, of the misused dies were destroyed. Obverses were saved because they contained the date. Thus, it is clear that the reverse dies of the 1804 dollar were destroyed along with the reverse of the 1827 quarter and possibly others. The Gobrecht dollar obverses and reverses were apparently retained and boxed because of their artistic beauty. There could be no more abuses of the 1804 dollar because the reverses were destroyed. The 1867 order of Director Linderman and the interview with Superintendent A. Loudon Snowden in 1880 thoroughly corroborate one another on these crucial points.

It should be noted that in the dates of the half cent dies in the foregoing May 18, 1867, schedule the die dated 1851 was apparently a misreading of 1831. Also the half cent die dated 1852 is repeated and the dates 1841, 1843, and 1845 are not in the group.

On becoming Chief Coiner in 1866, A. Loudon Snowden found in a vault under his jurisdiction a collection of over seven hundred old hubs and dies dating from about 1800 through 1854. These punches and dies are not to be confused with those dies which Director Linderman had in his vault. In 1869 A. Loudon Snowden discussed with Linderman the importance of destroying them, and they were heated and defaced by sledge without one impression being made from any of them. This was immediately reported to numismatists on behalf of A. Loudon Snowden by Edward Cogan.[108] Linderman then had all dies in his vault destroyed, but had four or five impressions struck from each of the pairs of dies in his vault. Snowden said that the

---

[107] *Numisma* (Nov., 1880), reprinted in *The Numismatist,* Vol. 50, No. 5 (May, 1937), p. 401, and in *The Numismatic Scrapbook Magazine,* Vol. 22, No. 3 (Mar., 1956), p. 389.
[108] *American Journal of Numismatics,* Vol. 4, No. 9 (Jan., 1870), p. 72.

Treasury Department had approved this action.[109] The 1804 dollar die was not used for such samples because there was no reverse. Linderman had obtained his own 1804 Class III dollar after the 1858 scandal, and added to his collection specimens of most of the patterns struck from those dies which he kept in his vault just before their destruction in 1869.

The A. Loudon Snowden correspondence is set forth in full:[110]

OFFICE COIN COLLECTORS' MAGAZINE, 139 NORTH NINTH STREET.

PHILADELPHIA December 12, 1871.

A. LOUDON SNOWDEN, Esq., Chief Coiner United States Mint:

DEAR SIR: There is an opinion prevalent among some numismatists that the regular coinage and experimental or pattern dies of past dates are now in the United States Mint, and that pieces are frequently struck off from them, thus entailing a loss (by depreciating values) upon collectors who possess cabinets of the different series of United States coins, etc.

Will you oblige by giving us the facts, so that we may judge of the truth of the complaints now so frequently heard in reference to the restriking of United States coins and other pieces at the Mint?

Yours, very truly,   E. MASON JR..

Editor of Mason's Coin Collectors' Magazine.

MINT OF THE UNITED STATES, CHIEF COINER'S DEPARTMENT.

PHILADELPHIA, December 14, 1871.

E. MASON, JR., Esq., Editor Coin Collectors' Magazine:

DEAR SIR: In reply to your communication of the 12th inst., I would state, for the information of all who may have any interest in the matter, that there are no regular coinage or pattern dies in the Mint, of any denomination whatsoever, except those dated 1871.

Shortly after my transfer to the position I now hold, I discovered in one of my vaults a large collection of old hubs and dies, which had been carefully labelled, with engraver's name and date of execution, by one of my predecessors, the late lamented Franklin Peale. This collection included hubs and dies for the various denominations of coin from about the year 1800 to 1855. It was not a complete series of dies, but it embraced either as hubs or dies all the rare pattern pieces executed by Mr. Gobrecht and others. Among the number were several from which no pieces are known to have been struck. Many of the devices were beautiful in design and exquisite in execution. This was peculiarly the case with a dollar and a half dollar hub by Gobrecht.

In the spring of 1869, I consulted with the Director, Dr. Linderman, as to the propriety, indeed importance, for various reasons, of having these hubs and dies destroyed. He fully concurred with me, and, acting under his authority, I had them all defaced by heating in the forge and use of the sledge. Of this large number of dies and hubs, not a single one was ever used to strike a single impression since I have held the office of Chief Coiner. About the same time that this destruction of dies was taking place, Dr. Linderman, to my knowledge, gave orders to the die sinker for the destruction of all the pattern hubs and dies of all dates, and all the regular coinage hubs of old devices and all coinage dies, except those dated 1869, that were then in his safe. This order was faithfully executed;

[109] Numisma (Nov., 1880); The Numismatist, Vol. 50, No. 5 (May, 1937), p. 401; The Numismatic Scrapbook Magazine, Vol. 22, No. 3 (Mar., 1956), p. 389.
[110] Mason's Coin Collectors' Magazine, Vol. 6, No. 1 (Jan., 1872), p. 15; The Numismatic Scrapbook Magazine, Vol. 8, No. 7 (July, 1942), p. 357.

so that when Governor Pollock was reappointed Director, in May of the same year, there was not a hub or die in the Mint except those in actual use upon the coinage for the then current year. Under his directorship (as has been customary for many years), all the regular coining dies used during the year are destroyed at the beginning of the following year, in the presence of the Chief Coiner and Engraver or their representatives.

Since Governor Pollock's reappointment there have been but two (2) series of pattern coins struck which were sold to collectors, viz: the silver halves, quarters and dimes (nine pieces), of reduced weight, dated 1869 and 1870.

The number to be issued was agreed upon between the director and myself before a piece was struck, and the dies were defaced when the number was reached.

Purely experimental dies, from which no pieces are sold, are also guarded with great care. But very few impressions are taken, and if the device, either in design or execution, is not satisfactory, the die is at once destroyed.

From all I can learn it was customary in former years to restrike a limited number of pieces from old dies to oblige collectors and others, and whilst there is no law against the practice it is liable to abuse, and perhaps it is well that the destruction of all the old dies and hubs has entirely removed this temptation.

The idea expressed in your letter that regular coinage and pattern dies of past years are now kept in the Mint, and frequently used, is without the semblance of truth to rest upon. I have answered your letter at some length in the hope that the erroneous impressions you speak of as being prevalent may be corrected.

I am, very truly,   A. LOUDON SNOWDEN.

Chief Coiner United States Mint.

It has been shown in Chapter V that the Class II and Class III 1804 dollars were struck at the same time. Although the Class II dollars which Mint employees released were destroyed by 1860, except for the example which the Mint retained, there was no indication of whether or not others had been made and were not then released. Those dollars which had not been sold by Mint employees were obviously concealed. Their edges still required lettering, and this was accomplished in due course along with the edge lettering of the 1801, 1802, and 1803 proof dollars. There was no possibility of coining any more pieces, because the reverse dies were destroyed. Nothing could be done with the 1804 obverse which was in special custody until its mutilation in 1869.

In 1869 J. N. T. Levick was offered a Class III 1804 dollar, but rejected it promptly as a "restrike."[111] It was not until 1875 that the first Class III 1804 dollar appeared in private hands. Then others followed. The 1801, 1802, and 1803 proofs appeared almost simultaneously. Coin dealer, John W. Haseltine, of Philadelphia, was the primary outlet for all of them.

The Class III 1804 dollars have been called "restrikes." The obverse die had been used in the year 1834, but the reverse die (Reverse Y) had never

---

[111] Edouard Frossard, *Numisma*, Vol. 9, No. 6 (Dec., 1885), p. 9.

been used before 1858. The use of the word "restrike" in this situation is more justifiable than the use of "original" as applied to Class I dollars. Yet the word "restrike," alone, when applied to 1804 dollar dies, is misleading in that it implies the reuse of bonafide dies. Actually, the Class II and Class III 1804 dollars are the result of reusing an antedated fantasy dollar obverse with an unused copy of a 1797–1803 type reverse.

The Mint did not request permission to restrike coins or to make antedated coins, because this would have naturally been denied. The report of the Director of the Mint for 1840 explored the matter somewhat as far as medals were concerned, and President Van Buren submitted the matter to the House of Representatives on January 22, 1841.

> Applications have been frequently made at the Mint for copies of medals voted at different times by Congress to the officers who distinguished themselves in the War of the Revolution and in the last war, the dies for which are deposited in the Mint: and it is submitted to Congress whether authority shall be given to the Mint to strike off copies of those medals, in bronze or other metal, to supply those persons making application for them, at a cost not to exceed the actual expense of striking them off.

This portion of the report was acted upon in Congress on January 25, 1841, and referred to the Committee on the Library. The matter was never reported out of that committee.

The Battle Begins

Specific reference to the individual specimens of the 1804 dollars appears to have begun in May, 1867,[112] when it was announced that the United States Mint, Stickney, and Mickley specimens were the only pieces known. This brought to light the fact that the Cohen specimen had been omitted.[113] However, in the *American Journal of Numismatics* for June, 1867, W. Elliot Woodward, the Boston coin dealer, alleged that there were five known pieces, adding the one sent to the Imaum of Muscat (see Chapter VIII). He also created a distinction between those dollars which were thought to be struck in 1804 and those which were thought to be subsequent restrikes from genuine dies. Woodward put his blessing on the Mickley and Cohen specimens and condemned as restrikes the U. S. Mint and Stickney specimens along with the alleged Muscat specimen.[114] Matthew Stickney, who was not then a subscriber to the newly founded *American Journal of Numismatics*, apparently received the text from Edward Cogan, the New York coin dealer, to stimulate a reply. The lines for the battle of misinformation were drawn. Stickney, in a letter dated July 2, 1867 (see Chapter X), asserted that his and the Mint specimen were original and indicated no knowledge of the authenticity of the others.[115] Mason, in October, 1867, agreed with Woodward's classification of originals and restrikes.[116] Then Woodward reconfirmed his thoughts in more specific terms in the Catalogue of the Sale of the Joseph J. Mickley collection on October 28, 1867, and stated that (1) the Mickley piece was "beyond question not only genuine, but original" and "supposed to be the only original one existing" until the Cohen specimen appeared; and (2) the U. S. Mint and Stickney pieces, "it was certain, were struck at a period subsequent to 1804."

All four of the pieces then located were identical in characteristics and in due course were all to be classed as both "originals" as well as "restrikes" as more erroneous rumors were added to the confusion.

When the Cohen 1804 dollar was first known to exist, the editor of the

---

[112] *Mason's Coin and Stamp Collectors' Monthly,* Vol. 1, No. 2 (May, 1867), p. 14.
[113] *Mason's Coin and Stamp Collectors' Monthly,* Vol. 1, No. 3 (June, 1867), p. 22; *American Journal of Numismatics,* Vol. 1, No. 4 (Aug., 1866), p. 32.
[114] *American Journal of Numismatics,* Vol. 2, No. 2 (July, 1867), p. 24.
[115] *American Journal of Numismatics,* Vol. 2, No. 4 (Aug., 1867), p. 41.
[116] *Mason's Coin and Stamp Collectors' Monthly,* Vol. 1, No. 7 (Oct., 1867), p. 60.

American Journal of Numismatics asked, "Is its history known? Is it original? Is it one of the few struck about 1838? Is it one of the batch issued from the Mint by one of the young gentlemen holding sway there a few years since, or is it from the celebrated factory in Ann St., N. Y.?"[117] This inquiry pointed out the choices as to whether it was struck in 1804, 1838, or 1858, or whether it was a skillfully hand-tooled alteration.

The Parmelee specimen, obtained by a lady during Polk's administration (1845–1848), was announced in May, 1868, as genuine and original, but at the same time it was pointed out that not only had lettered edge restrikes, perhaps fifty in number, been struck, but in addition, plain edged restrikes (see Chapter XI) had appeared and been recalled.[118]

On November 1, 1881, John W. Haseltine, of Philadelphia, who succeeded his father-in-law, William Idler, in the coin business, published the *Haseltine Type Table Catalogue*, which was the first classification of die varieties of U. S. dollars, half dollars, and quarters. It is remarkable that he should list only one variety of 1804 dollar and that the one he listed had reverse Y (Class III) with a leaf pointing to the left side of the base of I in AMERICA. This was the variety William Idler owned. In spite of two different varieties available for examination in the Mint collection in Haseltine's own city, and continual publicity, controversy, and comment on 1804 dollars, he failed to record that the 1804 dollar with reverse X (Class I) was different in that, among other things, the leaf points to the center of the base of I in AMERICA. This was a deliberate omission made to conceal the die differences between his coin and the Class I pieces.

Edouard Frossard, commenting in his inflammatory pamphlets, *Numisma*,[119] noticed that the illustration of the 1804 dollar in the catalogue of the sale conducted by the Berlin dealer, Adolph Weyl, on October 13, 1884, had differences from the Parmelee specimen, which Frossard described as "a genuine U. S. Mint restrike." He recognized that more than one set of reverse dies had been used but felt that the photograph was from an electrotype. Chapman Brothers acquired the coin from Weyl and reauctioned it on May 14, 1885, pointing out for the first time that there were two different reverses on 1804 dollars.[120] On this occasion, Frossard charged that it was a different coin than Weyl illustrated. He asserted that A. M. Smith had offered $400 to Weyl if Weyl would guarantee that 1804 dollar as genuine, but Weyl refused to do so, and the coin sold for about half of that amount in the auction. Frossard continued as follows: "Let's hope that some Philadelphia dealer will soon publish in full the whole truth concerning the secret and scandalous issue of 1804 dollars made in 1868 or 1869 by former employees of the U. S. Mint." The finger was thereby pointed particularly at John W. Haseltine as

---

[117] *American Journal of Numismatics*, Vol. 1, No. 5 (Sept., 1866), p. 40.
[118] *American Journal of Numismatics*, Vol. 3, No. 1 (May, 1868), p. 7.
[119] *Numisma*, Vol. 8, No. 6 (Nov., 1884); Vol. 9, No. 4 (July, 1885); reprinted in *The Numismatist*, Vol. 50, No. 7 (July, 1937), p. 615.
[120] Reprinted in George G. Evans, *Illustrated History of the United States Mint* (Philadelphia, 1885, etc.), p. 64; in *The Numismatist*, Vol. 50, No. 7 (July, 1937), p. 614; and in *Selections from The Numismatist* (Racine, 1960), Vol. I, p. 128.

well as at his former employees, the Chapman Brothers, to tell what they knew, but silence reigned supreme.

The real truth about the mix-up of the photographs can be reconstructed with a little imagination. The Chapmans needed a foreign source for a newly acquired 1804 dollar to aid its legitimacy, for the initial appearance of one in Philadelphia would further embarrass Mint officers and would detract from its selling price. It could be sent to a foreign dealer for pretended inclusion in an auction and bought back by the owner. It would then have a fancy foreign pedigree. Electrotypes of the Idler 1804 dollar with Reverse Y had been made in or just prior to 1875 (see Chapter XVI) and were available. Apparently, the electrotype was sent to Weyl to avoid sending the real coin. Weyl took the picture of the electrotype for his catalogue. Imagine the Chapmans buying a "rare" coin of this nature without seeing it in Europe or having it sent to America before the sale. They merely gave Weyl authority to top the highest bid. The worst that could happen would be that a high artificial price would be established. The Chapmans wanted the prestige of auctioning the coin at a later date themselves.

The Berg 1804 dollar also had a foreign commercial origin allegedly appearing for the first time in 1875 in Vienna along with other United States silver coins. (See Chapter XIX.) The same inferences can be drawn from its debut. Such unusual foreign origins did not escape the notice of the editors of the *American Journal of Numismatics*, but they drew no conclusions from the situation.[121]

In the Chapman sale of May 14, 1885, a careful listing of the owners of "originals" and of "restrikes" was undertaken. Seven "originals" were named as were two "restrikes." Six of the "originals" were actually Class I pieces, but the Davis specimen (Class III) was included in error. Chapman's listing of "originals" was then republished by Scott and Co., in July, 1885.[122]

As 1804 dollars appeared, John A. Nexsen of Brooklyn became intensely interested in the history of the 1804 dollar and devoted at least twenty years to "straightening out" the data. He listed ten pieces in 1887,[123] declaring that the Mickley, Cohen and Spiers pieces "are without doubt original Dollars coined in 1804." He declared all the others as uncirculated restrikes struck since 1838, stating that there were at least two separate restrikings. He pointed out that when Alexandre Vattemare visited the U. S. Mint in 1838, there was no 1804 dollar in the collection.[124] He did distinguish the second U. S. Mint specimen as having a plain edge but was not aware that the Adams, Davis, Spiers, and second Mint specimen had different reverses from the Mickley, Cohen, Parmelee, Stickney, Dexter, and first Mint specimen. He also did not know that the Spiers piece was an electrotype (see Chapter XVI).

[121] *American Journal of Numismatics*, Vol. 38, No. 3 (Jan., 1904), p. 92.
[122] *Coin Collector's Journal*, Vol. 10 (July, 1885), p. 111.
[123] *American Journal of Numismatics*, Vol. 21, No. 4 (Apr., 1887), p. 87.
[124] No verification of this assertion has been found. Vattemare collected American coins and studied their history. See Alexandre Vattemare, *Collection de Monnaies et Medailles de L'Amerique du Nord* (Paris, 1861). He went to see the Stickney 1804 dollar (Class I) in 1847.

In April, 1888, he noted the existence of the Linderman specimen,[125] which had been auctioned earlier in the year after the government had blocked the sale by Lyman H. Low of certain of Linderman's patterns because they were standard coin types struck in the wrong metal (see Chapter XIV). In April, 1891, the list with the addition of the Berg specimen was republished primarily to show change of ownership. The same assertions made in 1887 were repeated. He now claimed that the Mickley and Cohen specimens "are universally conceded to be ORIGINAL, being the only ones reclaimed from circulation, and without doubt were coined in 1804." He changed the Spiers specimen (an electrotype) from an original to the restrike category. He added that the Watters (misspelled as Walters), Forman, and Walther specimens, which were claimed to be genuine by their owners, were believed to be alterations.[126] His information about the Watters specimen came from an inquiry addressed to Ebenezer Locke Mason on March 31, 1890. Mason, who had made a special trip to Liverpool, England, in 1879 to buy the Watters piece, said that he had offered $1200 for it and declared it an original and not a restrike in articles published in 1890 in the Boston *Herald* newspaper and his own magazine.[127] Actually, he never saw the coin or Mr. Watters on his European trip, for Watters was not in Liverpool at the time, but he subsequently had obtained an impression of the coin.[128] Yet when Nexsen asked for specific data about it, Mason changed his position and said that in 1879 he thought that the Watters piece was an 1859 restrike, but in 1890 he now believed that it was an alteration.[129] The contradiction of stating that it was an original in one breath and either a restrike or alteration in another, shockingly enough appears in two separate articles five pages apart in the same issue of his own magazine. This gives rise to the speculation that Mason condemned the Watters piece in his second article in 1890 because he wished to frighten off others so that he might finally be successful in buying what he sincerely felt and hoped would be an "original." The Watters 1804 dollar is as "original" as an 1804 dollar can be and probably was the Imaum of Muscat's specimen. The alteration was in Mason's story, not in the coin.

In trying to confuse Nexsen and others, Mason had started a rumor that there was another Class II 1804 dollar in England. S. H. Chapman spread the tale in the Lyman Sale Catalogue, and the mythical coin finally ended up supposedly in the British Museum Collection.[130]

In 1893 Nexsen recognized that the Spiers dollar was not silver, but was silver plated; yet he believed it was a Mint-struck piece. In 1894 Nexsen added the history of the acquisition of the Rosenthal 1804 dollar to his previously published data.[131]

---

[125] *American Journal of Numismatics*, Vol. 22, No. 4 (Apr., 1888), p. 89.
[126] *American Journal of Numismatics*, Vol. 25, No. 4 (Apr., 1891), p. 98.
[127] *Mason's Coin Collectors' Magazine*, Vol. 13, No. 1 (June, 1890), p. 5.
[128] *Mason's Coin Collectors' Herald*, Vol. 1, No. 3 (Dec., 1879), p. 24; *Mason's Coin Collectors' Magazine*, Vol. 13, No. 1 (June, 1890), p. 9.
[129] *Mason's Coin Collectors' Magazine*, Vol. 13, No. 1 (June, 1890), p. 10.
[130] *The Standard Catalogue of United States Coins*, p. 172 of later editions.
[131] *American Journal of Numismatics*, Vol. 28, No. 1 (July, 1893), p. 23; Vol. 28, No. 4 (Apr., 1894), p. 92.

By July, 1897, Nexsen began to change his conclusions abruptly by pointing out:[132]

1. The U. S. Mint, Stickney, and Parmelee specimens all made their appearance between 1842 and 1846.

2. Beading and flat borders on 1804 dollars are not on the dollars of 1803 and prior thereto.

3. The beading is similar to that found on the 1836 dollars.

4. The 1804 dies were cut between 1836 and 1842.

5. Stickney should have questioned the 1804 dollars as being originals because they were brilliant proof specimens.

Nexsen received vigorous backing in his position from the editors of the *American Journal of Numismatics*, Lyman H. Low, and William T. R. Marvin. They expressed their opinion that the dies were the experimental work of a Mint engraver after 1835. In summation, they said, "In the mean time the Journal confidently asserts that there is no dollar of 1804 which was struck in that year by the U. S. Mint."[133]

No researcher deserves more praise for courage than John A. Nexsen, for in a final article published in April, 1905, he admits, "No one now believes that they were coined in 1804. I must therefore repudiate all that I said in these articles about originals and restrikes."[134]

He adds the Rosenthal specimen to his list, making a total of thirteen known pieces, and mentions that two reverse dies were used. He still erroneously believed that the Watters piece was false and that the Spiers piece was genuine. The Idler specimen was still concealed by Haseltine and the Siam specimen was not publicly known until its disclosure in 1962. However, for the first time Nexsen brings out the fact that there were some different relative positions of obverse and reverse dies. He also points an accusing finger at Haseltine, through whom he noted that both the Adams and Davis 1804 dollars made their appearance in 1877. Aided by others, Nexsen had earnestly announced, amended, and modified his findings on the 1804 dollar, leaving subsequent researchers a heritage of invaluable background on which to build final conclusions.

[132] *American Journal of Numismatics*, Vol. 32, No. 1 (July, 1897), p. 10.
[133] *American Journal of Numismatics*, Vol. 32, No. 3 (Jan., 1898), p. 70; Vol. 34, No. 1 (July, 1899), p. 30; Vol. 36, No. 4 (Apr., 1902), p. 122.
[134] *American Journal of Numismatics*, Vol. 39, No. 4 (Apr., 1905), p. 102.

Affidavits and Opinions About the 1804

The Dexter Dollar in the Dunham Collection was sold at B. Max Mehl's sale on June 3, 1941, and one of the features of the catalogue was the inclusion of a group of reproductions of authenticating affidavits written in February, 1887, by A. Loudon Snowden, former Superintendent of the United States Mint; Jacob B. Eckfeldt, Assayer of the United States Mint; R. A. McClure, Curator of the numismatic collection of the United States Mint; and Patterson DuBois, former Assistant Assayer of the United States Mint. These officials state in their affidavits (full text in Appendix A, B and C) that:

1. The Dexter 1804 dollar has absolutely the same figures, characteristics, lettering, edging, etc., as the specimen in the United States Mint Cabinet, except that the latter is one-half grain lighter.

2. Both the Dexter and the Mint Cabinet 1804 dollars are genuine and were coined at the same time from the same dies and collar.

Snowden, however, is the only one of the four who stated that the Mint specimen of the 1804 dollar "was coined in that year." The others carefully avoided that assertion, saying that the Mint specimen "is and has always been considered a genuine silver dollar." This alone is enough to arouse justified suspicion. Not one of these four highly experienced officials was sufficiently informed to realize that each of them destroyed the validity of his opinion by mentioning that a collar was used in the preparation of the coin. Each concluded that the edge lettering was produced in a collar die in spite of the fact that the collar die was first used at the Mint long after 1804 and edge lettering could not be produced in such a collar. The Chapman Brothers also had not hesitated to guarantee the 1804 Dexter dollar as genuine in the 1885 sale of the "Chapman Collection"[135] (the coin belonged to them), just as they had guaranteed the false Good Samaritan Shilling and other fabrications in the June 2, 1882, sale of the Bushnell Collection.[136]

In the sale catalogue of the Fairbanks Collection by Stack's on December 10, 1960, two handwritten statements as to the Davis 1804 dollar are illustrated. The first is a guaranty of genuineness dated October 23, 1877, written

---

[135] *The Chapman Collection Sale Catalogue*, Philadelphia, May 14, 1885, p. 24, catalogued by S. H. and H. Chapman.
[136] Eric P. Newman, "The Secret of the Good Samaritan Shilling," *Numismatic Notes and Monographs No. 142* (New York, 1959), p. 30; Edouard Frossard, "The Bushnell Sale," *Numisma*, Vol. 6, No. 3 (May, 1882); John J. Ford, Jr., "Numismatica Americana," *Coin Collector's Journal*, Vol. 18, No. 2 (Mar., 1951), p. 41.

by the Philadelphia dealer, John W. Haseltine, in connection with the sale of the coin. The second is from William E. DuBois, whose book first disclosed the existence of the 1804 dollar. The text of this letter is as follows:

United States Mint, Philadelphia, Penn.
Assay Department
Septr 17, 1878

In compliance with the request of Mr. R. Coulton Davis, I have made a critical examination of the *Dollar of 1804*, in his Collection.

Upon comparison with the specimens in the Cabinet of the U. S. Mint, I have no doubt that *this Dollar* is one of the *original issue*—and not a "restrike" from Mint dies.

Wm. E. DuBois
assayer
& in charge of the Mint Cabinet

It will be noted that DuBois pluralizes the word "specimens." DuBois merely compared the Davis specimen with the two coins in the Cabinet and concluded that it was of the same issue as the first known piece. He used the words "original issue." The date of the original issue was not implied. Whether or not the original issue was genuine was not stated. When the dies were made was not stated. His letter is correct as far as it goes, but DuBois carefully avoided the pertinent facts with which he was thoroughly familiar, namely that the dies and the first strikings of the 1804 dollar were both made during his tenure.

T. L. Comparette, Curator of the Mint Cabinet, commented about the Watters Class I 1804 dollar when he wrote on U. S. Treasury Department stationery on August 23, 1917:

To Whom it May Concern;
This is to certify that the specimen of 1804 Dollar shown me this day by Mr. Henry Chapman is from the identical die as a specimen in the Mint Collection, the latter being the specimen of the coin usually regarded as one of the original issue.

The foregoing merely confirms a comparison and gives no opinion of his own. He throws no light on the ambiguous phrases, "original issue" or "usually regarded."

The 1804 dollar owned by and named after Dr. Henry R. Linderman, Superintendent of the United States Mint, as the first owner, has the affidavit of his widow, Emily Linderman, to support it. This document, executed in 1887, is set forth in Mehl's sale of the Atwater collection, and in it the affiant swears that her husband told her that his dollar "was an original," that there were only "twelve or fourteen struck," that "he had paid for it in installments, not feeling able to pay for it all at one time."[137] (See Appendix E.)

The Linderman dollar, having the second reverse and being of Class III, is at best a "restrike," as distinguished from what is called an "original," as Mehl pointed out. How could Linderman, omitting the deliberate bypass of

---

[137] *Catalogue of the Sale of the James Ten Eyck Collection* by B. Max Mehl on May 2, 1922, item 394.

"unlucky thirteen," have known how many were struck if the dollar were really an original? He could have been aware only that such a number were known. The fact that Linderman's collection consisted almost entirely of restrikes and patterns which were made at the Mint and available to him at the intrinsic metal value, leads to the conclusion that this time payment story is not without "interest." His May 18, 1867, notation (see Chapter XII) showed that he had charge of many dies including the 1804 dollar and his collection had many restrikes and patterns from those dies, such as half cents dated 1831, 1836, 1844, 1846, 1847, 1848, and 1852; two 1827 quarters; dollars of 1836, 1838, 1839, 1851, and 1852; and a large assortment of patterns.[138] He had been in the employ of the Mint intermittently from 1853 to 1878 and was Chief Clerk during the scandal of 1858. His enthusiasm for coins and his position enabled him to collect "rarities" produced during that era. When he flipped his 1804 dollar in front of his wife, it must have landed on "tales."

The Rosenthal 1804 dollar (Class III) is accompanied by an official letter of certification which defies all truth. On the stationery of the Mint of the United States at Philadelphia is a letter written February 15, 1894, to James W. Ellsworth in Chicago, by O. C. Bosbyshell, Superintendent of the Mint, with written confirmations endorsed upon it by Charles E. Barber, Mint Engraver, and Robert A. McClure, Curator of the Mint Cabinet.[139] It stated that "this dollar has been subjected to the most severe scrutiny in the Mint, and all of the experts are entirely satisfied that it is [a] genuine dollar struck in the year 1804." It goes on to say, "Our Curator Mr. Robert A. McClure is thoroughly convinced of this—as is also our Engraver, Mr. Charles E. Barber. Mr. Jacob B. Eckfeldt, Assayer, is a Numismatis[t] of experience, and is entirely satisfied of its genuineness. Hon. A. Loudon Snowden has also added the weight of his opinion to those already quoted." The opinions of these five Mint officials is interesting in view of the fact that both the Mint Class I specimen and the Mint Class II specimen were available for examination and had different reverses. The Rosenthal dollar had the reverse of the Class II piece, which was well known to have been struck during the Mint scandal of 1858; none of these officials even admitted that, at best, the Rosenthal dollar was a "restrike." Jacob B. Eckfeldt, just as he did in the Dexter dollar affidavit, was careful to free his conscience by ignoring the statement that the coin was struck in 1804 and, in addition, neither he nor Snowden signed the Bosbyshell letter as the others did. The pedigree of the Rosenthal coin is given in the Bosbyshell letter as having been owned by a freed slave, because it was either the date of his birth or the date of his freedom, and having then been passed to the freeman's son, who held it for forty years, etc. Bosbyshell stated that he was promised "a more circumstantial account" of its background, which we are still awaiting. This pedigree, like many other pedigrees, seems to have been tailored to justify the coin's validity,

---

[138] *Catalogue of the Sale of the Henry R. Linderman Collection* by The Scott Stamp & Coin Co. on February 28, 1888; Catalogue by Lyman H. Low of the proposed sale on June 28, 1887, of the same collection; Farran Zerbe, "Pattern Pieces Seized," *The Numismatist*, Vol. 23, No. 6 (July, 1910), p. 166.
[139] Manuscript in the Chase Manhattan Bank collection.

for Bosbyshell was the agent of Ellsworth in the purchase of the coin according to the February 15, 1894, letter (full text in Appendix D).

It can be sincerely said that there seem to be more inaccuracies concerning 1804 dollars in affidavits and opinions of Mint officials than there were in producing the 1804 dollars themselves; this suggests a consistent effort to whitewash the background.

The truest statement about the 1804 dollar is too humorous to omit. DeWitt S. Smith, an eminent collector, said about the 1804 dollar, "One thing I have noticed, when anyone (dealer or collector) has one to sell he thinks it is genuine, but when some other party has one to sell, the same man will discredit it."[140]

John W. Haseltine in writing to his customer about the Idler Class III dollar said,[141] "Now in closing, I will stake my reputation that the Idler 1804 Dollar is a genuine and original dollar struck from dies at the United States Mint." There is nothing which can be suggested at this time, except to pull up the stake.

David Proskey, in an advertisement of the N. Y. Coin & Stamp Co., Inc., was concise when he said,[142] "The notorious 1804 die was not cut until 1835, by Gobrecht and used when occasion and influence required until about 1860."

Geoffrey C. Adams read a paper before the Chicago Numismatic Society and stated[143] "that the genuine 1804 Dollar is a myth, originated by unscrupulous coin dealers, and fostered by an ignorant press, and all numismatists should take warning and refrain from encouraging such chicanery, and relegate the 1804 Dollar (?), the 1823 cent restrike (?) and the 1795 Jefferson Cent (?) to the melting-pot or junk box where such fakes and frauds properly belong."

Ebenezer Locke Mason in 1884 felt that[144] "The 1804 dollar, in the silver series, is a restrike from the original dies," but W. Elliot Woodward in 1885 remarked,[145] "The 1804 dollar has long been considered, numismatically speaking, as the king of coins. To this distinction it is no longer entitled. It is a fact that the collector who can stand the charge can now obtain at any time an 1804 dollar with certainty and with but little delay. *** What man has done man may do."

Lyman H. Low, at the time of his sale of the Dexter 1804 dollar (Class I) on October 11, 1904, said that he had not consummated his theories sufficiently on the 1804 dollar to let them be known, but that he intended to do so. Instead, he urged the support of the contention that the 1804 dollar was "a bona fide issue and production of the United States Mint" out of respect for the opinions of the owners of the coin. He said: "*** we should take into

---

[140] *Catalogue of the Sale by B. Max Mehl of the H. O. Granberg Collection on July 14, 1913*, p. 17.
[141] *The Numismatist*, Vol. 22, No. 4 (Apr., 1909), p. 105.
[142] *The Numismatist*, Vol. 40, No. 11 (Nov., 1927), p. 703.
[143] *The Numismatist*, Vol. 17, No. 9 (Sept., 1904), p. 275.
[144] *Mason's Monthly Illustrated Coin Collectors' Magazine*, Vol. 1, No. 2 (July, 1884), p. 26.
[145] *Catalogue of the Sale of the Wight Collection* held February 24, 1885; reprinted in *The Numismatist*, Vol. 51, No. 1 (Jan., 1938), p. 19.

consideration the standing and experience of those eminent American collectors who have admitted the piece into their cabinets. The judgment of such men as Stickney, Mickley, Sanford, Appleton, Parmelee, Lilliendahl, Cohen, Reed and Ten Eyck must be respected, and more can be said of them than their wealth enabled them to possess the piece. They were connoisseurs as well as collectors."[146] Suffice it to say that none of these men, assuming that they had no natural bias as owners, seem to have written their opinions except Stickney (see Chapter X). Low himself had previously agreed in 1899 that no 1804 dollars were struck in 1804 and that the owners of 1804 dollars "will be reluctant to accept these opinions is to be expected."[147] Thus, Low seems to have changed his estimate of the value of the opinion of owners between the time he was an editor in 1899 and the time he was privileged to offer an 1804 dollar for sale in 1904. Low's intentions to enlighten the public further remained unfulfilled, for he couldn't carry water on both shoulders.

Edouard Frossard in 1885 stated with respect to J. Colvin Randall that "Mr. Randall has had repeated opportunities of purchasing 1804 dollars, as many as four specimens of the restruck coin, such as was lately sold by Chapman Bros., having been offered him at once, and at nominal prices, but he never yielded to the temptation of giving this bogus issue a quasi endorsement by adding it to his cabinet."[148]

Opinions, assertions, hunches, theories, assumptions, guesses, challenges, or pretensions by collectors, dealers, fence straddlers, iconoclasts, optimists, amateurs, experts, or public relations specialists, whether self-serving or altruistic, are without real value in numismatics unless supported by facts. Some have based their thoughts on stated facts; others may have had some facts but failed to disclose them. Some have prejudged the issue, and others have deliberately clouded the problem. Some have blinded themselves to facts; others have disbelieved the facts. It is only by facts that a reader may form his own opinion, and for that reason, this book is considerably detailed.

---

[146] *The Numismatist*, Vol. 17, No. 10 (Oct., 1904), p. 307.
[147] *American Journal of Numismatics*, Vol. 34, No. 1 (July, 1899), p. 32.
[148] *Numisma*, Vol. 9, No. 4 (July, 1885).

What Are the Proof 1801, 1802, and 1803 Dollars?

The question remains as to when and under what circumstances the proof 1801, 1802, and 1803 dollars were struck. There is no mention in any literature or catalogues of these unusual coins before 1876, yet if some were struck in the 1834–35 period and released to collectors, there would have been. The Mint Cabinet has never owned any of these proof dollars, yet they would have been in that collection if the coins were struck at the time of the striking the Class I 1804 dollar or if they had been struck legitimately. If specimens of the 1803 (B-7) had been struck when the dies were cut in the 1834–35 period, there would not have been evidence of heavy rust in the die. Since it has been shown that the 1801 (B-5) and the 1803 (B-7) were coined at the same time it is sound to conclude that the proof 1801, 1802, and 1803 dollars were struck long after the dies were made. A comment concerning the sale of a set by Haseltine in 1879 confirms this position by alleging that they "are suspected to be part of the surreptitious restrikes that have come to light again."[149] Edouard Frossard agreed when he said: "It is now also positively known that dollars of 1801, 1802, and 1803 were restruck by the same parties who restruck the 1804 dollar."[150]

The evidence points to their coinage in 1858, because of (a) the superimposed edge letters, as found on some Class III 1804 dollars, caused by the improper use or improper adjustment of the Castaing edge lettering device, (b) the edge lettering being bungled rather than crushed, (c) the immediate open accusation of surreptitiousness, (d) the superbly beautiful proof surface, and (e) the evidence of rust on one die, etc.

Edouard Frossard, at the time of the Jewett Sale on January 24, 1876, was shown an 1801, 1802, and 1803 proof dollar by John W. Haseltine, along with an 1804 dollar. Frossard describes the incident as follows:[151]

> At the time of the Jewett sale, and while awaiting the hour of business, we had the pleasure, in common with several collectors present, of inspecting four American dollars, dates 1801, 1802, 1803 and 1804. The first three named are not particularly rare dates, and are generally found in collections, but what gave them very great value in the eyes of all present, was their perfectly uncirculated, in fact, proof condition. It is

---

[149] *American Journal of Numismatics*, Vol. 13, No. 4 (Apr., 1879), p. 101.
[150] *Numisma*, Vol. 9, No. 6 (Dec., 1885).
[151] *The Coin Collector's Journal*, Vol. I (Mar., 1876), p. 63.

pretty well known that in the early days of the Republic but few coins were placed in collections in this country, hence a very limited number of proofs were struck. ° ° ° The remarkable coins alluded to, came from England, where they formed part of a private collection, and where they probably would have remained, had they not been discovered by that indefatigable hunter of American coins, Mr. J. W. Haseltine of Philadelphia. At the time when Americans paid but little attention to collections of coins, there were as eager collectors in England among our transatlantic cousins, as can be found among us today, and hence many choice specimens of the early American coinage found their way into English cabinets and private collections. ° ° °

In this deceptive manner, the 1801, 1802, and 1803 proof dollars were first introduced to the numismatists of America. As in the case of certain of the 1804 dollars, Haseltine had to resort to tales of foreign acquisition of the proof dollars in order to conceal the fact that he or his father-in-law, William Idler, had received them directly from Mint officials. He continued to sell sets of these three coins from time to time thereafter. No English collections ever seem to have contained these coins. Their derisive name of "proofs from abroad" remained with them.[152]

Chapman, in the Lyman Sale, states that the 1801, 1802, and 1803 proof dollars were being offered for sale by Mint officials in May, 1876, when he entered the coin business. He takes no position on the date of the making of the dies when he describes the proof of one of them as being "from a discarded, unused die or from a new die made in the mint about 1870 to 1876." Auction sales beginning in 1877 contained these proof dollars, usually in sets.[153] If the 1801, 1802, and 1803 proofs were struck in 1858 at the same time as the 1804 Class II dollars, they would have had plain edges by being struck in smooth collars. When the "scandal" of the Class II 1804 dollars took place, it would have been the exercise of discretion for the parties involved to conceal the 1801, 1802, and 1803 dollars just as they concealed the balance of the 1804 Class II dollars. None of the 1801, 1802, or 1803 proof dollars had apparently been distributed, for their sale price was minimal. Since the plain edges of the three 1804 Class II dollars which got into private hands were recognized as tell-tale defects, no more dollars struck from antedated dies could be sold with that deficiency. It was just as necessary to letter the edges of the 1801, 1802, and 1803 proofs as it was to letter the edges of the 1804 Class II dollars which had not come to light. When this was done is difficult to guess, since the coins could not be disposed of for many years after 1860 without great risk. By the manner in which edge lettering was done (see Chapter IV), it can be said that the 1804 Class II dollars were converted into 1804 Class III dollars, and that the 1801, 1802, and 1803 proofs

---

[152] Edouard Frossard, *Numisma*, Vol. 9, No. 6 (Dec., 1885).
[153] Haseltine (6/11/77) Lot 338; Haseltine (1/15/79) Lots 282–4; Haseltine (6/24/80) Lots 982–3; Chapman (Cleaneay 12/9/90) Lots 944, 949, 959, all illustrated; Chapman (Wilcox 11/6/01) Lots 323–4; Elder (Mougey 9/1/10) Lots 961–2, 965, two illustrated; S. H. Chapman (Lyman 11/7/13) Lots 13–15, illustrated; *Numismatic Scrapbook Magazine*, Vol. 6, No. 5 (May, 1940), p. 280; *Numismatic Gallery* (World's Greatest Collection 1/20/45) Lots 112, 119 and 125, illustrated; Kosoff (Higgy 9/10/43) Lot 817, illustrated; Mehl (Dunham 6/3/41) Lot 1055, illustrated; Mehl (Roe 6/12/45) Lots 426–8, one illustrated; Wayte Raymond, *The Standard Catalogue of United States Coins*, 16th edition, et seq., p. 172.

received their necessary edge lettering at the same time. The participants in the 1858 incident apparently did not feel any embarrassment, for they merely waited for about seventeen years for time to dull memories. Then they began to sell the 1801, 1802, and 1803 proofs at the same time as they began to sell the 1804 Class III dollars for their personal benefit.

The 1801, 1802, and 1803 proofs are commonly referred to as "restrikes." If we accept the fact that their dies were made in the 1834–35 period, then they should be called "Mint struck copies, or "novodels." If fabricated on more than one occasion, these would be restrikes of Mint struck copies, but there is no evidence of such restriking. In any event, the reference to them as restrikes should no longer be used, because it implies bonafide original dies or striking at the time of their dating, which is certainly not the case.

Alterations and Other Fakes

Because of the high selling prices of dollars dated 1804 in the last part of the nineteenth century and because of the belief by many that those dollars were either genuine or restrikes from genuine dies, thoroughbred fakes began to appear and reappear. In the Catalogue of the Seavey collection published in 1873, the second plate has an illustration of the obverse of an 1804 dollar (Item 337). The 4 has a crosslet, and the base and upright are joined by a gradual curve on each side; the coin has radials extending to the circumferential edge and is a well-executed alteration of a genuine 1803 (B-6) dollar. Lorin G. Parmelee, who owned the Seavey collection, must have had this fact promptly called to his attention, for he acquired one replacement for it at the Sanford Sale on November 27, 1874, and another at the sale of the Henry S. Adams collection on November 1, 1876.

John A. Bolen (1826–1907), who fabricated copies of early American coins between 1862 and 1869, could not resist the temptation of trying his skill in

Dollar with date altered to 1804 by J. A. Bolen (1826–1907) and his name stamped on edge.

fabricating an 1804 dollar, but it is to his credit that he stamped his name on the alteration of the 1803 (B-5) which he produced and which is now in the American Numismatic Society collection (see illustration).

Even Sylvester S. Crosby was deceived by an alteration of an 1803 (B-6) dollar into an 1804 over 1803 dollar. He believed that the die itself was overdated at the Mint and stated:[154]

> I have seen a dollar of 1804, which I believe to be genuine, struck from a die altered from 1803, with both figures plainly showing; and as half dollars of 1805 are found, struck in a die altered from 1804, the existence of a half dollar die of 1804, and the fact that alterations were made in dies for that year, are both proved.

He also declared a second specimen of the overdate as genuine. Based upon this authentication, Frossard, in his catalogue for the sale of the A. H. Salt-marsh collection on April 13, 1892, illustrated and listed the 1804 over 1803 dollar (Item 290) as genuine, but it fortunately was withdrawn as an altera-tion before the sale took place.[155]

Whether an "1804 dollar" was genuine or false was asserted to have come before a court in Philadelphia in 1895, when Felix Schultz, as owner, became involved in litigation.[156]

To add a little humor to the matter of alterations, the *American Journal of Numismatics* inserted an article from a Boston newspaper which stated that an 1804 dollar had been altered from an 1806 dollar, but that the assist-ant curator of the U. S. Mint collection, not having a sense of humor, felt that numismatists should have been told by the editors that no 1806 dollars exist.[157] However, a subsequent author suggested that dollars dated 1805 and 1806 may come to light.[158]

Even the date of a dollar with a hole through it was altered to 1804.[159] This is inexplicable, except for the possibility that the conniver was only prac-ticing.

Coins which are altered into 1804 dollars do not seem to lack romantic and fascinating pedigrees to back their authenticity. Whether plowed up in a field, inherited from an ancestor, found in an old tobacco can, given to the owner's grandmother by Abraham Lincoln, located in a group of other old coins, or discovered in an early American site, each of such new 1804 dollars has been given a burst of momentary glory before sinking back into the status of an alteration.[160]

B. H. Collins, an employee of the United States Treasury Department, reported that by 1899 there was an epidemic of 1804 dollars. He indicated that John E. Kennedy of Lowell, Massachusetts, was removing the last 0 from 1800 dollars, covering the entire coin with wax, carving the wax away in the shape of a figure 4, and plating on a figure 4 of silver with a galvanic current. These altered dollars were then sold by men dressed as tramps who

---

[154] Sylvester S. Crosby, "U. S. Coinage for 1804," *American Journal of Numismatics,* Vol. 25, No. 4 (Apr., 1891), p. 101; see also *The Numismatist,* Vol. 51, No. 1 (Jan., 1938), p. 18.
[155] *American Journal of Numismatics,* Vol. 28, No. 1 (July, 1893), p. 23.
[156] *Mehl's Numismatic Monthly* (May, 1910), p. 66.
[157] Vol. 22, No. 1 (July, 1887), p. 20; Vol. 22, No. 2 (Oct., 1887), p. 48; Vol. 27, No. 4 (Apr., 1893), p. 93.
[158] Charles H. Schmall, *The Numismatist,* Vol. 45, No. 11 (Nov., 1932), p. 691.
[159] *American Journal of Numismatics,* Vol. 32, No. 3 (Jan., 1898), p. 70.
[160] "Another 1804 Dollar," *The Numismatist,* Vol. 43, No. 6 (June, 1930), p. 377; *American Journal of Numismatics,* Vol. 12, No. 3 (Jan., 1878), p. 80; Vol. 22, No. 2 (Oct., 1886), p. 47; Vol. 25, No. 1 (July, 1890), p. 20; Vol. 27, No. 4 (Apr., 1893), p. 93; Vol. 28, No. 1 (July, 1893), p. 23; Vol. 28, No. 3 (Jan. 1894), p. 63; Vol. 28, No. 4 (Apr., 1894), p. 92; Vol. 36, No. 1 (July, 1901), p. 29; Ted Hammer, "The Keokuk 1804 Dollar," *Numismatic Scrapbook Magazine,* Vol. 3, No. 12 (Dec., 1937), p. 277.

said they had spent all of their money except the rare 1804 dollar which was in their family. Saloon keepers were either the most gullible for these schemes or the most willing to stir the imagination of those they served.[161] Edouard Frossard had called this to public attention in the November, 1884, *Numisma*, but said that the coins before alteration were 1801 dollars as well.

In *Alexander & Co.'s Hub Coin Book* (Boston, 1900) both a "genuine" and an altered date 1804 dollar are illustrated inside the title page and the public is warned that "1801 Dollars are often altered to 1804 with intent to defraud."

The Secret Service made an arrest on the basis that an 1804 dollar was counterfeit, only to learn that the figure 1 had been removed from a genuine 1801 dollar and a figure 4 attached with glue in its stead.[162]

The 1804 dollar belonging to C. A. Watters of Liverpool, England, was said to be an alteration at the time Nexsen[163] was revising his list of what were thought to be genuine pieces (see Chapter XIII), but this was not true.

An amusing story relates how an 1804 dollar was dug up in a field by a farmer who had a $900 mortgage on his farm. A banker coming to collect the payment spotted the coin casually lying on the table. The banker, concealed the fact that he was a numismatist and stated that he wanted the coin because his great grandfather's birthyear was 1804. He offered $1.50 for the coin, but slowly increased his offer to the amount of the mortgage, when the farmer finally and very reluctantly agreed to make the exchange. The banker promptly took the coin to a dealer and offered to sell the coin for $2000. The dealer pointed out that the 4 in the date was soldered on. The banker thereupon accused the farmer of being a cheat.[164]

A workman in New Haven, Connecticut, in excavating for a Yale ice rink, dug up a snuff box with eighteenth century paper money and coins among which was an 1804 dollar with lettered edge.[165] This was obviously a planned hoax.

An Indiana collector reported that he not only had one altered 1804 dollar, but had two of them.[166]

B. Max Mehl offered and illustrated an 1804 dollar in his H. O. Granberg sale of July 14, 1913. Mehl stated that it was a genuine 1804 dollar struck in 1804. H. O. Granberg, the owner of the coin, gave his opinion that it was authentic and had been obtained from the Pinkerton Detective Agency, from the body of a sailor who was found washed up on the beach in Chesapeake Bay. Although it was from different dies than known 1804 dollars, it was tested in 1906 at the Mint by being brought to white heat in an effort to dislodge the 4, but the 4 remained fast. In spite of these assurances, certifica-

[161] *Numismatist*, Vol. 12, No. 3 (Mar., 1899), p. 56; reprinted Vol. 50, No. 7 (July, 1937), p. 614; reprinted in *Selections from The Numismatist* (Racine, 1960), Vol. I, p. 128; see also L. A. D. Montague, 35, No. 1 (Jan., 1922), p. 25; *American Journal of Numismatics*, Vol. 32, No. 3 (Jan., 1898), p. 70; *The Numismatist*, Vol. 11, No. 3 (Mar., 1898), p. 64.
[162] *American Journal of Numismatics*, Vol. 36, No. 4 (Apr., 1902), p. 116.
[163] *American Journal of Numismatics*, Vol. 25, No. 4 (Apr., 1891), p. 98.
[164] Dudley Butler, "An 1804," *The Numismatist*, Vol. 55, No. 11 (Nov., 1942), p. 795.
[165] "1804 Silver Dollar Found at New Haven?," *The Numismatist*, Vol. 27, No. 2 (Feb., 1914), p. 62.
[166] "The 1804 Dollar," *The Numismatist*, Vol. 50, No. 11 (Nov., 1937), p. 1022.

tions, and ballyhoo, it was pointed out before the sale that the coin had an altered date, and it was marked "withdrawn" when the price list was divulged.[167] Granberg still refused to believe that his 1804 dollar was an alteration,[168] and in 1937 was hoping to have some "able, fair-minded writer" authenticate it.[169] It is an alteration of an 1800 (B-1) dollar.

Even the die for the 1804 dollar was alleged to have been an old 1801, 1802, or 1803 die surreptitiously altered into an 1804 by employees in the Mint in 1838.[170]

Dr. Charles Spiers of San Francisco had many people confused about his 1804 dollar for a long time. He was alleged to have acquired an 1804 dollar in 1846, when he was a medical student in Philadelphia. He gave this piece to the Society of California Pioneers, who placed it in the San Francisco Mint. It was listed as genuine from 1887 to 1927, even though it was 46 grains underweight and was a silver-plated electrotype with a plain edge and copper showing through.[171] In addition, it was first listed as a pattern (A-W 26) in 1913, but properly delisted in 1959 in J. Hewitt Judd's revision.[172] Spiers kept for himself another 1804 dollar which, when he sold his dollar collection to Alexander Jay Cartwright, Jr., turned out to be an alteration, as was the 1794 dollar in that collection.[173]

It was pointed out in 1890 that numerous dollars altered to 1804 were seen in England and that it was difficult to detect them because one variety of the 1801 dollar (B-1 and 2) bore a close resemblance to the 1804 dollar, except in the date.[174] M. H. Bolender, in his "The United States Early Silver Dollars from 1794 to 1803," published in 1950, points out that the 1800 (B-20) dollar has its upper right star close to the Y and has therefore often been used as a candidate for alteration into an 1804 dollar, for the Mint-made dollars dated 1804 have the same characteristic.

In 1939 an 1804 and an 1805 dollar were sent to London from the West Indies for authentication and sale. American opinions indicated that both dollars had altered dates.[175] They were acquired by Farran Zerbe as such. In June, 1961, after extensive research, the Zerbe 1804 and 1805 dollars were asserted to be authentic, and to have been struck from unknown dies cut at the time the coins were dated.[176] The 1804 dollar was soon thereafter shown to be an alteration of an 1802 over 01 (B-4) and the 1805 to be an alteration

[167] Lot 320 in Granberg Collection Catalogue; see also "The 1804 Dollar," *The Numismatist*, Vol. 26, No. 10 (Oct., 1913), p. 555.
[168] *The Numismatist*, Vol. 26, No. 10 (Oct., 1913), p. 555.
[169] *The Numismatist*, Vol. 50, No. 9 (Sept., 1937), p. 815.
[170] "The Silver Dollar of 1804," *The Numismatist*, Vol. 45, No. 12 (Dec., 1932), p. 773.
[171] *American Journal of Numismatics*, Vol. 21, No. 4 (Apr., 1887), p. 87; Vol. 25, No. 4 (Apr., 1891), p. 99; Vol. 28, No. 1 (July, 1893), p. 23; Vol. 39, No. 4 (Apr., 1905), p. 103; B. Max Mehl, Reprint of "Haseltine Type Table Catalogue" (Fort Worth, 1927), p. 76; Wayte Raymond, *Standard Catalogue of United States Coins*, 16th edition, et seq., p. 172.
[172] J. Hewitt Judd, *United States Pattern, Experimental and Trial Pieces* (Racine, 1959), p. 17.
[173] *The Numismatist*, Vol. 50, No. 11 (Nov., 1937), p. 1022.
[174] *Mason's Coin Collectors' Magazine*, Vol. 13, No. 1 (June, 1890), p. 10.
[175] *The Numismatist*, Vol. 52, No. 10 (Oct., 1939), p. 799; Vol. 53, No. 1 (Jan., 1940), p. 24; see Lynn Glaser, "Some Undiscovered Coins," *Numismatic Scrapbook Magazine*, Vol. 26, No. 9 (Sept., 1960), p. 2514; Walter Breen, "Silver Coinages of the Philadelphia Mint," *Coin Collector's Journal*, 1958, p. 17.
[176] Alfred J. Ostheimer, III, "Contemporary 1804 and 1805 Silver Dollars Authenticated." *The Numismatist*, Vol. 74, No. 6 (June, 1961), p. 723; *Numismatic Scrapbook Magazine*, Vol. 27, No. 6 (June, 1961), p. 1457; *Coin World*, June 9, 1961, p. 12; *Numismatic News*, June 19, 1961, p. 6.

of an 1803 (B-6); the points of certain stars on each obverse having been reaimed by alteration in an attempt to make the dies appear to differ from all other dollar obverse dies regardless of date. The other stars, the bust, the lettering, and the first three numerals of the date, as well as die cracks and die imperfections, correspond identically in the Zerbe pieces and the above mentioned unaltered obverse die varieties.[177] M. H. Bolender, author of the standard reference on early U.S. dollars, promptly agreed with this position on being advised of the evidence, but A. Kosoff in a subsequent publication, entitled *An Illustrated History of United States Coins* (Encino, Calif., 1962), p. 10, did not wish to take a position on the matter.

By 1842, the Mint had made a negative electrotype of the Stickney 1804 dollar (Class I), because the Joseph Saxton medal-ruling machine required such a model[178] to produce the illustrations for the Eckfeldt and DuBois book. In 1873 a copper electrotype appeared as Item 338 in the Seavey collection. The sale of the Mendes I. Cohen collection on October 25, 1875, included an electrotype of the Idler 1804 dollar (Lot 387); this appears to be the first mention that the Idler 1804 dollar (Class III) was in existence. Numerous electrotypes were made from it, and John W. Haseltine in 1909 stated that his father-in-law, William Idler, in 1869 had insisted that Haseltine promise to keep the existence of the Idler dollar a secret because it was being used to make electrotypes.[179] Actually, a better reason for keeping it a secret was to avoid the embarrassment to the Mint employees of having a third 1804 dollar appear publicly for the first time in Idler's hands. Electrotype copies were also made by the Mint of the Class II 1804 dollar in its collection (see illustration), the electrotype first being described as a pattern (A-W 26) but subsequently being delisted by Judd as a false piece made by DuBois.

Electrotype Copy of Class II 1804 Dollar

Altered 1804 dollars have been listed as altered pieces in auction catalogues of the past,[180] but in recent years the sale of alterations at auction has

---

[177] Eric P. Newman, "Diagnosing the Zerbe 1804 and 1805 Dollars," *The Numismatist*, Vol. 74, No. 10 (Oct., 1961), p. 1315; *Numismatic Scrapbook Magazine*, Vol. 27, No. 10 (Oct., 1961), p. 2576; *Coin World*, Sept. 1, 1961, p. 3 and editorial p. 4; Oct. 6, 1961, p. 12; *Numismatic News*, Sept. 4, 1961, p. 1; Oct. 2, 1961, p. 4.
[178] *A Manual of Gold and Silver Coins* (Philadelphia, 1842), p. 189.
[179] *The Numismatist*, Vol. 22, No. 4 (Apr., 1909), p. 105.
[180] W. Elliot Woodward's sale of the J. G. Ralston collection on October 16, 1882, of the Winslow Lewis collection (Lot 140) on May 2, 1883, of the Heman Ely collection (Lot 105) on January 8, 1884, and of J. Colvin Randall collection (Lot 290) on September 15, 1885; New York Coin Co. sale of the Robert C. Davis collection (Lot 453) on January 20, 1890.

been frowned upon and generally discontinued.

As stated in 1899, there are 1804 dollar casts, electrotypes, and alterations scattered throughout the land in profusion, some so cleverly executed that it requires careful study to detect them.[181] This situation has not changed, and so long as altered and other fake coins make the rounds, there will be reappearances of them as genuine coins from time to time. Two such 1804 dollars were illustrated and described in the April 20, 1961, issue of the *Coin World,* and another with a pretense of genuineness in the issue of April 6, 1962.

---

[181] "The 1804 Dollar Again," *Numismatist,* Vol. 12, No. 3 (Mar., 1899), p. 55.

The 1804 Half Dollar Alteration

If the saga of 1804 alterations is to be truly complete, the half dollar should not be omitted.

From the fact that the Mint records showed that half dollar production in 1804 was 156,519 pieces and from the existence of two obverse varieties of overdates of 1805 over 1804 half dollars (Beistle 1 and 2), it is logical (though erroneous) to assume that genuine 1804 half dollars existed. In 1867 W. Elliot Woodward was respectful to this thought when he said that the Mickley collection "probably contains the only perfect set of U. S. silver to be found together, and even this lacks the half dollar of 1804; a specimen of which is claimed for a fine collection in the Empire State, but concerning the genuineness of which opinions are divided."[182] The 1804 half dollar referred to made its appearance in an inventory prepared in 1861 for the private sale

Half dollar with date altered to 1804.

of the collection of the father of George W. Rice. George W. Rice, an able numismatist in his own right, often heard his father mention this coin and state that L. M. Marshall, a coin dealer of Oswego, New York, (the issuer of Civil War Store Cards H-G 6330 and 6332) had pronounced the coin genuine.[183]

Edward Cogan, the well known coin dealer of New York City, straddled the issue of the genuineness of this coin by stating, "The only one that I have ever seen and which was pronounced original by several excellent authorities

---

[182] *American Journal of Numismatics*, Vol. 2, No. 2 (June, 1867), p. 25.
[183] George W. Rice, "Errors and Inconsistencies in the United States Mint Records," *The Numismatist*, Vol. 8, No. 11 (Nov., 1895), p. 268.

is in the possession of Col. E. Jewett, of Utica, who many years ago sent it to me to ascertain whether it was genuine."[184]

Woodward sold the same piece as genuine in the Ferguson Haines sale on October 13, 1880, (Lot 569), the J. E. Burton sale in October, 1881, (Lot 520), and the Winslow Lewis sale on May 2, 1883, (Lot 169, illustrated).[185] Finally, B. Max Mehl "discovered" the piece in 1933 and proclaimed his discovery in an open letter to *The Numismatist* to be "a real honest-to-goodness 1804 half dollar."[186] It is merely a clever alteration of an 1806 half dollar (Beistle 4a-Ha) and is among the oddities in the Eric P. Newman collection (see illustration).

[184] Edward Cogan, "Table of Gold, Silver and Copper Coins Not Issued by the United States Mint," (New York, 1871), p. 4.

[185] Walter Breen, "Research in the Archives," *Coin Collector's Journal*, Vol. 18, No. 4 (July, 1951), p. 87.

[186] "Mr. Mehl Discovers an 1804 Half Dollar," *The Numismatist*, Vol. 46, No. 11 (Nov., 1933), p. 706.

Summary

With respect for all bonafide opinions and conclusions reached in the past concerning the 1804 dollars and their affiliated pieces, the following conclusions are drawn by the authors:

1. The dies for the 1804, 1801 (B-5), 1802 (B-8), and 1803 (B-7) dollars were cut at the U. S. Mint in the 1834–35 period, the principal evidence for this conclusion being:

(a) Their raised flat border and dentilation was of a style first adopted at the U. S. Mint in 1828.

(b) They lack radials, which other coins of 1804 have.

(c) Some figure punches used on the dates of the 1801 (B-5) and 1802 (B-8) dollars were of a style not adopted until 1820.

(d) The missing curl tip on the 1801 (B-5) and the 1804 obverses shows that the dies were cut after the 1802 (B-8), which has a complete curl tip. The missing curl tip is not found on any other U. S. dollars and the last dies cut with the bust punch were not cut in normal chronological order.

(e) The figure 4 punch in the 1804 does not have a crosslet as it should have.

(f) Coinage dies slightly smaller in diameter than the finished coin were necessary to use with the collar die device under development for the new Mint in the 1833–36 period. Dies larger in diameter than the finished coin were in use during the 1804 period.

(g) Proof dollars were struck in 1834–35 to include in presentation sets.

2. The Class I 1804 dollars were struck at the U. S. Mint in the 1834–35 period, the principal reasons for this conclusion being:

(a) The edge lettering is crushed by a plain collar die which was not in use in the 1804 period and was being developed in the 1833–36 period.

(b) They are proofs and coinage of proofs did not commence at the Mint before 1817.

(c) If the dies were not made prior to the year 1834, the coins could not have been struck earlier.

(d) The first disclosure of the existence of an 1804 dollar was an illustration published in 1842.

(e) They were struck for and included in presentation sets ordered in 1834 and 1835.

3. The Class II and Class III 1804 dollars were struck at the Mint in 1858, the principal reasons for this conclusion being:

(a) Rust on Reverse Y shows that the die was used long after being cut.

(b) The only remaining Class II dollar is struck over an 1857 coin.

(c) Reverse Y was loose in its die stake, causing double striking on all specimens.

(d) The obverse and reverse were out of line when all the coins were struck.

(e) The recall of the Class II coins in 1860.

(f) The contemporary correspondence concerning the incident.

(g) The destruction of the reverse dies by the Mint in 1860 and the deposit of the 1804 obverse die in safekeeping in 1860.

4. The 1801 (B-5), 1802 (B-8), and 1803 (B-7) dollars were struck at the same time, in 1858, the principal reasons for this conclusion being:

(a) The 1801 (B-5) and 1803 (B-7) have a common mark from a sliver adhering to the reverse die.

(b) Their uniform sharpness indicates striking on a steam-driven lever press.

(c) They were coined with a plain edge at first, as were the 1804 Class III dollars.

(d) The 1803 obverse has a severe rust spot, showing that it was struck long after the die was made.

(e) None was known by collectors until after 1875 when they appeared in sets along with the Class III 1804 dollars and through the same sources.

(f) The wire rim is similar to that found on some Class II and Class III 1804 dollars.

(g) The dies were destroyed in 1860 instead of being deposited in safekeeping at that time.

5. The edges of Class III 1804 dollars were lettered a year or more after striking, the principal reasons for this conclusion being:

(a) The coins slipped in the Castaing machine, causing defective lettering and doubled lettering.

(b) The coins are dished, showing that too much side pressure was applied by the Castaing machine.

(c) The plain edged Class II pieces which were first released in 1858 were readily shown to be unnatural.

6. The edges of the 1801 (B-5), 1802 (B-8), and 1803 (B-7) were lettered after striking, the principal reasons for this conclusion being:

(a) The wire rim resulting from striking is folded inwardly by the Castaing machine.

(b) The coins slipped in the Castaing machine, causing defective edge lettering and double edge lettering.

(c) The edge lettering is not crushed but merely applied poorly.

7. The dollar coinage which took place prior to March 27, 1804, was from dies dated 1803 or prior thereto.

8. There was no authorized silver dollar coinage after March 27, 1804, until the Gobrecht pattern dollar of 1836. The cutting of dies for and striking of dollars dated 1804 in 1834 was unlawful and not authorized by the orders for presentation sets.

9. An error in published official coinage records made William E. DuBois, Jacob R. Eckfeldt, and other Mint officials assume that dollars dated 1804 existed.

10. Mint officials were collecting coins by date before the formation of the Mint Cabinet in 1838.

11. All principal punches for cutting dies for draped bust dollars were available at the Mint in 1834.

12. Extra specimens of the 1804 dollar enabled DuBois to have "rare" pieces to exchange with collectors for specimens to be added to the Mint Cabinet collection.

13. Stickney knew that the 1804 dollar he received was not coined when dated.

14. The distribution of Class I 1804 dollars was cautious because it was being pretended that the dies were legitimate and that the coins were made in 1804.

15. From 1840 to 1854 national medals were restruck from Mint dies for collectors and others, on request and without control or proper records.

16. The surge in numismatics in 1858 made the high price obtainable for an 1804 dollar tempting to those who controlled the dies.

17. In 1858 there was an unauthorized general practice of restriking patterns and certain regular issues in various metals, and of making mulings.

18. The Class II dollars struck in 1858 were for the personal profit of one or more Mint employees.

19. After the scandal of 1858 was exposed, the edges of the 1801 (B-5), 1802 (B-8), 1803 (B-7), and the Class III 1804 dollars were lettered. The coins were then concealed by one or more Mint employees until 1869 when one was offered to J. N. T. Levick and quickly rejected as a restrike. By 1875 it was thought safe for Mint employees to offer them for sale through John W. Haseltine and the Chapman brothers.

20. Jacob R. Eckfeldt, William E. DuBois, James R. Snowden, Henry Linderman, A. Loudon Snowden, and many others in Mint service knew that the 1804 dollars were artificial but felt it expedient not to expose the situation for the good of the Mint and the Mint employees.

21. The 1804 eagle without a crosslet on the 4 is struck from dies cut at the same time and for the same purpose as the 1804 dollar dies and the proof 1801, 1802, and 1803 dollar dies. Cutting the dies for and striking proofs of an 1804 eagle late in 1834 was in violation of coinage laws and was not authorized by the orders for presentation sets.

22. The 1833, 1834, and 1835 proof half dollars with crushed edge lettering were struck during the 1835–36 period from dies prepared in connection with the attempted transition of the border detail of the half dollar from radials to a raised flat border with low inside dentils. The King of Siam did not receive a proof 1834 half dollar of this type.

23. There are no genuine 1804 dollars and those struck from Mint-made dies which bear that date are antedated fantasies. The "King of American Coins" is an impostor, but was made for a King.

The Pedigree History

The first comprehensive listing of the provenience of each specimen of the 1804 dollars was compiled by S. H. and H. Chapman and appeared in connection with the sale of a Class I 1804 dollar at their auction sale of May 14 and 15, 1885. In this listing the Chapmans named each of the then current owners and gave a pedigree history of nine specimens. For the first time, the differences between the "originals" and the "restrikes" were pointed out. The 1804 dollars with the first known reverse (Reverse X) were described as original coins issued by the Mint in 1804 and it was claimed that restrikes with another reverse (Reverse Y) were made in 1858 with a plain edge and again between 1860 and 1869 with lettered edges. Most of this account was repeated in the 1885 and subsequent editions of *The Illustrated History of the United States Mint* by George G. Evans.

John A. Nexsen, who since 1887 was publishing and revising the pedigrees of the coins, was asked by Lyman H. Low in 1904 to prepare a list of current owners, pedigrees and sales records for each of the then known specimens. This list was included in the auction catalogue of the sale of the H. G. Brown collection on October 11, 1904.

A final tabulation by John A. Nexsen was published in the *American Journal of Numismatics* in April, 1905. It was essentially an expanded version of his previous listings. This material has been generally copied by most subsequent writers and catalogers. It was used as a source of information by B. Max Mehl in adding such a listing to his 1927 reprint of John W. Haseltine's, *Type Table of U. S. Dollars, Half Dollars and Quarter Dollars.* Most of the recent auction sales containing an 1804 dollar have included some sort of listing of owners based on these publications.

Many of the older sources of 1804 dollar information were reprinted in the July, 1937, *Numismatist* along with available photographs to illustrate the named specimens. This touched off a rash of claims about unrecorded specimens which were made in the September and November issues of the magazine. All of the unrecorded 1804 dollars turned out to be coins with altered dates.

A pedigree history of the 1804 dollars was included in *American Numismatic Society Notes and Monographs, Number 95*, entitled "The Silver Dollars of the United States of America" by Arthur D. McIlvaine, 1941, but the proof Watters and Siam specimens (Class I) were at that time still undisclosed. A few of the Class III specimens were mentioned in the McIlvaine study, but no attempt was made to give a listing of all their owners.

The pedigree record which follows is an assemblage of information taken from every available source believed by the authors to be reasonably accurate. In many instances the auction sales gave an invaluable background. Stories concerning the initial appearance of each specimen have to be taken with a grain of salt. At best, they are the fanciful "original" stories fabricated from the same cloth as the dollars themselves.

The name of each specimen used in this list is based on traditional usage and usually is the name of the first prominent collector who owned the coin. The pieces are listed in their respective Class according to their order of appearance. The recorded weights were taken from several sources which are believed to be accurate.

PEDIGREE HISTORY
OF
EVERY KNOWN SPECIMEN
OF THE
1804 DOLLAR

Photograph courtesy of the Smithsonian Institution

Proof condition; has been carefully cleaned in recent years; minor nicks and friction spots. Normal die alignment. Edge lettering crushed.

The 1804 dollar was first illustrated in *A Manual of Gold and Silver Coins,* June 1, 1842, by Eckfeldt and DuBois; Plate II, No. 3. It was identified simply as, "Dollar, 1797–1805." The picture was created by a medal ruling machine invented by Joseph Saxton, which mechanically produced a drawing from an electrotype of a coin.

The 1804 dollar pictured in their book was not the present Mint specimen, but a duplicate piece which was traded to Matthew A. Stickney in 1843. The existence of the Mint specimen was first reported by Stickney after he obtained his coin.

The U. S. Mint Cabinet specimen is now part of the National Collection in the Smithsonian Institution, Washington, D. C. It was listed as number 568 in the *Catalogue of the U. S. Mint Collection,* 1912, etc.

The Mint Cabinet collection of coins and minerals began in 1838, and a formal appropriation of $1000 was voted by Congress for this purpose on March 3, 1839, but in subsequent years the amount was cut to $300 per year. Director Patterson turned over the development of the collection to William E. DuBois who retained jurisdiction over it until his death in 1881. Samples of earlier U. S. coinage called "Master Coins" had been previously accumulated by Adam Eckfeldt before the formal creation of the Mint Cabinet. Foreign coins could be obtained at intrinsic metal value by mere selection from the large quantities of foreign specie continuously deposited in the Mint for recoinage.[187] They could be then held in the bullion account.

In the records of the Mint Cabinet (1838-9), Director Patterson wrote, "But as the appropriation will not be more than $800 (if that much) the deficiency is intended to be met by selling off some of the superfluous pieces to Roper, Morris and others."[188]

---

[187] James R. Snowden, *A Description of Ancient and Modern Coins in the Cabinet Collection at the Mint of the United States* (Philadelphia, 1860), p. iii; *American Journal of Numismatics,* Vol. 8, No. 3 (Jan., 1874), p. 65; "The Life of William DuBois," *American Journal of Numismatics,* Vol. 16, No. 2 (Oct., 1881), p. 44.
[188] Walter Thompson, "What the Archives Reveal About 1804 Dollars," *The Numismatic Scrapbook Magazine,* Vol. 27, No. 8 (Aug., 1961), p. 1990.

Henry Chapman photograph

Cleaned, impaired proof; slight "cabinet friction." Normal die alignment. Edge lettering crushed.

Obtained by Matthew A. Stickney at the Mint, May 9, 1843, it being a duplicate, in exchange for "Pine-tree money and rarities not in their collection, one piece of which, has since proved to be exceedingly rare: the 'Immune Columbia' in gold, 1785." The gold piece was overstruck on an English 1775 guinea.

The dollar remained in the Stickney collection until after his death in 1894, when it passed to his daughter. It was subsequently sold by Henry Chapman on June 25–29, 1907, as Lot No. 849 in the famous sale of the Stickney collection. Several pages of description and history of the dollar are included in this sale, with a photograph on Plate XI.

The coin was purchased at this auction by Col. James W. Ellsworth of New York for $3,600. In 1923 Wayte Raymond bought the entire Ellsworth collection, and in March of 1923, he sold the dollar to William C. Atwater of New York City.

B. Max Mehl conducted the auction sale of the Atwater collection on June 11, 1946. The coin, Lot No. 213, was well described and included the complete description given in the 1907 Chapman catalogue. It was illustrated with a halftone reproduction. The piece sold for $10,500, the buyer being Louis Eliasberg. The coin is presently in his collection.

U. S. Mint ....c. 1842–1843
Matthew A. Stickney 1843–1894
Stickney estate 1894–1907
Col. James W. Ellsworth 1907–1923
Wayte Raymond 1923
William C. Atwater 1923–1946
Louis Eliasberg ....1946–present owner

S. H. and H. Chapman photograph

*Very fine; has been circulated and has many nicks and scratches. Normal die
alignment. Edge lettering crushed.*

This dollar was said to have been received in 1865 over the counter by Edward Cohen, who was keeping an Exchange office in Richmond. It was
passed from him to his uncle, Colonel M. I. Cohen of Baltimore, whose collection was sold by Edward Cogan, October 25–29, 1875. The piece was
described as follows, and a photographic reproduction of the obverse was
shown on Plate I:

> No. 535.   1804   This extremely rare Dollar was procured from Rich-
> mond, Virginia, where it was known to Colonel Cohen to exist for many
> years before it came into his possession. It has been more circulated than
> either of the two previously sold at Auction, and has every appearance of
> having been struck in the year of its date, and is guaranteed to be
> original.

It was purchased at this auction by Henry S. Adams of Boston for $325.
It was sold when the Adams collection was auctioned by Bangs, Merwin &
Co., N. Y., November 1, 1876, to L. G. Parmelee, of Boston, for $500. H. G.
Sampson obtained it from Parmelee in 1878 for $600 and sold it later in 1878
to William B. Wetmore, of New York, for $625.

The Wetmore collection was sold at auction by S. H. & H. Chapman on
June 27–28, 1906. A photograph is on Plate III of the catalogue and a rather
lengthy history of the 1804 dollars was given:

> No. 208.   Lettering on edge lightly struck, and invisible on part of the
> periphery as in all the other six specimens. Weight 410¼ grs., which is
> correct, as the difference between this and the average weight of the very
> fine specimens, 415.8 grs., legal standard 416 grs., has been lost by wear,
> as it has evidently been much circulated, sufficiently to have caused it to
> have lost this difference of about five grains. It has evidently been in actual
> circulation and bears no appearance whatever of a piece rubbed pur-
> posely to make it look old. It is the only specimen that shows having been
> in circulation.

The Chapmans purchased the dollar for $720 at this auction and sold it to James H. Manning for an undisclosed amount in July of 1906.

The coin was next offered as Lot No. 778 when B. Max Mehl auctioned the Manning collection on May 17, 1921. Mehl's halftone illustration, however, was actually the Stickney specimen and not the Cohen coin. The coin was bought by Elmer S. Sears for $2,500 plus 5 per cent. Later, in 1922, Mehl sold the coin for Sears to Lammot DuPont for $3,200. The coin now belongs to Lammot DuPont's family in Wilmington, Delaware.

Edward Cohen 1865
Col. M. I. Cohen 1865–1875
H. S. Adams 1875–1876
L. G. Parmelee 1876–1878
H. G. Sampson 1878
William B. Wetmore 1878–1906
S. H. & H. Chapman 1906
James H. Manning 1906–1921
Elmer S. Sears 1921–1922
Lammot DuPont 1922–1952
Lammot DuPont family ....1952–present owner

K. E. Bressett photograph

Very nearly uncirculated, nice steel gray tone, slight friction on high points. Normal die alignment. Edge lettering crushed.

First offered in the sale of the Joseph J. Mickley collection on October 28, 1867, by W. Elliot Woodward, Cataloguer:

> No. 1696.   This piece is regarded by all American collectors as the gem of Mr. Mickley's collection. It has been in circulation, but it is still in the finest condition, retaining its brilliancy of surface, and being entirely uninjured. It was obtained many years ago from the Bank of Pennsylvania and is beyond question, not only genuine, but original. Of the four specimens known, two, it is certain, were struck at a period subsequent to 1804, and till one was recently obtained by Col. Cohen, from Richmond, this was supposed to be the only original one existing; scarce.

This dollar is said to have been received on deposit over the counter (about 1850) by the Bank of Pennsylvania; Henry C. Young being the teller who received it. Young was later a cashier of the Commonwealth Bank, Philadelphia. Joseph J. Mickley of Philadelphia, obtained it from the bank, and it remained in his possession until the sale of his coins in 1867, when it was bought by W. A. Lilliendahl for $750; from him Edward Cogan obtained it for $675 cash and some coins in February, 1868, and immediately sold it to William S. Appleton, of Boston, for duplicates from his collection valued at $775. Appleton in 1905 gave it to the Massachusetts Historical Society, Boston, Massachusetts.

Henry C. Young ....c. 1850
Joseph J. Mickley ....before 1859–1867
W. A. Lilliendahl 1867–1868
Edward Cogan 1868
William S. Appleton 1868–1905
Massachusetts Historical Society ....1905—present owner

Photograph courtesy of Omaha Public Library

Sharp, perfect impression. Stars nearly all flat or rounded. Normal die alignment. Edge lettering crushed.

It has been stated that a lady obtained this dollar from the Mint during the period of President Polk's administration (1845–1849), and hearing of the high price paid for Mr. Mickley's piece ($750, October 28, 1867), she turned her coin over to her son who sold it to Mr. Sanford about April, 1868.

First offered at auction in the sale of the E. H. Sanford collection held by Edward Cogan in New York City, November 27, 1874:

> No. 99.   This Dollar I guarantee is original and a remarkably fine impression, and is known to be one of, if not the most rare piece in the American series, not more than four or five being known to collectors in the United States.

The piece was sold to Lorin G. Parmelee for $700 and was offered at the sale of his collection by Messrs. Bangs and Co., June 25–27, 1890. A photographic reproduction of the obverse appears on Plate Eight of the catalogue:

> No. 817.   (1804) Dollar: stars nearly all with rounded centers, otherwise a sharp perfect impression of this most famous coin: a light crack in die connects the tops of letters in LIBERTY. This piece is from the "Sanford Sale."

At the Parmelee sale, in 1890, it was purchased by Byron Reed, of Omaha, for $570. Prior to the sale it had been offered for sale by Edouard Frossard in *Numisma* of June, 1890, for $750.

Byron Reed bequeathed his collection to the city of Omaha in his will on his death on June 6, 1891. The dollar is now in the collection of the Public Library in Omaha, Nebraska.

Lady .... c. 1845–1868
E. H. Sanford 1868–1874
Lorin G. Parmelee 1874–1890
Byron Reed 1890–1891
City of Omaha .... 1891—present owner

B. Max Mehl photograph

Brilliant proof. Second or third finest preserved specimen. Normal die align-ment. Edge lettering crushed.

Originally said to be the property of Adolph Weyl. The coin was purchased at the sale of the Weyl collection (Lot No. 159) in Berlin, Germany, by S. H. and H. Chapman, October 13, 1884, for $216. Next offered in the Chapman sale of May 14 and 15, 1885, where it was described as Lot No. 354: "In superb, extremely fine condition, with beautiful proof surface, as fine as, if not the finest of the seven known. We guarantee it genuine." It was purchased for James V. Dexter of Denver, Colorado, by J. W. Scott (Scott Stamp & Coin Company) with a floor bid of $1,000.

After Dexter's death the coin was sold by Roland G. Parvin, the executor of the estate, to H. G. Brown of Portland, Oregon, for a reported $2,000 on November 5, 1903. Lyman H. Low, however, claimed that the price was $1,500. The piece was next offered for sale in Low's auction of the H. G. Brown collection, October 11, 1904:

> No. 431.   Extremely fine, with a brilliant, proof-like surface, and un-impaired since its last public appearance at an auction sale in Philadelphia in May, 1885, when it was purchased on an order from J. B. Dexter, for $1,000. Plate.

The plate (Plate I) was a rather poor halftone reproduction, for which the cataloguer apologized. The coin was sold for $1,100 to William F. Dunham of Chicago.

It was sold as Lot 1058 at the sale of the Dunham collection by B. Max Mehl on June 3, 1941, to C. H. Williams of Cincinnati, Ohio, for $4,250. The dollar was thoroughly described and illustrated with a halftone reproduc-tion as well as one full page enlargement. Prospective buyers received a pho-tographic enlargement on request.

In 1950, Harold Bareford purchased the coin for a reported $10,000 through Sol Kaplan and A. Kosoff.

Photograph courtesy of R. Green

Perfect brilliant blue proof. All stars on obverse weakly struck. One of the finest preserved specimens. Normal die alignment. Edge lettering crushed.

This specimen was first publicized in *Mason's Coin Collectors' Magazine* in June, 1890. In several contradictory articles, E. Locke Mason, Jr., claimed that the piece was owned by a Mr. Walters [*sic*] who was a wealthy corn merchant of Liverpool, England, and that Watters saw it in a pawn broker's window in Liverpool and bought it for twelve shillings. Mr. Watters supposedly carried the coin as a pocket piece and refused to part with it at any price. Mason later asserted that the coin was an altered date piece and convinced Nexsen that it should not be included in his pedigree listing.

Watters' collection, including the 1804 dollar, was auctioned by Glendining of London, the American portion being sold on June 14, 1917. The sale also included a proof 1834 half dollar, quarter, and half dime (and possibly a proof 1834 dime, cent, and half cent), making it probable that these proofs and the 1804 dollar were from the Imaum of Muscat's set. The dollar was described as follows and illustrated with a collotype reproduction of the obverse:

> No. 227.   AR, Dollar, 1804, excessively rare, in perfect condition, considered one of the finest specimens known. See plate. Shows the same slight flaw in die at top of the letters of Liberty as the Parmelee specimen.

This coin was purchased by Henry Chapman for £330 ($1,603.80) who sold it June 20, 1918, to Virgil M. Brand of Chicago for $2,500.

After Brand's death, the coin was inherited by his brother, Armin, and later sold through dealer R. Green of Chicago in 1945 for $5,000 to C. F. Childs of Chicago. The coin now remains in the Childs' family.

Imaum of Muscat 1835–
C. A. Watters ....before 1879–1917
Henry Chapman 1917–1918
Virgil M. Brand 1918–1926
Virgil M. Brand estate 1926–1937
Armin W. Brand 1937–1945
C. F. Childs and Childs family ....1945—present owner

Photograph courtesy of D. F. Spink

Perfect brilliant proof. Nearly all of the design and most of the stars are sharply struck. One of the choicest specimens. Normal die alignment. Edge lettering crushed.

This was the last of the Class I dollars to come to light. Its existence was first disclosed in a talk by David F. Spink at the 1962 Educational Program of the American Numismatic Association Convention in Detroit.

It is evident that this specimen is part of the set of coins prepared in the Philadelphia Mint late in 1834 and delivered on April 5, 1836, to the King of Siam. This presentation set, in the original yellow Morocco case, is still preserved intact except for two coins.

The casket originally contained a complete set of proof coins dated 1834 and the 1804 proof dollar and 1804 proof eagle. The 1834 half dime and 1834 quarter eagle with motto were presumably lost or removed from the case at some time during its mysterious history. No facts have been disclosed concerning how the set left Siam or where it has reposed over the years.

This dollar is identical in all respects to the other Class I specimens and it is certain that all eight of these dollars were struck at the same time. The Watters specimen is the only other piece traceable as part of a presentation set and was undoubtedly the dollar included in the set given to the Imaum of Muscat.

The King of Siam 1836–
Undisclosed ....1962–present owner

Photograph courtesy of the Smithsonian Institution

Sharp, brilliant proof. The finest preserved and sharpest of the dollars with Reverse Y; all others being those of Class III and weakly struck at the center of the reverse side. Plain edge, high wire rim. Reverse shows spots from slightly rusted die at U of UNITED. The 0 in the date is aligned with the second T in STATES.

The plain edge dollar was undoubtedly placed in the Mint collection shortly after its manufacture in 1858 or 1859. Its existence, however, was generally unknown until it was exposed by H. P. Newlin as a restrike in his 1883 book on half dimes,[189] where he correctly condemned the piece on the basis of information given to him by one of the custodians of the Mint Collection. The restrike issue was first widely publicized in Chapman's 1885 auction sale catalogue and later repeated in Evans' history of the U. S. Mint.[190] It was catalogued as No. 569 in the *Catalogue of the U. S. Mint Collection,* 1912, etc.

The Mint specimen is the only remaining plain edge 1804 dollar. It was struck over a Five Frank Shooting Thaler of Bern, Switzerland, dated 1857. The undertype clearly shows on both sides of the coin. Several copper and silver plated electrotype copies of this specimen exist. One of these is the noted Dr. Spiers' specimen and was listed as No. 26 in the book by Adams and Woodin, *United States Pattern, Trial and Experimental Pieces,* where it was thought to be unique.

The Mint specimen now reposes in the National Collection in the Smithsonian Institution, Washington, D. C.

---

[189] Harold P. Newlin, *The Early Half Dimes of the United States* (Philadelphia, 1883), p. 8.
[190] S. H. and H. Chapman, *The Chapman Collection Sale* on May 14, 1885, No. 354; George G. Evans, *Illustrated History of the United States Mint* (Philadelphia, 1885, et seq.), p. 64.

Photograph courtesy of Johns Hopkins University

Extremely fine condition. The reverse shows evidence of the die having rotated slightly during striking, giving a doubled impression to most of the design. Edge lettering blundered and doubled in places. The 0 in date is aligned with the second T in STATES.

O. H. Berg of Baltimore is said to have obtained this dollar in 1875 from Messrs. Koch & Co., of Vienna. The Berg collection was sold May 23–24, 1883, by Bangs & Co., catalogued by John W. Haseltine.

> No. 568. 1804 Dollar. Obverse, evenly and handsomely struck. Reverse, slightly double struck. Although a little worn by circulation, it is Very Fine. About as fine as the one in the Sanford sale, and considerably finer than that sold in the Cohen collection. I will here state, for the benefit of collections who might be deceived by alterations, that one great evidence of the genuineness of an 1804 dollar is that the upper right star is very close to the "Y" in LIBERTY; barely escapes touching it, while the upper star on left is very far from "L." This dollar was obtained about eight years ago (1875) from Messrs. Koch & Co., of Vienna, with a large number of other United States silver coins. Guaranteed genuine.

The coin was sold to Thomas Harrison Garrett of Baltimore for $740 and remained in his collection until his death in 1888. His collections of books, prints, coins, art, etc., were held intact for awhile, since he left no will. On his widow's death in 1921, his two sons, John and Robert, split up their father's collections, according to their own interests, John taking the books and coins. John W. Garrett kept the 1804 dollar until his death, June 26, 1942. By his will, all of his coins were given to the Johns Hopkins University, Baltimore, Maryland.

Koch & Company .... –1875
O. H. Berg 1875–1883
T. H. Garrett 1883–1888
T. H. Garrett estate 1888–1921
J. W. Garrett 1921–1942
Johns Hopkins University .... 1942—present owner

S. H. Chapman Photograph

Extremely fine, weakly struck at center, several nicks in hair. Fairly well lettered edge. The 0 in date is aligned with the second T in STATES.

John W. Haseltine, the Philadelphia dealer, sold this piece to Phineas Adams of Manchester, New Hampshire, for $550 some time around 1876. The first time that Haseltine exhibited this coin was while waiting for the beginning of the sale of the Jewett collection in New York City, January 24–28, 1876. He offered his coin for $600 and said that it came from an old collection in England.

Adams in turn sold it to Henry Ahlborn of Boston, from whom it passed into the hands of John P. Lyman of Boston, with a full set of dollars for $1,800, c. 1880. S. H. Chapman sold the Lyman collection November 7, 1913. The dollar appeared as Lot No. 16 where it was described as being very fine, not fully struck up. The reverse is slightly double struck and the edge lettering is complete, without repetition. Chapman then goes on for six pages reciting his views about the 1804 dollars and defending his opinion that the Lyman specimen represents a unique striking made after the "originals" but before both the plain edge restrikes and the restrikes with errors in edge lettering.

Waldo Newcomer of Baltimore was the purchaser at $340. B. Max Mehl sold the United States portion of the Newcomer collection at private sale in 1932 to Col. E. H. R. Green, son of Hetty Green, the noted "witch of Wall Street." When the Green collection was split up, about 1940, the dollar was sold to A. J. Allen of Plainfield, New Jersey, for a reported $3,200.

Allen sold the coin to F. C. C. Boyd of East Orange, New Jersey, in 1946 and later that same year A. Kosoff sold it for Boyd to Percy A. Smith of Portland, Oregon.

This coin next appeared in B. Max Mehl's Golden Jubilee Sale of May 23, 1950, where it was consigned by Smith as Lot No. 804 and was sold for $3,250 to Amon Carter, who still owns the coin.

John Haseltine .... –1876
Phineas Adams 1876–1880
Henry Ahlborn .... c. 1880
John P. Lyman .... c. 1880–1913
Waldo Newcomer 1913–1932
Col. E. H. R. Green 1932–1940
A. J. Allen 1940–1946
F. C. C. Boyd 1946
Percy A. Smith 1946–1950
Amon Carter .... 1950–present owner

Photograph courtesy of Stack's

Extremely fine, sharp strike although weak at center. Edge lettering blundered and doubled in places. The 0 in date is aligned with the second T in STATES.

Dealer John W. Haseltine sold this specimen to R. Coulton Davis on October 23, 1877, for $500. In the bill of sale, Haseltine guaranteed the coin to be genuine.

In 1883 Haseltine repurchased the piece for $1,050 and later sold it to George M. Klein of Vicksburg, Mississippi, for $1,200. When next offered at the sale of the Klein collection (95th Woodward sale, May 21–25, 1888, Lot No. 1940) it was accompanied by a letter from the Mint Assayer, William E. DuBois, stating that it was a dollar of the "original issue" and not one of the restrikes. R. C. Davis purchased the coin at this sale for $660 with J. Colvin Randall acting as purchasing agent.

Shortly after Davis' death in 1888, it was bought by John N. Hale of Phillipsburg, Pennsylvania, for $850. It remained in the Hale estate until 1950.

This dollar was sold at auction in New York City by the Parke-Bernet Galleries on May 11, 1950, for $3,400 to Mrs. Fullerton, the daughter of Henry P. Graves. It was subsequently sold by Stack's as Lot No. 1333 in the Davis-Graves sales of April 8–10, 1954, for $8,000 to a gentleman reported to be from Fairbanks, Alaska.

The coin was next sold by Stack's as Lot 576 at the "Fairbanks Collection" auction on December 10, 1960, to Samuel W. Wolfson of Jacksonville, Florida, for $28,000.

J. W. Haseltine	–1877
R. Coulton Davis	1877–1883
J. W. Haseltine	1883
George M. Klein	1883–1888
R. Coulton Davis	1888
John N. Hale	1890–1897
Hale family	1897–1950

Photograph courtesy of A. Kosoff

Sharply struck; perfect proof. Blundered edge lettering.

Henry R. Linderman was employed at the Mint in many capacities between 1853 and 1878, and undoubtedly received his dollar directly from the Mint. His collection was catalogued for sale by Lyman H. Low, scheduled for June 28, 1887. Government authorities did not allow the sale to take place and removed several pieces from the collection. A new catalogue of the remainder was prepared by Scott Stamp and Coin Company without illustrations and the sale was held February 28, 1888.

> No. 40.   Dollar, 1804. A beautiful sharp proof, evenly centered, edge lettered. The finest known specimen of this valuable coin. This piece has the advantage over the few existing specimens, in being the property of the late Director of the Mint, Dr. Linderman, which alone is a guarantee of its being struck in the U. S. Mint; it is from the same dies as that in the Mint Cabinet. The edge lettering on this is distinct; ° ° ° HUNDRED CENTS ° ° ONE ° ° DOLLAR ° ° OR UNIT. The latest impressions are said to have plain edges, and others have muddled inscriptions, but this is of neither sort. At previous sales, inferior specimens have sold for $1,000 and $1,200. The perfection of the one now offered should command a large advance on all preceding offers.

The dollar was sold for $470 to James Ten Eyck of Albany, New York. Ten Eyck died July 28, 1910, and his collection was sold at auction by B. Max Mehl, May 2, 1922. The dollar appeared as Lot No. 394 and was illustrated with a halftone picture on Plate IV.

> No. 394.   The Dollar of 1804! Proof, nearly in full brilliancy. Excessively rare and valuable. Plate.

The coin is then described in some detail on the next page and one-half, where it is described as a restrike, even though it was accompanied by a statement from Henry Linderman's widow that it was an original.

The coin sold for $840 to Lammot DuPont. On his death, it passed to his family.

Photograph courtesy of Chase Manhattan Bank Museum of Moneys of the World

Very fine condition; appears to have been in circulation. Edge lettering blundered and doubled in places. The 0 in date aligned with the second T in STATES.

A freed slave was said to have given this coin to his son who held it for over forty years. W. Julius Driefus of Alexandria purchased it for $100 in 1893 and sent it to Messrs. Joseph Rosenthal's Sons (Isaac Rosenthal), scrap iron dealers of Philadelphia, in payment of a debt of $500.

James W. Ellsworth purchased it from them through O. C. Bosbyshell, Superintendent of the Mint, accompanied by a letter attesting as to its genuineness and so endorsed by R. A. McClure, Curator, and Charles E. Barber, Engraver, in 1894. Ellsworth kept the coin until March, 1923, when Wayte Raymond purchased his entire collection.

When Wayte Raymond split up this collection, the Rosenthal dollar was consigned to Guttag Brothers and purchased by Farran Zerbe in 1924; it went into the Chase National Bank collection with the Zerbe collection purchased by them in 1929. It is now the property of the Chase Manhattan Museum of Moneys of the World.

W. Julius Driefus	1893
Isaac Rosenthal	1893–1894
James Ellsworth	1894–1923
Wayte Raymond	1923–1925
Farran Zerbe	1925–1929
Chase Manhattan Bank (formerly Chase National Bank)	1929—present owner

Photograph courtesy of A. Kosoff

Extremely fine, weakly struck at the centers. The clearest edge lettering of any 1804 dollar. The 0 in date is aligned with the second T in STATES.

The existence of this specimen was first made known when the collection of William Idler, of Philadelphia, was dispersed in 1908 by John W. Haseltine, his son-in-law. H. O. Granberg of Oshkosh, Wisconsin, was the purchaser.

In a letter to Granberg, dated October 19, 1908, Haseltine described the coin as being slightly convex on one side and concave on the other. He also said that Idler had the coin forty years ago (1868) but that Idler bound Haseltine to secrecy in reference to it, as Idler had made electros from it. The first of these electrotype copies were noted in 1875.[191]

This dollar next appeared in the sale by B. Max Mehl of the William C. Atwater collection on June 11, 1946, where the coin sold as Lot 214 to Will W. Neil for $2,875. It was illustrated with a halftone picture and a full page description.

Once again B. Max Mehl handled this coin when he sold it as Lot No. 31 of the Neil collection on June 17, 1947, to Edward Hydeman for $3,125. It was illustrated with the same halftone plate and a similar description as was used in the Atwater sale.

The dollar remained in the Hydeman collection until 1961, when it was offered at public auction by A. Kosoff, March 3–4, 1961. A new record price of $29,000 was announced, but the name of the buyer was not disclosed.

William Idler 1868–1908
H. O. Granberg 1908–
William C. Atwater .... –1940
William C. Atwater family 1940–1946
Will W. Neil 1946–1947
Edwin Hydeman 1947–1961
Undisclosed .... 1961–present owner

[191] M. I. Cohen sale, October 25, 1875, Lot No. 387 ($10.00)

APPENDIX

—A—

STATE OF PENNSYLVANIA.

City and County of Philadelphia.

I, A. LOUDON SNOWDEN, of the City, County and State aforesaid do hereby certify and declare as follows:

That I was Register, Chief Coiner and Superintendent of the United States Mint located in the City, County and State aforesaid from May 7. 1857 until July 1. 1885, with the exception of two years in which I was Post Master of the said City of Philadelphia, and am thoroughly familiar with the affairs thereof;

I have a very full and thorough knowledge of the Coins preserved by the said Mint and now forming what is termed the "Mint Cabinet of Coins", among which is a certain Silver Dollar of the year 1804 coined in that year, which Silver Dollar has been in the possession of the authorities of said Mint for more than Forty five years;

I have also seen and examined a certain other Silver Dollar of the said year 1804 sold by the Chapman Brothers of the City, County and State aforesaid to one James V. Dexter, of Denver, Colorado, and am sufficiently familiar with it to express an opinion, and do hereby certify and declare that a comparison of said last mentioned Coin with the one in the Mint first above described, shows that the figures, characters, lettering, edging, etc., etc., on said Coins are absolutely the same, and that the Coin belonging to Mr. Dexter is a counterpart of the one now in the Mint;

I do hereby further certify and declare that in my judgment both of said Coins are genuine Coins, coined at the same time and from the same dies and collar, and that no differences exist between them with the slight exception of the weight, in which respect the Mint Dollar is about one half grain lighter than the one now owned by Mr. Dexter and which is within the legal tolerance allowed by law.

Given under my hand this Tenth day of February A. D. One Thousand eight hundred and eighty seven.

A. Loudon Snowden

–B–

STATE OF PENNSYLVANIA.
City and County of Philadelphia.

We, the undersigned, being respectively the Curator and Assayer of the United States Mint located in the City, County and State aforesaid, do hereby certify that we have compared a certain Silver Dollar of the year 1804 now belonging to Mr. James V. Dexter of Denver, Colorado, with the one now in the said Mint and which is and has always been considered a genuine Silver Dollar, and that said Silver Dollars both as regards lettering, edging, characters, figures, etc., etc., are almost identical, the only difference being in the weight of said Dollars, concerning which the Dollar in the Mint is about one half grain lighter than the Dollar belonging to Mr. Dexter; and we do hereby certify further that in our judgment and to the best of our belief, both of said Coins are genuine and were struck from the same dies and collar and at the same time.

Given under our hands this Eleventh day of February A.D. one thousand eight hundred and eighty seven.

Jacob B. Eckfeldt
Assayer U.S. Mint
R. A. McClure
Curator

–C–

STATE OF PENNSYLVANIA.
City and County of Philadelphia.

To all persons to whom these presents may come,_____greeting:

I, Patterson DuBois of the City, County and State aforesaid do hereby certify that I was Assistant Assayer of the United States Mint located in the City, County and State aforesaid, and while such Assistant Assayer compared a certain Silver Dollar of the year 1804 now belonging to Mr. James V. Dexter of Denver, Colorado, with the one now in the said Mint and which is and has always been regarded as a genuine Silver Dollar of that year, and that said Silver Dollars both as regards lettering, edging, characters, figures, etc., etc., are almost identical, the only difference being in the weight of said Dollars, concerning which the Dollar belonging to Mr. Dexter is about one half grain heavier than the one in the Mint; and I do hereby further certify that, in my judgment and to the best of my belief, from such examination and comparison, both of said Coins are genuine and were struck from the same dies and collar at the same time.

Given under my hand this Fourteenth day of February A.D. one thousand eight hundred and eighty seven.

Patterson DuBois
Late Asst. Assayer
US Mint
Phila.

139

—D—

The Mint of the United States at Philadelphia

Superintendent's Office

Feb'y 15, 1894

James W. Ellsworth, Esq;
  Chicago, Ill.
My dear Sir;

The 1804 Silver Dollar purchased by me, for you today, from Mr. Isaac Rosenthal of 190 Berks Street, this City, came into his possession in the following manner: A Mr. Julius Driefus, Nos. 3 & 4 South Wharves, Alexandria, Va., does business for Mr. Rosenthal, and borrowed money from him. Mr. Driefus met with a colored man who had this dollar for forty years, that he received it from his father, who was a freedman—the father kept the dollar because it either was the date of his birth, or the date he became a freedman—Mr. Rosenthal cannot remember which. I am promised a more circumstantial account, and will transmit it to you as soon as I receive it. This dollar has been subjected to the most severe scrutiny in the Mint, and all of [the] experts are entirely satisfied that it is [a] genuine dollar struck in the year 1804. Our Curator, Mr. Robert A. McClure is thoroughly convinced of this—as is also our Engraver, Mr. Charles E. Barber. Mr. Jacob B. Eckfeldt, Assayer, is a Numismatis[t] of experience, and is entirely satisfied of its genuineness.

Hon. A. Loudon Snowden has also added the weight of his opinion to those already quoted.

Personally I have not the least doubt in the world regarding the genuine character of this coin, and I heartily congratulate you upon possessing so rare a numismatic treasure.

Very truly yours
  O. C. Bosbyshell
    Superintendent

I critically examined the above coin and pronounce it genuine and an original dollar of 1804
R. A. McClure
Curator

I examined the above coin and quite agree with all that is said in this letter
Chas. E. Barber, Engraver

"State of Pennsylvania ⎱ SS.
Monroe County ⎰

Personally appeared before me a Justice of the Peace in and for said County of Monroe, Emily Linderman, widow of the late Dr. Henry R. Linderman, director of the Mint, who being duly sworn according to law deposes and says, "that the said Dr. Linderman told deponent that he had obtained the 1804 Dollar in his collection, that it was an original, that it was of great rarity, there only having been twelve or fourteen struck, that it was one of the finest, if not the finest specimen in existence, that he had paid for it in installments, not feeling able to pay for it all at one time". He then showed the specimen to deponent afterward locking it in his office safe with his collection".

(Signed) Emily Linderman.
Sworn and subscribed before me this first day of July A. D. 1887.

Charles W. Holbrook,
Justice of the Peace.

Department of State
Washington City
December 2d 1834

Sir

As the object of the Department in procuring the boxes for
containing the coins intended to be sent as presents to Siam and
Muscat is not only to preserve them from being soiled, but to
show them to greater advantage, the color of the interior lining
and the form of construction are left to your discretion. It is also
thought best upon reflection, that the whole of the work which
is designed to be done upon the caskets should be executed at
Philadelphia. After they have been prepared, therefore, in the
way directed by a former letter from the Department, you will
please to have them decorated on the exterior with some suit-
able device in gilding displaying the national emblems, the
Eagle, stars, &c., in such manner as may be agreeable to your
taste, or that of the artist employed. For the additional expense
thus incurred, which it is presumed will not be considerable, you
will be at liberty also to draw on the Department. If the articles
are received here by the 20th of December, they will be in time
to answer the purpose for which they are designed.

I have the honor to be, Sir,

Very Resp.
John Forsyth

To Doct Samuel Moore
Director of the Mint

Samuel Moore, Esq.
Director of the Mint, Phila.

Department of State
W. 31 March 1835.

Sir,

I will thank you to cause to be prepared two sets of the coins
of the United States in caskets, similar to those already prepared
for this Department. It is desired that they should be ready in
time for the sailing of the United States sloop of war Peacock.
That ship is now at New York under sailing orders, but her de-
parture will, probably, be delayed until the 10th of April. As
soon as they are ready, you will send them addressed to Edmund
Roberts Esq. under cover to the collector of the customs. The
colours of the caskets and of the linings is left to your own taste.
It is hoped that all practicable despatch will be used in the ful-
filment of this request.

I am, Sir, your obedt. Servt.
John Forsyth

INDEX OF NAMES

(Excluding bibliographical references)

AFTERWORD

The book you now hold is a commemorative reissue of *The Fantastic 1804 Dollar*. As authors Eric P. Newman and Kenneth E. Bressett relate in the preface, collaboration on its manuscript began in 1959. Newman and Bressett shared ideas and theories, assisted in their research by various members of the numismatic community, including several owners of the coins. Newman wrote most of the text, with Bressett working on research and pedigrees and coordinating photographs. The book was finally published in 1962, by Whitman Publishing Company of Racine, Wisconsin.

Since then, this groundbreaking work of scholarship has taken its place as a classic in the canon of numismatic literature. Whenever the remarkable Draped Bust dollars of 1804 are discussed, whenever a specimen stirs up excitement at auction, *The Fantastic 1804 Dollar* is mentioned.

As befits a classic book about such a romantic and famous coin, the story behind *The Fantastic 1804 Dollar* is one of the most dramatic in numismatic publishing.

"Stop the Presses!"

The Fantastic 1804 Dollar originally was scheduled to be printed and bound in time for advance copies to be shipped from Whitman (in Racine) to the August 1962 convention of the American Numismatic Association (in Detroit).

Coauthor Eric Newman had already shaken up the numismatic community the year before, at the August 1961 ANA convention in Atlanta. There he gave a presentation on the theory that the 1804-dated dollars were *pièces de caprice*—"fantasies" deliberately made decades after 1804, probably in the 1830s. Their design details and manufacture, Newman reasoned, were suspiciously different from those of pre-1804 coins. Newman was not the first researcher to suggest the coins were struck post-1804; as numismatic historian Q. David Bowers recalls, "What Newman did was put it all together to make logical sense."

Newman and Bressett were convinced that the coins, though dated 1804, were not from that year. After months of careful research, by the time *The Fantastic 1804 Dollar* went to press in August 1962, they were equally convinced that the "diplomatic presentation set" theory was a dead end—that the coins were *not* struck as gifts to accompany foreign trade-and-amity missions. Chapter IX of their manuscript was entitled "The Diplomatic Gift Delusion."

The authors' conclusions were radically altered by a surprise at the 1962 ANA convention in Detroit—the very place where the book was scheduled to debut.

In an educational seminar, numismatic researcher James C. Risk announced the existence of the "King of Siam Proof set" and its 1804 dollar. Not only that, he displayed the actual set itself! It was owned by coin dealer David J. Spink of London, who had purchased it from two elderly ladies believed to have been descendants of Anna Leonowens, the teacher of the king's wives and children. Here was physical evidence that Newman and Bressett had lacked in their thorough search of Mint records, State Department letters, and other historical archives. This evidence immediately rendered their book—in the process of being printed, 350 miles away—obsolete.

Bressett quickly went to a telephone after the seminar and called Whitman headquarters to stop the presses. The pages that had already been printed were ordered destroyed, and Newman and Bressett went to work revising their manuscript with new research based on the

King of Siam set. Two months later their dramatically updated final manuscript was published, to widespread acclaim.

In the October 20 and October 27, 2008, issues of *Coin World,* journalist Paul Gilkes interviewed Bressett and Newman about their experience with *The Fantastic 1804 Dollar.* "Although [Bressett] was able to stop production of the book," writes Gilkes, "the collector side of his personality ensured copies of the original work would survive. Bressett said he asked for fewer than two dozen copies of the page proofs from the printing of the original manuscript to be bound in the same cover as was intended for publication of the original manuscript" (the same binding used for the published version). "[Some] of those bound copies of page proofs were delivered to Bressett in Detroit at the convention. . . . [Bressett], Eric Newman, Breen and Glaser all received copies, with the remaining copies distributed to some of the contributors as well as some of the 1804 dollar owners who cooperated with the authors during the research phase." On the rare occasions they appear on the market, unsigned copies of these bound proofs sell for about $600, and autographed copies for $1,000 or more.

THE EXCITEMENT CONTINUES

In 1987 Newman and Bressett prepared a synopsis of all the new information published about the 1804 dollar since their book's debut. They presented this "25th Anniversary Follow-Up" as a lecture for the Coinage of the Americas Conference (COAC) at the American Numismatic Society in New York City. Their goal was to satisfy the hobby community's growing interest in the famous coins and their ongoing saga. By then many of the known specimens had been sold and resold, garnering excitement and publicity as each sale came up.

In October 1987, the King of Siam set was offered for sale at public auction by Bowers and Merena, Inc. A comprehensive description of the set and its known history was prepared by Bressett and included in the catalog, along with a list of the pedigrees and known owners of each of the 15 pieces.

In July 1989, RARCOA auctioned the Dexter specimen for $990,000. In October 2000 it would be sold again, this time by Stack's Rare Coins, for $1,840,000.

In April 1997, Stack's and Bowers and Merena Galleries sold the Stickney specimen for a record-breaking $1,815,000—the highest price ever paid for any coin at a public auction.

In 1999, in the foreword to Q. David Bowers's *The Rare Silver Dollars Dated 1804 and the Exciting Adventures of Edmund Roberts,* Eric Newman and Kenneth Bressett wrote:

> Much has been written and discussed about the phenomenal origin and history of
> the United States silver dollars dated 1804. It is quite likely that more attention
> has been paid to these mysterious coins than to any other single numismatic item.
> In 1960 when we jointly tried to determine once and for all exactly why, when,
> and how these pieces were made, there were many theories but few verifiable facts.
> What today is recognized as common knowledge was at most only speculation at
> that time.
>
> Learning the truth about the origin of the 1804-dated dollars was a formi-
> dable task for several reasons. The most daunting was the reluctance of U.S. Mint
> officials over the years to explain when or why the coins were struck. In some cases,

when questioned in the 1860s the officials simply did not know. Others, including those who were parties to the original or subsequent minting, were reluctant to divulge any information that might implicate their associates, predecessors, or the Mint Department in a possible scandal.

Other obstacles further clouded the truth. Records were lost or non-existent. Legends, myths, and tall tales were widely circulated and were designed to shield anyone from the responsibility for distributing the coins to collectors and make the coins appear to be normal government issues. Every possible cover was used to obfuscate the truth. Human nature being what it is, many of the stories were believed, exaggerated, perpetuated, and so firmly ingrained that few people wanted to hear or believe anything else.

As the story of the genesis of the 1804-dated dollars unfolded, it became apparent that their existence was even more complex and fraught with connivance than originally thought. It was no secret that the coins were not made in 1804. Learning exactly when and why the coins had been minted became the primary objective of our search through all available records. It was a search that in time revealed stories of intrigue, mystery, and romance. It was a tale unlike that of any other coins in the annals of United States numismatics, and one worthy of the coins being referred to with the often used title "The King of American Coins."

Since publication of *The Fantastic 1804 Dollar* in 1962 there have been several attempts by various journalists to add to or challenge the known information about these coins. In most cases little new or undisclosed material has come to light, and the fundamental conclusions presented in the book have been accepted. There are now [in 1999] estimated to be more than 1,000 references to the 1804-dated dollar in numismatic literature. The record is unparalleled by any other coin.

On August 30, 1999, the year that Bowers's book was published, his firm of Bowers and Merena Galleries auctioned the Sultan of Muscat presentation specimen (called the "Watters Specimen" by Newman and Bressett). Once again an 1804 dollar set a world-record auction price for a single coin: it changed hands for $4,140,000.

In March 2008 the Mickley specimen—which last had sold in 1993 for $475,000—made international headlines when it was auctioned for $3,737,500.

As of press time, 1804 dollars hold seven of the first fifty records of the "Top 250 Coin Prices Realized at Auction" (compiled annually in the *Guide Book of United States Coins*). The Sultan of Muscat specimen still stands as the most valuable silver coin ever auctioned, anywhere. The famous 1804 dollar—the "King of U.S. Coins"—shows no sign of relinquishing its courtly title.

The legendary King of Siam Proof set.

A REMEMBRANCE
WITH THE AUTHORS

Looking back on how the 1804 dollar book was written always gives me a chuckle. It is not that the project was anything other than a dedicated, intensive endeavor on our part, and our contributors'. What is so amusing is how we ever had the courage to undertake such a project at a time when there was very little reliable data available to us, few informational resources to draw upon, and none of the electronic equipment that we have come to use so liberally today.

—*Kenneth E. Bressett*

"About half a century ago," Eric Newman and Ken Bressett recall, "when we longed to know more about the origin and background of the mysterious 1804 dollars, there was a veil of secrecy surrounding every aspect of how these coins came to be, when and why they were made, and even how many were known to exist."

The authors think back to the most generally available source of information at that time, a short paragraph in Wayte Raymond's *Standard Catalogue of United States Coins*. It said, succinctly, "1804. The first dollar of this date was acquired from the mint about 1845. The dies being extant several others were struck between that time and 1878. Later strikes are from the second die. Of those struck from the first die only six are known." The pieces were listed in the pricing section of the catalog along with other Bust dollars, with the notations "First Reverse. Ex. Rare," and "Second reverse. Very Rare."

Similar vague information was found in the specialized work of M.H. Bolender in his classic 1950 book, *The United States Early Silver Dollars from 1794 to 1803*, and its later editions. "His comment about the 1804 dollars was quite remarkable," says Bressett. Bolender wrote, "The few rare and famous silver dollars of 1804 are so well-known to collectors, that it was the intention of the author to omit this paragraph." He then went on to paraphrase nearly the same details that were found in the *Standard Catalogue*.

R.S. Yeoman's *Guide Book of United States Coins* (the "Red Book") was still in relative infancy at that time, but it was a forerunner in its attempt to shed light on these esoteric coins. The book explained that two theories about the origin of the dollars were fashionable:

1. The "originals" were made in 1804 as shown in Mint reports and other official statements, and "restrikes" were made at a later date from dies found in the Mint.
2. Pieces were made between 1836 and 1842 using equipment and techniques not available prior to that time.

Bressett, who would later work for Yeoman as the Red Book's editor, says, "The closing sentence in its description gave inspiration to the investigative work undertaken by several of us who wanted to determine the true origin of these pieces."

The 1804 dollar has been and probably will continue to be a subject of much discussion. Unless some new evidence is uncovered the mystery of its existence or disappearance will always be a matter of speculation for the numismatic fraternity.

—*A Guide Book of United States Coins*

Over the years, after the coins first entered numismatic collections, countless articles, statements, theories, and conjectures were published supporting one theory or another in an attempt to explain their origin. By the 1940s it was widely believed that six "original" coins existed, and seven "restrikes." They were referred to as Type I and Type II, and it was felt that they were not made in 1804. Exactly when they were made and how they came to be was the lingering mystery.

"My interest in learning the true origin of the 1804 dollars began around 1956," says Bressett. "Locating reliable information and articles on the subject was a challenge." Fortunately, he was able to learn bits and pieces from old-timers such as B. Max Mehl, Abe Kosoff, R. Green, and others who had actually sold some of the coins. A pedigree history that had been constructed by Arthur D. McIlvaine, entitled "The Silver Dollars of the United States of America," was published in the 1941 *American Numismatic Society Notes and Monographs,* Number 95. Bressett was also fortunate to be able to examine the specimens in the Smithsonian Institution, the Johns Hopkins University, Chase National Bank, and the Massachusetts Historical Society.

> We soon learned that others were just as enthusiastic in the quest to uncover the truth about the coins. Through correspondence and occasional conversations at coin shows, it became clear that sharing information was the surest way to bring our individual research together and form some logical conclusions.

Both Bressett and Newman were advancing along the same line of reasoning, and "combining our research was a major breakthrough."

> Working together was a pleasant experience that will never be forgotten. It was an exciting time of discovery, only hampered by the limiting communications of that day. Correspondence was hammered out on a typewriter and sent by mail. Pictures and weights had to be taken mostly by trial and error on improvised equipment. Note-taking and recording material was extremely time-consuming without the convenience of today's copy machines. We both spend countless hours searching through every available book and document to locate even fragments of information about coins of the early U.S. Mint.

A CONTROVERSIAL SUBJECT

In the June 1961 issue of *The Numismatist* appeared an article entitled "Contemporary 1804 and 1805 Dollars Authenticated," by Alfred J. Ostheimer III of Philadelphia. "He had just acquired these two coins for $30,000," says Newman, "to add to his excellent collection of early U.S. dollars."

Newman had agreed to give an educational forum presentation for the annual American Numismatic Association convention, to be held in Atlanta that August. He had not undertaken much research on 1804 dollars, but "I thought Ostheimer's conclusions might be an intriguing subject to research and to speak about," he says. By examining U.S. Mint records and available images, it seemed to Newman that the topic would hold the attention of a sophisticated audience. Not only that—"I felt that Ostheimer was in error." Ostheimer was informed that the talk would be contrary to his position. "He brought his attorney and his metal expert to listen," Newman recalls. "The talk was given and extensively published. Ostheimer stated that he had determined to file suit against the speaker and any publisher for defaming the genuineness of the coins involved. No greater stimulus could have been provided for me to plow further and more thoroughly into the subject. Ken and I found consolidated thinking was the best choice. The litigation never occurred."

The write-up of his talk, although correct, "was a substantial embarrassment to me," says Newman, "because I learned months afterward that the subject had been previously published in detail in the January 1940 *Numismatist.*" It went unnoticed because it was erroneously listed in the journal's own 1959 *Index to The Numismatist* as "More Information on the 1904 and 1905 U.S. Dollars (D.F. Spink)," rather than 1804 and 1805.

THE SPIRIT OF COOPERATION

The two researchers recall that amid the laborious research and writing effort that went into their book project, there were times of exhilaration and mirth that made it worthwhile. There was an outstanding sense of collaboration among everyone involved. "Time spent working with Eric Newman in his home was priceless," says Bressett. "Interviewing owners of several of the coins was a novel experience. Untangling the mystery was the ultimate satisfaction that provided a feeling of accomplishment."

When Newman asked Amon Carter Jr. of Fort Worth, Texas, about his 1804 dollar, Carter's response was to mail not only his 1804 dollar but also his 1801, 1802, and 1803 "restrikes" for study. "When this surprise parcel arrived," says Newman, "I soon noticed that the tip of the curl on the left side of the top of the hair of Liberty was clearly formed on the 1802 and 1803 coins, but was missing on the 1801 and 1804 pieces. A close timeframe of preparation of the dies was thus indicated for all of them, but the order in which the dates were punched onto the obverse dies was not specifically determinable. It certainly was not chronological. At least it led to the conclusion that obverse die preparation was part of the same abnormal endeavor, as no other known dollars of the period had such a missing tip."

Newman emphasizes that the 1804 dollars were struck in violation of federal law, because they do not contain the date in which they were struck.

> Section 10 of the Act of April 2, 1792, specifically provided as to United States coinage that "Upon one side of each of said coins there shall be an impression emblematic of Liberty and the year of the coinage. . . ." This provision was in force in 1834 and was even reaffirmed in Section 13 of the Act of January 18, 1837. No U.S. Mint employee, no federal official including the president or anyone else, had the right to do or instruct another to do otherwise. Thus even if Andrew Jackson as president had ordered the minting of dollars or eagles for diplomatic presents they would have been required to be dated 1834, as were other U.S. coins in the diplomatic sets. As has often been pointed out, there were no U.S. silver dollars or gold eagles in circulation for almost three decades prior to the 1834 request for diplomatic sets, making the inclusion of these two denominations an inappropriate action by U.S. Mint officials. Their instructions specified coins "of each kind now in use, whether gold, silver, or copper."

The coauthors note that, "In spite of these minor technical violations, the popularity of the 1804 dollar and eagle have never diminished, and the zeal people have to own them, see them, and read about them has spread."

LOOKING TO THE PAST, AND THE FUTURE

Newman and Bressett didn't rest on their laurels after their landmark publication. Since 1962, they have both continued to study and write about the fantastic 1804 dollars. Their "25th

Anniversary Follow-Up," presented in 1987, has already been mentioned. In 1993 came Newman's "A Restated Opinion on the Origin of the 1804 Dollar and the 1804 Eagle Proofs," published in *America's Silver Dollars: Coinage of the Americas Conference* (American Numismatic Society, New York, October 30, 1993). In 2007 Bressett authored "The Nature and Use of Electrotype Reproductions" (published in the American Numismatic Association's *ANA Journal: Advanced Studies in Numismatics,* Volume 2, Number 1, Spring 2007).

The making of *The Fantastic 1804 Dollar*, like every substantial research project, had its share of tedious work and drudgery. Today, with those tribulations far in the past, Newman and Bressett look back on the many friendships they cultivated, the new experiences that were shared, and the unexpected incidents they encountered. Naturally they remember the last-minute discovery of the King of Siam set as being one of the most important. "Such events brought us together because of the mutuality of our numismatic research, writing, and goals," says Newman. "They developed our lifelong cooperation and friendship."

"Another experience that still keeps me laughing," Bressett says, "was the time that I examined the Sultan of Muscat specimen, then owned by the Charles F. Childs family."

> After spending a pleasant day examining Childs's collection at his home in Chicago, we decided to go out for a bite to eat. As a "security" measure he placed the dollar in hiding on top of a china cabinet. A couple of months later I received a frantic call from Mr. Childs, saying "Ken, I can't find my dollar anywhere. I think it is missing." Remembering the odd hiding place, I asked, "Have you checked on top of your china cabinet?" Yes, it was right there—and we both got a good laugh out of the great protection that had been given to a coin that eventually sold for more than $4 million.

While reminiscing is pleasant, both Newman and Bressett look forward to perhaps someday solving a few more parts of the mystery surrounding the 1804 dollars and other pieces that were very likely made in the Mint at the same time and by the same people. High on that list are the Proof 1804 gold eagles with their odd 200-reed edges that are so different from normal coins made in 1804. Many questions still remain unanswered about the quantity made of the Proof "restrike" dollars of 1801, 1802, and 1803. "The quest goes on," say Newman and Bressett, "and the entire story may someday be revealed—if not by us, then surely by researchers of another generation."

The King of Siam 1804 presentation dollar.

APPENDIX A:
THE 1804 DOLLAR IN THE 1947 *GUIDE BOOK OF UNITED STATES COINS*

In late 1946, when the first edition of the *Guide Book of United States Coins* (the "Red Book") was published, solid facts about the 1804 dollars were scarce. The coins' existence had been known for more than a hundred years, and most of the specimens that we know today had already been discovered (six of the eight "originals," and all seven "restrikes"). Still, the coins' origins, their date or dates of issue, and their authenticity were all shrouded in mystery.

With little more than a few U.S. Mint and State Department records to rely on, numismatists of 1946 were left to infer, opine, and conjecture about the 1804 dollars. Even so, in the first Red Book's seven paragraphs we can see the germination of ideas that would finally bear fruit in the early 1960s.

1803 Small 3	20.00	30.00
1803 Large 3	17.50	25.00

THE 1804 DOLLAR

This famous piece has been called the King of United States Coins. There are specimens known as originals (type 1) of which six are known, and re-strikes (type 2) of which seven are known.

Opinion is divided regarding the origin, date of issue and authenticity of this coin. Those who adhere to the belief that these coins were struck in 1804 point to such evidence as the letter written by Robert Patterson, Director of the Mint, to President Thomas Jefferson. This letter stated that no dollars had been minted "during the last two years." Inasmuch as the letter was dated April 2, 1807, they infer that dollars were struck during 1804.

Mint records show that 19,570 silver dollars were coined in 1804 and that these coins were struck after March 28, 1804. Years later a die with the date 1804 was found at the mint among discarded dies.

It is a matter of record that Director Boudinot stopped the coinage of silver dollars in 1804 to prevent their exportation because their face value was less than their bullion value. It can be logically supposed that the coins were never released, but thrown back into the melting pot. The record also shows that seven 1804 dollars were reserved for assay. These may well be the 1804

[129]

SILVER DOLLARS

original type silver dollars now held by museums and collectors.

Some numismatists believe that the 1804 dollars were struck at the mint between 1836 and 1842, during the period when Christian Gobrecht was creating his well known patterns in preparation for the new issue of silver dollars. The first known specimen, a proof, was obtained from a mint officer by Mr. Stickney on May 9, 1843, in exchange for an "Immune Columbia" piece in gold. Proponents of the theory that these pieces were struck during the later period, base their contention on the fact that the 1804 dollars differ from issues of 1803 or earlier and conform more closely to those struck in 1836 to 1842 — their edges or borders having beaded segments and raised rim, not elongated, denticles such as are found on the earlier dates.

Although the mint records state that 19,570 dollars were coined in 1804, in no place does it mention that they were dated 1804. It was the practice in those days to use old dies as long as they were serviceable with no regard in the annual reports for the dating of the coins. It is entirely possible that the 1804 total for dollars may actually have covered coins which were dated 1803.

The 1804 dollar has been and probably will continue to be a subject of much discussion. Unless some new evidence is uncovered the mystery of its existence or disappearance will always be a matter of speculation for the numismatic fraternity.

TYPE 1

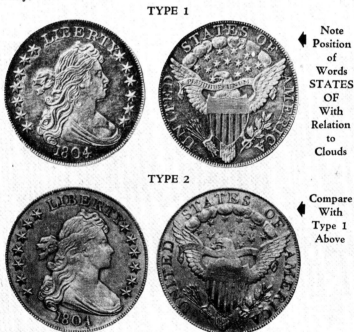

Note
Position
of
Words
STATES
OF
With
Relation
to
Clouds

TYPE 2

Compare
With
Type 1
Above

1804 Type 1, Original (Brand specimen sold for $5,000.00; Stickney specimen sold for $10,500.00).
1804 Type 2, Restrike (Idler Specimen sold for $2875.00).

[130]

APPENDIX B:
EDMUND ROBERTS AND THE DIPLOMATIC COINS

In his 1999 book *The Rare Silver Dollars Dated 1804 and the Exciting Adventures of Edmund Roberts* (from which much of this appendix is drawn), Q. David Bowers provides a wealth of information on the American diplomat who took the fantastic 1804 dollars to Asia.

Edmund Quincy Roberts (1784–1836) was a native of Portsmouth, New Hampshire, the son of a U.S. Navy lieutenant who died when Edmund was a small child. His mother passed away when he was 16, leaving Edmund and his biological sister in the care of their unaffectionate stepfather. The latter, a merchant seaman, died at sea the following year when he was swept overboard in a storm. He had bequeathed his wife's children nothing from his estate.

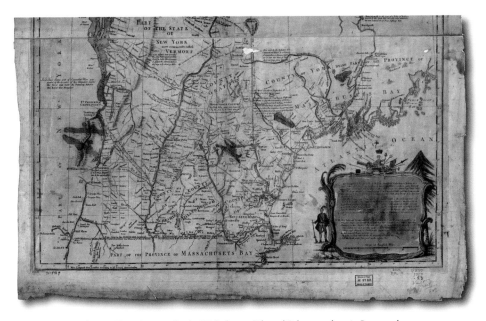

The New Hampshire coastline in 1784, the year Edmund Roberts was born in Portsmouth.

Edmund spent much of the next eight years at sea under the tutelage of a bachelor uncle, Captain Josiah Joshua Roberts (known as "Joshua"), who taught him the ins and outs of merchant shipping. The elder Roberts was a successful import/export trader associated with a British firm in Argentina. Their main ports of call were in South America, and included Buenos Aires, Montevideo, and Rio de Janeiro. For a time in 1804 Edmund tended to his uncle's business interests in London, then went back to sea, where he managed cargos and transactions. Bowers describes the division of responsibilities aboard a typical merchant ship of the time:

The hired captain directed the crew of one to two dozen sailors and the navigation of the ship, while the supercargo [the management position Edmund Roberts held] determined at which ports to call, how long to stay there, and what was to be taken aboard or offloaded. Sometimes the supercargo himself was an entrepreneur who arranged financing. Other times, a trading company out of an American port would hire a supercargo on a profit-sharing basis. Still other times, as with Joshua Roberts and his nephew Edmund, the maritime trade would be a family business. Captains and ships could be hired and dismissed at will, although some of the larger trading companies operated their own small fleets. It seems that uncle Roberts had several ships.

Edmund Roberts in 1804, at the age of 20 (from a wax miniature portrait).
He wrote from London to his sister: "It is a beautiful mode of taking likenesses,
but as such things are apt to do, mine, I think, rather flatters me."

When his uncle died around 1806, Edmund inherited his prosperous shipping company and a large fortune. He moved the firm's headquarters from Buenos Aires to his native Portsmouth, New Hampshire—not the busiest North American harbor, but a profitable commercial center.

The number of vessels arriving in Portsmouth from foreign ports dropped from 80 in 1807 to only 25 in 1808. To blame were various U.S. shipping embargos enacted because of the war between Napoleonic France and Great Britain. Congress passed the Embargo Act of December 1807 to forbid ships registered in the United States and presently in American ports from trading anywhere except at other American ports. The number of Portsmouth-bound vessels, compiled from customs records, doesn't account for any illegal trading in sheltered coastal inlets outside of the town's official wharves. Such trading did take place, but it would have been kept clandestine and "off the books" if it broke the Embargo Act. Even if illegal trading added a few ships' worth of commerce to the total, the loss of regular business was hard felt. It put an estimated 1,500 sailors out of work in Portsmouth. A few years later, the War of 1812 damaged the city's maritime trade even further.

The ship Roberts *sailed for New Orleans from Portsmouth in December 1808.*
With the Embargo Act in effect, trade with foreign ports was forbidden.

Despite such international complications, Edmund Roberts continued to invest in shipping and ran a busy fleet of trading vessels out of Portsmouth from 1807 to 1823. In 1808 he married; his beloved bride was a niece of New Hampshire's governor. Of their eleven children, eight daughters would live to adulthood. During the War of 1812, Roberts is believed to have engaged in a limited run of privateering—essentially, government-sanctioned pirating of enemy ships. His 101-ton brig the *Mars,* with seven guns and a crew of about 125, is not known to have captured any treasure from its lone privateering venture in December 1814. Roberts and his business partners lost one ship to the British during the war, but acquired three captured enemy ships, later using them for commerce.

Roberts was also active in banking during the war, serving as a director of the Rockingham Bank in Portsmouth starting in 1814. He was on the board of directors of the New-Hampshire Fire and Marine Insurance Office.

Despite this robust and varied business activity, Roberts's success as an entrepreneur was precarious. Investment and shipping losses cut into his inheritance, as did some unwise underwriting of the transactions of friends and relatives, and other unfortunate business deals.

In late 1820 he sought to expand his horizons through a government appointment. "Seeking a more stable source of income in face of his reduced assets," writes Bowers, "and desiring to develop his business in a foreign port, on December 28, 1820, Edmund Roberts wrote to United States Senator John F. Parrott in Washington asking him for assistance."

> Dear Sir,
>
> I wrote to Mr. Eustis a short time since and requested him to make an application to obtain for me the Consulate or Commercial Agency at Havana. By his answer of the 15th inst. he says it appeared there it is already between two candidates. However, not deeming it altogether desperate, he should make known my request.
>
> Will you do me the favor to add your influence to that of Mr. Eustis and Mr. L.L. Hill to obtain me this office. The latter gentlemen I have written to this day from the subject. I am partially acquainted with the Spanish language and could soon perfect myself in it, which would be of great service to me in case I succeeded to the office.

If recommendations from here would be of service or from Boston, N. York, &c., I can easily procure them. In case the office is disposed of, I do not wish any person to know I have made an application.

I remain with much esteem and respect, your obt. St.

Edmund Roberts.

[Note at bottom by Parrott: Answered 14th Jan 1821.]

After months of lobbying, Roberts's efforts paid off, and in March 1823 he was appointed to a consular post at Demerara, in eastern South America, part of what would later become British Guiana. Demerara consisted mainly of a vast inland jungle and several coastal towns, with products of sugar, rum, cotton, indigo, and exotic woods. It is uncertain whether Roberts actually took up his post there; if he did, it was not for long. He is known to have attended a gala in Portsmouth on May 21, 1823, celebrating the bicentennial of the area's settlement. A year later, he was involved in preparations to welcome the Revolutionary War hero Lafayette as he visited Portsmouth on his tour of America.

Bowers relates that through the 1820s Edmund Roberts's business activities were curtailed by lack of capital.

> Economic times were difficult not only for Roberts, but for others in the maritime trade out of Portsmouth. It seems that he traveled extensively in search of opportunities. During this time he may have sailed across the Indian Ocean to Bombay, India. Alternatively, he may have had conversations with traders out of Salem or some other port who had engaged in the Bombay trade. Bombay, whose commerce was under the control of the British who had granted a franchise to the Honourable East India Company, served as a busy depot for the import and export of many goods, including opium which was an especially valuable trading article

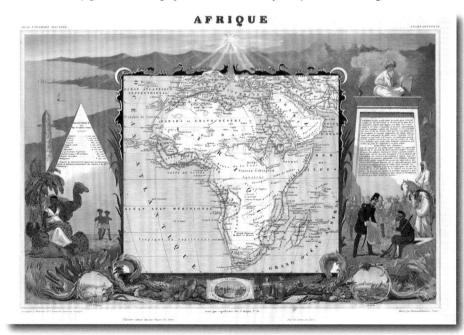

Africa in the mid-1800s. Edmund Roberts would be drawn to Zanzibar, off the eastern coast.

with distant China. In any event, by 1826 he had heard many enticing stories about the potential of trade at Mozambique, Zanzibar, and other places on or near the east coast of the African continent.

Levi Woodbury—New Hampshire senator, and, later, secretary of the Navy—would help launch Roberts's diplomatic career.

In 1827 Roberts took up with some friends and started an African trading company. He left for Zanzibar that October, full of high hopes, but his landing brought a series of misadventures and frustrations. At every turn he was confounded and cheated by port officials and by the agents of the sultan of Muscat (the influential Asian potentate who controlled the region). Instead of spending ten to twelve days at the port, as expected, Roberts was delayed there for four months! Finally, in a turn of good fortune, he was introduced by a well-connected French businessman to the sultan himself, who happened to be making his first visit to Zanzibar while Roberts was mired there in red tape. A friendship developed. Roberts encouraged the sultan to expand trade relations with the United States (a nation the ruler admired). The sultan assisted Roberts by smoothing out his Zanzibar difficulties. (Even with the sultan's help, the mission was, in Roberts's words, "a disastrous affair" in terms of profit.)

In the ensuing years Roberts pursued various other business opportunities in the United States. He also prodded friends in business and politics, trying to encourage American diplomacy with Muscat. His angling met with no success. In October 1830 his wife died at age 42, leaving Roberts a widower with eight daughters. "Family finances remained difficult," writes Bowers, "but hopes and affection remained strong." Not eight months later, in May 1831, a relative by marriage—New Hampshire senator Levi Woodbury—was named secretary of the Navy in Andrew Jackson's administration. From this influential position Woodbury lobbied for Roberts's appointment to a diplomatic post. On January 26, 1832, Edmund Roberts was officially designated a "special agent" of the United States government, charged to negotiate treaties with Muscat, Siam, and Cochin-China.

*The sultan of Muscat (after a mid-1800s painting by Henry Blosse Lynch),
and the silver dollar presented to him in 1834.*

President Andrew Jackson approved of the mission to Asia. He is seen here on an 1833 inaugural medalet, and in a circa-1845 daguerreotype.

Bowers quotes the letter of commission from Secretary of State Edward Livingston to Roberts:

> [To Edmund Roberts]
> [From the] Department of State
> Washington,
> January 27, 1832
>
> Sir:
>
> The President having named you his agent for the purpose of examining in the Indian Ocean, the means of extending the commerce of the United States by commercial arrangement with the powers whose dominions border on these seas, you will embark on board of the United States sloop of war, the *Peacock,* in which vessel (for the purpose of concealing your uniform from powers whose interest it might be to thwart the objects the President has in view) you will be rated as Captain's Clerk. Your real character is known to Captain Geisinger, and needs not be to any other person on board, unless you find it necessary for the purpose of your mission to communicate it to others.
>
> As you will enter the Indian Ocean from the eastward, the first place at which your duties will begin will be Cochin-China. Here you will proceed to the capital of the country Hué, sometimes called Huefoo, or such other of the royal cities as the king may reside at. You will in your passage to this place, inform yourself minutely of the trade carried on between the kingdom and the countries—the nature of the products of the country, whether natural, agricultural, or manufactured—the maritime and military strength, and of the articles of merchandise of personal consumption or demanded for their own commerce with other nations of the favors granted to or exactions made upon the commerce of the various nations who trade with them.
>
> On your arrival you will present yourself to the King with your power and the letter addressed to him. You will state that the President having heard of his fame for justice and desire to improve the advantages of commerce for the good of his people has sent you to inquire whether he is willing to admit our ships into his harbors with such articles of merchandise as will be useful to him and his people, and to receive in return the products of their industry or of their soil. That we manufacture and can bring arms, ammunition, cloths of cotton and wool, glass, &c. (enumerating all the articles that you find they usually import), that we can furnish them cheaper than any other nation because it is against the principles of our nation to build forts or make expensive establishments in foreign countries, that we never make conquests, or ask any nations to let us establish ourselves in their countries as the English, the French, and the Dutch have done in the East Indies.
>
> All we ask is free liberty to come and go for the purpose of buying and selling, paying obedience to the laws of the country while we are there. But that while we ask no exclusive favor, we will not carry our commerce where we are treated in any degree worse than other nations. We will pay all the duties that are required by the King's authority, but we will not submit to pay more than any other nation does, nor will we bear the exactions of any of his subordinate officers, that the President is very powerful, has many ships of war at his command, but that they are only used to protect our commerce against imposition, that the King wishes

to secure the advantages of our trade, he may enter into a treaty by which the above stipulations must be secured to our merchants, that as soon as this is known, our ships will resort to his ports, enriching him by the duties that he will receive, and his subjects by their commerce.

An important point is to obtain an explicit permission to trade, generally, with the inhabitants, for it is understood that at most, or all of the ports, the Mandarins or other officers, now monopolize the commerce, permitting none of the inhabitants to trade with foreigners.

You will be furnished with a power to conclude a treaty if one can be obtained on the terms above specified and such others as shall hereafter be mentioned, and to promise, which you may do verbally or in writing, that the usual presents shall be made on the exchange of the ratification of which you may settle a list of such things as may be most agreeable, not exceeding ten thousand dollars in value for each power.

Your compensation will be six dollars per diem, and all necessary personal expenses, which last can only be in unforeseen cases, as your subsistence on board the ship is provided for. An advance will be made to you of one thousand dollars on account of your pay, and two hundred dollars for such presents as may be necessary to gain an audience.

The above instructions will govern you in your missions to Siam and the powers of Arabia on the Red Sea where you will also be conveyed.

You are authorized to draw on the Department for the amount of your allowance as it becomes due, after deducting the advance now made to you and for your necessary expenses to be certified by the commander of the vessel in which you sail.

I am, Sir, very respectfully,
Your obedient servant,

Edward Livingston

P.S.—Your compensation will commence on the 9th January 1832, the day of your leaving your residence to proceed on your mission.

As noted by Newman and Bressett (see page 63), Edmund Roberts carried a generous supply of American gifts for the rulers and dignitaries he was destined to meet in Asia. Roberts noted in a letter that "*presents* are *widespread* in these countries, & are considered as a mark of respect. They render the donor of more or less consequence according to their *magnitude*. Both in C. China & Siam, among the first questions asked was 'What presents have you for the king?'"

DIPLOMATIC SUCCESS AT LAST

In Cochin-China, Special Agent Edmund Roberts was unable to meet with the emperor, and lengthy wrangling with his ministers failed to bring about a treaty. However, any disappointment was overshadowed by the success of the rest of his 26-month voyage of negotiation. With Siam and with Muscat Roberts crafted the first diplomatic trade treaties the United States had ever arranged in Asia.

On October 7, 1833, the sultan of Muscat wrote a letter to "the most high and mighty Andrew Jackson, President of the United States of America, whose name shines with so much brilliancy throughout the world." In glowing prose the sultan wrote:

> Your Highness's letter was received by your faithful and highly honorable representative and ambassador Edmund Roberts, who made me supremely happy in explaining the object of his mission, and I have complied in every respect with the wishes of your honorable ambassador, in concluding a treaty of friendship and commerce between our representative countries, which shall be faithfully observed by myself and my successors, as long as the world endures.
>
> And his Highness may depend that all American vessels resorting to the ports within my dominions, shall know no difference, in point of good treatment, between my country and that of his own most happy and fortunate country, where felicity ever dwells.
>
> I most fervently hope that his Highness the President may ever consider me as his firm and true friend, and that I will ever hold the President of the United States very near and dear to my heart, and my friendship shall never know any diminution, but shall continue to increase till time is no more. I offer, most sincerely and truly, to his Highness the President, my entire and devoted services, to execute any wishes the President may have within my dominions, or within any ports or places wherein I possess the slightest influence.

In early May 1834 Roberts returned to Washington and reported to the president: The treaty of amity and commerce with Siam (March 20, 1833) freed American trade from governmental monopoly and from all export and import duties. The treaty of amity and commerce with Muscat (September 21, 1833) granted the American consul extraterritorial powers, fixed duties at five percent, and granted the United States most-favored-nation status.

Jackson, his cabinet, and Congress were all pleased with the success of Roberts's mission. A second voyage was planned, to exchange treaty ratifications with the sultan of Muscat and with Siam, and to make renewed overtures to Cochin-China. Japan was mentioned by Secretary of State John Forsyth as a potential interest, as well.

It was for this second trip that the 1804 dollars were ordered as part of "complete sets" of "specimens of each kind [of coin] now in use" in the United States. According to Bowers:

> The budget for gifts—which had been $3,000 for the first voyage—was moved up to $5,000 for starters, plus an additional $10,000 if a trade treaty could be arranged with either Cochin-China or Japan. [Roberts's] salary was elevated to that of a chargé d'affaires and was set at $4,400 (raised to $5,000 at Roberts's request), plus reimbursement for expenses. Although Roberts had hoped to be given a diplomatic rank or at least designated as an envoy, he remained only as a "special agent." This may have been an expediency or ploy on the part of President Andrew Jackson and the State Department, for the actions of an official envoy or ambassador would have been subject to the advice and consent of the United States Senate, whereas no particular legislative notice had to be taken of a "special agent." Interestingly, years later when the State Department distributed Edmund Roberts's report, he was referred to as "Special Envoy" Roberts. The word *envoy* was used throughout the State Department text! One later historian designated him as *envoy plenipotentiary extraordinaire*, a title which, no doubt, would have pleased Roberts immensely.

The Proof coins given by Edmund Roberts to King Rama III of Siam, in their original presentation case of yellow leather and blue velvet. Two pieces—the 1833 gold inaugural medal of President Andrew Jackson, and the half dime—were not in the set when it turned up in the late 1950s; they were added by later owners.

Bowers notes the following listings of diplomatic gifts for Japan, Muscat, and Siam in 1835 and 1836. The listings are from State Department records. They are abbreviated from those originally given to Edmund Roberts, do not include gifts for Cochin-China, and do not include coins in the gifts for Japan. (The order of the boxes and the irregular sequence are from the original manifest. *Nankeens* are trousers.)

List of Articles for Presents to Siam

5 [No. 1 to 5]: 10 pairs rich cut-glass 2-light vase lamps, with new form cut shades to each burner.

1 Cask: 2 dozen chimneys, extra to fit lamps. · 4 new form cut shades to match. · 6 Gross lamp wicks. · 294 yds. Super Carpeting.

5 Boxes [as follows]:

Box No. 7: Bale 100 Short pieces American nankeens. · 1 Bale 50 long American nankeens.

Box No. 8: Bale 100 Short pieces American nankeens. · 1 Bale 50 long American nankeens.

Box No. 9: Bale 100 Short pieces American nankeens. · 1 Bale 50 long American nankeens.

Box No. 10: Bale 100 Short pieces American nankeens. · 1 Bale 50 long American nankeens.

Box No. 11: Bale 100 Short pieces American nankeens. · 1 Bale 50 long American nankeens.

2 large Scarlet Shawls.

1 Map U. States, with richly gilt rollers and upper frames, with 2 descriptive memoirs in morocco.

Box No. 14: Rich velvet dress with gold cord. · Satin stripe dress with satin underdress. · Satin coat with brandenburghs. · 3 Super embroidered pocket handkerchiefs. · 3 pairs silk hose. · 3 pairs gloves. · 3 pairs shoes. · White velvet opera hat, with 2 Birds of Paradise. · Blonde dress hat. · Hat and veil.

Box No. 13: 1 Super blue cloth uniform coat. · 1 Super blue cloth Trousers. · 1 Purple Dahlia dress coat. · 1 Buff Cassimere pantaloons. · 1 Embossed satin vest. · 1 Black suit, coat, vest and trousers. · 1 Chapeau, for Major General. · 1 Plume, for Major General. · 1 pair fine gold Epaulettes, for Major General. · 10 Nankeen suits.

Box No. 17: 1 Silk American Flag, with silk cover. · 2 Swing gilt glasses (mirrors). · 2 chased, gold-mounted swords in velvet scabbards.

2 Cases: 100 papers, Native American Forest tree seeds.

2 Cases: 100 papers, Herbaceous flowers and plants.

1 Case: One set of coins of U. States, with duplicate quarter-eagle.

List of Articles for Presents to Muscat

3 Cases [Nos. 1, 2, and 3]: 2 sets richly mounted cut-glass Lamps, with new form shades to suit, and extras.

Box No. 5: Bale: No. 20, 50 long; 25, 100 short; 29, 100 short American Nankeens.

Box No. 6: Bale: No. 28, 50 long; No. 12, 50 long; No. 33, 50 long American Nankeens.

Box No. 7: Bale: No. 2, 50 long; No 10, 50 long; No. 11, 50 long American Nankeens.

1 Map U. States, with richly gilt rollers and upper frames, with 2 descriptive Memoirs in morocco.

Box No. 8: Rich satin dress, richly trimmed. Blonde & Gold cord & tassel. · Embroidered lace dress with satin underdress. · Satin faced Thibet dress. Pelerine trimmed with down. · 3 Super. Embroidered Pocket handkerchiefs. · 3 pairs silk hose. · 3 pairs Gloves. · 3 pairs Shoes. · Corded skirt. · Rich satin hat and veil. · Cherry opera hat. · Blonde dress hat.

Box No. 4: 1: Super. Blue cloth Uniform coat. · 1 Super. Blue cloth Trousers. · 1 purple dahlia dress coat. · 1 Buff Cassimere pantaloons. · 1 Embossed Satin Vest. · 1 Suit black, coat, vest and trousers. · 1 Chapeau, for Major General. · 1 Plume, for Major General. · 1 pair fine gold Epaulettes, for Major General. · 10 Nankeen suits.

Box No. 9: 1: Silk American flag with silk cover. · 1 Chased gold mounted sword & 1 dirk or Attaghan in velvet scabbards. · 1 Patent rifle, highly finished with fine gold inscription plate. · 1 Patent Carbine, finished as above.

1 Case: One set of Coins U. States, with duplicate quarter-Eagle.

List of Articles for Presents to Japan

Ten merino Sheep, of the finest wool, viz., 2 bucks and 8 ewes.

Four canisters, say 50 lbs., of English Saffron, of the best quality.

One Repeating Gold Watch, with heavy gold chain, 8 ft. long, seals and key.

One Musical Box.

Five pieces Broadcloth, superior quality, 1 red, 1 yellow, 1 green, 1 dark blue, 1 light blue, full width, 20 yards each.

Elegant Cut Glassware, dessert set, to match, large size.

A Map of the United States.

A Set of Prints of the Naval Victories of the United States.

Trunk of Assorted Specimens of American Cotton Manufacturers.

Splendid Sabre, crescent form, with belt, One Rifle and One Shot Gun with percussion locks and a large supply of percussion caps.

One Pair of Pistols in case.

Coins of the types presented as diplomatic gifts on Edmund Roberts's mission.
(Pictured are the Proof coins from the King of Siam presentation set.)

As Newman and Bressett relate, Roberts's records show that he successfully delivered one set of coins to the sultan of Muscat (on October 1, 1835) and another to the king of Siam (on April 5, 1836). Unfortunately, while in Siam the groundbreaking diplomat contracted dysentery, and he died at Macao on June 12, 1836. Eighteen days later Edmund P. Kennedy, commodore of the squadron that took Roberts to Asia, wrote to Washington: "I have directed that the [diplomatic] presents be forwarded to the United States by the first vessel directed to the State Department." Undoubtedly among those gifts returned were the coins originally intended for the emperors of Cochin-China and Japan.

Edmund Roberts died in service to his nation. As the first U.S. diplomat to secure treaties with the courts of Asia, he helped pave the way for the ambitious and important voyages of Commodore Matthew Perry not 20 years later. Back in Portsmouth, the *Journal of Literature and Politics* ran an obituary five months after Roberts's death. Its 700-plus words include the following tribute:

> Thus has fallen in a strange land, and thus has been by strangers honored and by strangers mourned, one of the most noble, generous, honest, and benevolent of our citizens, a fond and devoted father, a true and zealous friend, an intelligent, energetic, honorable and enterprising man. Thus has fallen a most able, judicious, and efficient public officer, who has long served his country most faithfully and successfully, in advancing her commercial interests, and also has now yielded his life in her cause.

APPENDIX C:
COMPLETE REGISTRY OF
KNOWN 1804 DOLLARS

This registry of the known silver dollars dated 1804 is based on research compiled by Q. David Bowers in his *Rare Silver Dollars Dated 1804 and the Exciting Adventures of Edmund Roberts.* In that work Bowers notes that "This registry is summarized and considerably finessed from Q. David Bowers' 1992 *Silver Dollars & Trade Dollars of the United States: A Complete Encyclopedia,* this in turn drawing upon various sources, the most important of which was information in the Newman-Bressett *Fantastic 1804 Dollar,* combined with these authors' follow-up paper presented at the American Numismatic Society's Coinage of the Americas Conference in 1987; and Walter Breen's 1988 *Complete Encyclopedia of United States and Colonial Coins.* Additional material is from the Bowers and Merena catalogue of the Louis E. Eliasberg, Sr. Collection, 1997, and from contributions received since that time including from those who have bought or sold 1804 dollars." He further notes that "the names and nicknames attached to the coins are those given by Newman and Bressett (among others) and typically refer to the first *well-known* person or entity who owned the specimen or who *may have.* Most early pedigrees are highly conjectural."

From this solid foundation the registry was updated in late 2008, having been reviewed by numismatic researchers P. Scott Rubin, Mark Borckardt, and Kenneth Bressett.

Note that the coins are illustrated at approximately 1.5x actual size.

CLASS I 1804 DOLLARS

So-Called "Originals" (Early Strikings Beginning in 1834)

1. Mint Cabinet Specimen
Newman-Bressett: "U.S. Mint Specimen"
(Smithsonian Institution coin)

Details of this specimen: Impaired Proof due to cleaning on multiple occasions, including with silver polish, this occurring generations ago, before enlightened curators were in charge.[1] 415.2 grains. The edge lettering is crushed, as on two of the 1802 Proof novodels. It bears nicks and friction spots.

This coin was illustrated in the 1842 book by Jacob R. Eckfeldt and William E. Dubois, *A Manual of Gold and Silver Coins of All Nations, Struck Within the Past Century,* providing the first notice collectors saw in print that an 1804-dated dollar existed, although fanciful pictures of such pieces had been published earlier in cambists (exchange rate publications). It was the engraving of this coin that attracted the notice of Matthew A. Stickney and led to his acquisition of No. 2 below.

> **1834–1838:** Struck sometime during this period, by or under the direction of Chief Coiner Adam Eckfeldt.
>
> **1838, June:** Believed to have been added to the Mint Cabinet formed at this time by Adam Eckfeldt and William E. Dubois, although Alexandre Vattemare, a numismatist visiting from France this year, did not report seeing it.[2] Perhaps it had been removed for some purpose, or had not yet been added to the display.
>
> **1842:** Illustrated by Jacob Reese Eckfeldt and William E. Dubois in *A Manual of Gold and Silver Coins of All Nations, Struck Within the Past Century.*
>
> **Later years, to date:** National Coin Collection (Mint Cabinet), Smithsonian Institution, earlier on display at the second and third Philadelphia mints. On display in 1893 in Chicago as part of the Treasury Department exhibit at the World's Columbian Exposition.
>
> **1945:** In the past, various Mint and government officials were willing to provide authentications, stories, etc., concerning 1804 silver dollars. However, this letter dated October 4, 1945, by J.E. Graf, of the Smithsonian Institution, to 1804 dollar owner C.F. Childs, Chicago, closes the circle: "Mr. T.T. Belote, Curator of History, has brought to my attention your letter to him of September 25 with reference to the 1804 dollar in the National Numismatic Collection. . . . We have no information whatever concerning the circumstances under which it was acquired by the Mint."[3]

2. The Stickney Specimen

(Eliasberg Collection coin)

Details of this specimen: Described as Proof-63 in the Eliasberg Collection catalog; later graded as Proof-65 by PCGS. 415.3 grains. The edge lettering is crushed. On the obverse a fine die crack begins at the outermost tip of star 6 and continues upward, through the tops of LIBERTY ending at the left side of the last letter. The reverse has a tiny crack beginning at the right top side of the I in UNITED, continuing across the body of that letter, through the tops of TED, and ending in the field to the right of the D. These are probably stress cracks that originated during the die punching and annealing process, and are believed to be common to all specimens of this variety, although the extent of the cracks varies.

Matthew Adams Stickney was the first numismatist to acquire an 1804 dollar. On May 9, 1843, he went to the Philadelphia Mint and received this coin in exchange for an IMMUNE COLUMBIA coin struck in gold and several other items, including examples of Massachusetts Pine Tree silver coins. At the time, Stickney was one of just a handful of American collectors who collected American silver coins systematically (by date sequence, hoping to acquire each and every one).

> **1834–1843:** Struck during this time, by or under the direction of Chief Coiner Adam Eckfeldt.[4] Most likely coined circa the mid-1830s along with the other Class I coins.
>
> **1843:** Mint Cabinet Collection duplicate.
>
> **1843, May 9:** Matthew Adams Stickney acquired the coin from the Mint Cabinet, where it was a duplicate (although not earlier publicized as such), by exchanging for it a 1785 Immune Columbia cent in gold and some other pieces, including "Pine-tree money."[5] The token was larger than a current $5 gold piece, and for gold value alone represented a profit of several hundred percent over the face value of the 1804. The origin of the 1785 Immune Columbia trade coin, struck over a 1775 British gold guinea, is surrounded by its own mystery and is thought by some to have been made as a numismatic delicacy (despite Stickney stating that he acquired it from a bullion dealer); however, the era is early, antedating such fantasy coiners as Edwin Bishop and Thomas Wyatt, who seem to have emerged in the 1850s. Concerning the Stickney visit, S. Hudson Chapman in his November 1913 catalog of the Lyman Collection commented: "The late Matthew A. Stickney informed me in conversations and by letter that in 1843 he saw two specimens in the Mint Cabinet and exchanged for one of them the unique Immune Columbia in gold and some Massachusetts silver coins. He also stated at that time only these two specimens were known." This recollection, if true, would seem to indicate that when Stickney made the exchange, the keepers of the Mint Cabinet assured him that the 1804 dollar was very rare and gave him no indication that others had been struck.
>
> **1843–1894:** Stickney Collection. Widely cited during his ownership, with numerous mentions in the *American Journal of Numismatics,* auction catalogs, and other printed material. This was the focal 1804 dollar for many years.
>
> **1894–1907:** Stickney's daughter.
>
> **1907, June:** Henry Chapman, auction of the Stickney Collection, June 25–29, 1907, Lot 849 ($3,600). This was one of Chapman's largest and most important sales and served to re-establish his numismatic importance about a year after the well-known partnership with his brother S. Hudson Chapman had been dissolved. Both Chapmans went on to conduct illustrious sales through the 1920s. In describ-

ing this 1804 dollar for sale in the Stickney collection, Henry Chapman wrote, in part: "This 1804 dollar has never been out of Mr. Stickney's possession and so carefully guarded by him that few persons were ever even allowed to see it. He always considered the 1787 New York Brasher doubloon and this coin his greatest numismatic treasures."

1907–1923: Colonel James W. Ellsworth. Displayed at the American Numismatic Society, 1914, and illustrated on Plate 17 of the catalog titled *Exhibition of United States and Colonial Coins, January 17th to February 18, 1914.* Ellsworth's 1804 dollar and selected other coins were part of a spectacular loan and reference display that included three other specimens of the 1804 dollar.

1923, March 7: Wayte Raymond and John Work Garrett via Knoedler & Co. The latter, a well-known dealer in paintings and art, controlled the sale of the collection. Garrett put up the money and thus had first pick of anything he wanted (but he already owned an 1804 dollar), and the remainder of the coins—constituting most of the collection—were marketed by Raymond, a dealer of excellent reputation whose star was rising rapidly.

1923–1940: William Cutler Atwater, New York collector.

1931, June: On the commission of Atwater, Wayte Raymond published a pamphlet describing the history of this specimen, noting in part: "Ownership and pride of possession contribute a large part of the pleasure of collecting, and Mr. William C. Atwater of New York is justly proud of owning the celebrated Stickney 1804 Dollar. This is by far the most famous pedigreed coin in America and is one of the outstanding pieces in his remarkable collection of United States coins. The pedigree of this splendid coin dates back to May 9th, 1843, when it was purchased from the cabinet of the U. S. Mint by Mr. Matthew Stickney of Salem, Mass. It remained in the Stickney Collection until after his death in 1894, and was finally sold at auction for his estate by Henry Chapman of Philadelphia in 1907. It thus remained in the possession of Mr. Stickney and his daughter for 64 years. It was purchased at the Chapman auction for $3,600.00 by Col. James W. Ellsworth of New York. In 1923 I bought the entire collection of Col. Ellsworth and Mr. Atwater acquired the Stickney dollar, as well as many other rare pieces, from me. The letters reproduced in this pamphlet speak for themselves and confirm the pedigree of this famous coin from the time it left the United States Mint eighty-eighty years ago." Several letters followed providing additional evidence of the pedigree of the "celebrated 1804 dollar."

1940–1946: William Cutler Atwater estate.

1946: B. Max Mehl, Atwater Collection, June 11, 1946, Lot 213 ($10,500). The Atwater Collection sale included examples of the Class I and Class III 1804 dollars.

1946–1976: Louis E. Eliasberg Sr. Widely exhibited at banks and at the Smithsonian Institution. The following was written by Eliasberg in 1956: "The dollar on exhibit is the only coin of this rare date that can be traced back to the United States Mint, where it was acquired by Mr. Stickney in 1843 in exchange for a gold IMMUNE COLUMBIA cent and several other pieces. There are six original 1804 dollars known to exist of which three including this specimen are in private collections. It is the most famous pedigreed coin in America and has only been in four collections in the past 113 years."

1976–1997: Louis E. Eliasberg Sr. estate.

1997, April 6: Cataloged and sold by Auctions by Bowers and Merena, Inc., in cooperation with Stack's. Realized $1,815,000, a record price for any coin ever sold in public competition.

1997: Spectrum Numismatics, Greg Roberts as bidder.

1997 to date: Private collection.

3. King of Siam Presentation Specimen

Newman-Bressett: "Siam Specimen"

Details of this specimen: Proof-65 (PCGS grade). 415.5 grains. The edge lettering is crushed.

This 1804 dollar is part of a cased presentation set struck in 1834 and believed to have been presented by Edmund Roberts on behalf of President Andrew Jackson to King Ph'ra Nang Klao (Rama III) of Siam in 1836. The set also contained the following: 1834 half cent; 1834 cent; 1834 dime; 1834 quarter dollar; 1834 half dollar; 1834 Without Motto $2.50 gold; 1834 Without Motto $5 gold; 1804 "restrike" $10 gold; and two other coins which are now missing. Later owners (Spectrum Numismatics), upon displaying the set, included an 1834 half dime (ex Floyd Starr Collection) and a gold Andrew Jackson inaugural medalet to take the place of the missing Proof 1834 With Motto $2.50.

The following pedigree is conjectural before circa the 1950s:

1834, November: Adam Eckfeldt, chief coiner at the Philadelphia Mint. Coined to the order of U.S. State Department, for inclusion in a set of specimen coins for diplomatic presentation.

1835: Placed aboard the USS *Peacock* in the custody of special agent Edmund Roberts.

1836, April 6: Presented by Roberts as a gift from President Andrew Jackson for King Ph'ra Nang Klao (Rama III) of Siam.

1836–1868: In the possession of the royal family of Siam, passing from Rama III to his half-brother, Rama IV, a.k.a. King Mongkut, who died in 1868. *The line of descent through the 1950s is conjectural.*

1869, October 18: Following the death of his father on this date, 15-year-old Chulalongkorn became king. Known as Rama V. King Chulalongkorn died on October 23, 1910.

19th century: Anna Leonowens, who was known as Anna of Siam (memorialized in the musical *The King and I*). Certain of her accounts of life in Siam, including certain aspects of her relationship with Rama IV, have been proved fictional by scholars.[6] Thus, the pedigree leap from this point to David F. Spink is highly conjectural. In 1962, Newman and Bressett commented (italics added): "No *facts* have been disclosed concerning how the set left Siam or where it has reposed over the years."

Late 1800s to mid-1900s: Believed to have descended through the Leonowens family.

1950s: Two older ladies, who were believed by David F. Spink to have been descendants of Anna Leonowens, brought the set to Spink & Son of London. The half dime and the With Motto 1834 $2.50 gold coin were missing from the set by this time. At the Spink office, one of the numismatic experts, Donald Crowther, met with the two ladies.[7]

1950s–1979: Owned by David F. Spink, personally, with no benefit to the firm (which caused some dissension among firm members). As Spink was an owner of the firm, he had the right to do this. Displayed at the American Numismatic Association Convention, August 1962, there becoming the center of much interest and attention.

1979: Lester Merkin, agent for David F. Spink. At the time, Lester received some criticism from Spink & Sons staff members, although Lester was simply acting as agent for David F. Spink. The price of the set was $1,000,000, although the eventual transaction also involved some coins taken in trade.[8]

1979–1989: Elvin I. Unterman, Garrison, New York. Exhibited at the Smithsonian Institution, 1983.

1987: Lester Merkin, agent for Elvin I. Unterman.

1987, October 14: Bowers and Merena, King of Siam Sale, Lot 2209. The set was reserved by the consignor; the reserve was not met.

1989, October 18: Stack's, agent for the owner. Sold on this date.

1989–1990: The Rarities Group (Martin B. Paul) and Continental Rarity Coin Fund I (Greg Holloway).

1990, May: Superior Galleries. Included in the catalog titled as the Father Flanagan Boys Town Sale, May 27–29, 1990, Lot 3364.

1990–1993: Iraj Sayah (Los Angeles investor and coin dealer; traded under the name Unigold) and Terry Brand (Los Angeles industrialist).

1993: Superior Galleries, auction of January 31 and February 1, 1993, Lot 1196. Sold to Dwight Manley, on the staff of and bidding for Spectrum Numismatics, Santa Ana, California.

1993 to 2005: Private Western collection. On public display as part of the Treasures of Mandalay Museum in the Mandalay Bay Resort & Museum in Las Vegas, Nevada, beginning on March 3, 1999 (grand opening date of the Resort).

2005 to date: Steve Contursi, Rare Coin Wholesalers, via Ira & Larry Goldberg Coins & Collectibles.

4. The Sultan of Muscat Presentation Specimen
Newman-Bressett: "Watters Specimen"
(Childs Collection coin; Pogue Collection)

Details of this specimen: Gem Proof-68 (PCGS). 416.7 grains. The edge lettering is crushed. The coin has blue and iridescent toning. It is lightly struck at certain star centers. On the obverse a fine die crack begins at the outermost tip of star 6 and continues upward, through the tops of LIBERTY, ending at the left side of the last letter. The reverse has a tiny crack beginning at the upper-right serif of the N in UNITED, continuing across the body of that letter, through the tops of TED, and ending in the field to the right of the D, about two thirds of the way to the next-to-highest feather at the bottom of the wing. The high state of preservation of this specimen permits the observation of certain die-crack details that might not be discernible on lower-grade pieces. All 1804 Class I dollars show this crack to one degree or another, thus providing a marker for authentication purposes.

This is the finest known 1804 dollar. It is believed to have been presented in 1835 by Edmund Roberts on behalf of President Andrew Jackson to the Sultan of Muscat, this being the very first 1804 silver dollar distributed outside of the Mint. The early pedigree is conjectural as no paper trail survives. The set turned up in England in the 1860s, where it could have come from Muscat (by a route unknown) or may have been part of a British collection (for the British were avid collectors of U.S. coins in the 1830s and 1840s, long before a comparable interest arose in America).

The title "Sultan of Muscat Presentation Specimen" was given by Q. David Bowers. In *The Fantastic 1804 Dollar,* Newman and Bressett titled it the "Watters Specimen."

The following pedigree is conjectural before circa 1867–1868:

1834, November: Adam Eckfeldt, chief coiner at the Philadelphia Mint. Coined to the order of the U.S. State Department, for inclusion in a set of specimen coins for diplomatic presentation.

1835: Placed aboard the USS *Peacock* in the custody of special agent Edmund Roberts.

1835, October 1: Presented by Roberts to the following:

1835–1856 (?): Sayyid Sa'id-bin-Sultan (a.k.a. the Sultan of Muscat) in cased presentation set of 1834. At the time the sultan (popularly but incorrectly called *Imaum* or *Imam*) of Muscat was the most prominent actor in commercial trade in the northern and western reaches of the Indian Ocean.

1856 to 1867 or 1868: Exact dates and intermediaries unknown. Possibly in the hands of a London numismatist by the latter time.

1867 or 1868 to 1917: Charles A. Watters, Liverpool, England. By this time the coins were no longer in their original presentation case.[9] Watters acquired the 1804 dollar in 1867 or 1868, possibly from a source in London, this per a letter from Watters, June 27, 1879, to Jeremiah Colburn (quoted in full under the Watters biography in Appendix II of *The Rare Silver Dollars Dated 1804 and the Exciting Adventures of Edmund Roberts*). A related letter from Watters, June 25, 1879, to Ebenezer Locke Mason Jr., of Philadelphia, mentions it. Leonard S. Forrer, London coin dealer, wrote to R. Green, April 30, 1946, in response to an inquiry about Watters and where the 1804 dollar may have been acquired: "Although I was at the war in 1917, I have some recollection of a discussion which took place then or earlier, as to where Mr. Watters had obtained the 1804 dollar, and to the best of my recollection and belief, it was said that he purchased it from a Mr. Eschwege of Liverpool. The latter gentleman was a foreign exchange dealer in Liverpool, who had a small numismatic business as well, and I believe that on inquiry from Mr. Eschwege he could not recollect from whom he had bought the coin, and alleged that it had turned up in an odd lot in Liverpool, which would not be at all surprising. As both these gentlemen are now dead, it is impossible to carry the information any further." However, it seems from Watters's 19th-century correspondence, which states a London source, that the involvement of Eschwege is questionable. Moreover, the contact Forrer had with Eschwege in 1917 was a half century after Watters obtained the 1804 dollar.

1917, June 14–15: Messrs. Glendining & Co., Ltd., London, sale of Part II the Watters Collection. Lot 227, the 1804 dollar, was sold on June 15 for £330. "Excessively rare, in perfect condition, considered one of the finest specimens known." Other silver coins representing a partial presentation set of 1834 were sold separately.

1917–1918: Henry Chapman. Displayed at the 1917 American Numismatic Association Convention in Rochester, New York. Sold by Chapman on June 20, 1918, for $2,500 to Virgil M. Brand.

1917, August 23: Letter furnished to Chapman by T. Louis Comparette, curator of the Mint Collection:[10] "To Whom It May Concern: This is to certify that the specimen of 1804 dollar shown me this day by Mr. Henry Chapman is from the identical die as a specimen in the Mint Collection, the latter being the specimen of the coin usually regarded as one of the original issue."

1918, June 20: Addendum to the Comparette letter: "June 20, 1919. The 1804 dollar which I this day sold to Mr. Virgil M. Brand is the identical dollar shown by me to Dr. Comparette and which he mentions above. Henry Chapman. No. 333 So. 16th. Philadelphia."

1918–1926: Virgil M. Brand.

1926–1933: Virgil M. Brand estate.

1932, November 18: Appraised at $3,500 by Burdette G. Johnson.[11] The coin was serial no. 86957 in the Virgil Brand estate and was located in "Rarities Box No. 8."

1933, November 1, to date unknown (by 1942): To Armin W. Brand on November 1, 1933, via the Brand estate division.[12]

1933 November, or later, but by 1942: Traded by Armin W. Brand to his brother, Horace Louis Philip Brand.

1942–1945: On consignment from Horace Louis Philip Brand to Charles E. Green and Ruth Green. Offered in *The Numismatist,* April 1942, p. 348, by R. Green (trade style of Charles E. Green; Ruth was his wife). However, the listing used a stock photograph and not an image of the 1804 dollar being offered.

1945, August 10: Sold by Horace Louis Philip Brand and his former wife Erna M. Brand to Ruth and Charles E. Green; price $3,150. Brand told Green that he sold it to raise money to give to its co-owner, Erna. The transaction took place in the Industrial National Bank, Chicago.[13] Advertised in *The Numismatist,* September 1945, p. 998 (illustrated; titled "Purchased by R. Green").

1945, September 29: After some discussion with Charles E. Green, Charles Frederick Childs contacted his son, Frederick Newell Childs, stating that he was uncertain about buying it for $5,000, as Green had offered it. C.F. Childs had been in touch with and had asked opinions of dealer Abe Kosoff (of the Numismatic Gallery, New York City), the Smithsonian Institution, and the Philadelphia Mint, but was still undecided. Green had given him an option until September 30, but extended it to October 1. Uncertain as to Childs's intentions, Green had informed Louis E. Eliasberg Sr., the Baltimore collector, of its availability.

1945, October 1: F. Newell Childs recommended that his father, Charles Frederick Childs, buy the coin. The decision was made in the early afternoon. In the meantime, Louis Eliasberg indicated he was ready to buy it for $5,000 if Childs did not. Sold by R. Green and C.E. Green to the following, for $5,000. Paid for the next day.[14] Later, Eliasberg purchased the Stickney specimen from Mehl's sale of the Atwater Collection.

1945, November: R. Green's advertisement in *The Numismatist* informed readers that the coin had been sold, "name of purchaser withheld by request."

1945 to 1952: Charles Frederick Childs for his son, Frederick Newell Childs; added to the collection (by date sequence) of U.S. coins formed by Walter H. Childs beginning circa 1870. C.F. Childs: "I acquired for my son the 1804 dollar out of the Virgil Brand Collection."[15]

1952: Given with the Childs coin collection to Charles Frederick Childs II, age eight, whose father, F. Newell Childs, acted as custodian.

1952–1999: C.F. Childs II and family.

1999, August 30: Walter H. Childs Collection sale, Auctions by Bowers and Merena, Inc. Sold to the following for a record auction price for any coin, $4,140,000. Held at the Park Lane Hotel, New York City, the Childs Collection sale drew hundreds of participants as well as worldwide television (ABC, CBS, NBC, CNN, Fox, Reuters, etc.) and press coverage.

1999, August 30, to date: Brent Pogue and his father, Mack Pogue, whose winning bid was handled at the sale by dealer David W. Akers.

5. Dexter Specimen
(Dunham Collection coin)

Details of this specimen: Proof-63. 415.8 grains. The edge lettering is crushed. There is a "D" counterstamped on a cloud on the reverse.

This dark bluish-steel toned Proof, known as the Dexter specimen, and which just as easily could be called the Dunham specimen or the Bareford specimen, set a then–record price for a coin sold at public auction in 1989. It just missed realizing a seven-figure price, a barrier that would not be broken until 1996 with the sale of the Eliasberg 1913 Liberty Head nickel.

The following pedigree is conjectural before circa 1884:

> **1834–1840s, circa:** Struck sometime during this period, by or under the direction of Chief Coiner Adam Eckfeldt. Most likely coined circa the mid-1830s along with the other Class I coins.

> **19th century:** Unknown intermediaries, perhaps someone connected with the Mint or, likely, a descendant.

> **1879, October 14:** Adolph Weyl sale, Berlin, Prussia, Lot 83. The 1804 dollar was included in a group with silver dollars dated 1794, 1795, 1796, 1797, 1801, 1803, 1804, 1836, 1838, 1839, 1851, 1852, 1854, 1855, 1856, 1857, and 1858. This was most probably the source for the auction appearance following. This reference was discovered by numismatic literature dealer George Kolbe in 2003 and published along with the sale of the auction catalog in Kolbe's 92nd Sale, November 13, 2003,

Lot 1115. Kolbe also reproduced on page 100 nine lots of U.S. coins offered for sale by Weyl in his sale of 1879.

1884, October 14: Adolph Weyl sale, Berlin, Prussia, Lot 159 ($216).

1884–1885: Chapman brothers, who bought their own coin, but now it had an exotic, if contrived, pedigree to a German cabinet.

1885, May 14–15: Chapman brothers sale, Lot 354 ($1,000). Described by the Chapmans as a "great gem."

1885: J.W. Scott, Scott Stamp & Coin Company. Per the Chapman brothers description in their 1885 sale: "S.H. and H. Chapman purchased October 1884, at a sale in Berlin, and resold to a Mr. Scott, a dealer in coins,[16] for $1,000 at their Philadelphia sale, in May 1885." Scott was agent for the following.

1885–1899: James Vila Dexter, Denver, Colorado. In his infinite wisdom, Dexter seems to have taken a "D" punch and counterstamped his initial on a cloud on the reverse. Apparently, he marked certain other of his coins as well.

1887, February 10: A. Loudon Snowden, former superintendent of the Mint, swore an affidavit stating that the Dexter specimen formerly sold by the Chapman brothers, and also the Mint Cabinet 1804 dollar [No. 1 in the present listing], were both (italics added) "of the year 1804 *coined in that year.*"

1899–1903: Dexter estate.

1903, November 5: Roland (a.k.a. "Rollin") G. Parvin, Union Deposit & Trust Co., Denver, executor of the Dexter estate. Sold on this date, after much correspondence with the numismatic community.

1903–1904: H.G. Brown, Portland, Oregon. *The Numismatist,* December 1903, noted that an 1804 silver dollar was sold by Roland G. Parvin, secretary and treasurer of the Union Deposit and Trust Company, Denver, for the sum of $2,000 with the buyer being H.G. Brown, of Portland, Oregon, according to a report. "The silver dollar made in 1804 is the gem of the United States coinage, and the price paid yesterday is the highest paid for an American coin. The story leading up to the sale is interesting: For some years past there has not been a mail that has not brought to Mr. Parvin inquiry in regard to the coin, and each contained a query as to what price to buy. Mr. Parvin would usually write down the first figure which came to his mind, because he did not wish to part with the coin. When he answered Mr. Brown's letter he placed the figure at $2,000 and forgot all about the matter. No sooner had the letter arrived and telegrams began to pour into the office of Mr. Parvin from Mr. Brown. The Denver man disliked to part with it, but in order to keep his word he sent the dollar today in receipt of the order for $2,000."

1904, October 11: Lyman H. Low, Part I of the Brown Collection, Lot 431 ($1,100). "Extremely Fine, with a brilliant, proof-like surface." In the same month, *The Numismatist* carried Lyman H. Low's defense of the 1804 dollar, which had been criticized in an earlier issue: "In my catalogue of the coming Brown sale I give what I believe to be the most complete account that has ever been published of this celebrated coin, with an accurate tabulated list of every genuine specimen that is known up to date—just 13 of them. . . . I have my theories, gathered from points which I have stored away from time to time, during the past 25 years, some of which I disclose in the Brown catalogue, but I have not consummated them sufficiently at the present time, to give them as freely as I would like to do; later I intend to do so. I regard it as very important, when considering the endorsement to be given to the coin as a bona fide issue and production of United States Mint, that we should take into consideration the standing and experience of those eminent collectors who have admitted the pieces into their cabinets. The judgment of such men as Stickney, Mickley, Sanford, Appleton, Parmelee, Lillienthal, Cohen, Reed, and Ten Eyck must be respected, and more can be said of them than that their wealth enabled them to possess the piece. They were connoisseurs as well as collectors, foremost in the ranks, and the adverse criticisms of today must be taken cautiously, and the source and object or aim of such, carefully considered." This was begging the question, as discussion in numismatic circles centered not upon whether such pieces had been struck at the Mint, but upon *when* they had been made.

1904–1939: William Forrester Dunham, Chicago. Exhibited by Dunham including at the February 4, 1910, meeting of the Chicago Numismatic Society, a group which at that time was one of America's most active numismatic clubs. *The Numismatist,* February 1905, commented that the Dexter specimen of the 1804 silver dollar, recently purchased by William F. Dunham of Chicago, "will remain forever" in that city, according to a four- page article that designated the piece as the "King of Rarities." The narrative continued: "For a century it has remained wrapped in silk and tissue paper, waiting all the time, says the present owner, to come into the possession of someone who never would part with it again. In a way the action of the present owner in buying the coin was a patriotic deed. He bought it for the city and says it shall never leave here. When the Field Columbian Museum is housed downtown he will give his collection to that institution. It will never again be for sale."

1939–1941: B. Max Mehl, who purchased the Dunham collection for his inventory. The reaction of the Field Museum was not recorded.

1941, June 3: B. Max Mehl, Dunham Collection, Lot 1058. Sold privately to Charles M. Williams for $4,250 before the "auction" took place. Williams had his pick of anything else he wanted from the Dunham sale beforehand; he also bought another rarity, the 1822 $5. Although an "auction catalog" was published, Mehl sold many things before the sale, often *long before,* but listed them in the catalog anyway, and later published the "prices realized." The numismatic community was none the wiser until in later years the story came to light through several channels. Q. David Bowers (in a study of the John Work Garrett papers), Donald M. Miller (of Indiana, Pennsylvania, who noticed the curious situation that multiple tokens were pedigreed to the same single Dunham sale lots, and in addition to this unusual situation, some had been invoiced prior to the Dunham sale), and Abe Kosoff (who told of Charles M. Williams having had his pick of the Dunham delicacies before the auction), were among those piecing together the story.

1941–1949: Charles M. Williams, Cincinnati, Ohio.

1949: Abe Kosoff (via Numismatic Gallery) and Sol Kaplan, purchasers from Williams.

1949–1981: Harold Bareford.

1981, October 22–23: Stack's, Bareford Collection, Lot 424 ($280,000).

1981–1985: RARCOA (Ed Milas), Chicago, Illinois.

1985–1989: Leon Hendrickson and George Weingart.

1989, July 7: RARCOA, Auction '89, Lot 247 ($990,000).

1989–?: American Rare Coin Fund, L.P., Hugh Sconyers, financial manager, Kevin Lipton, numismatic manager.

1990s, early: Northern California collector.

1993, July: Superior Galleries sale, Lot 551. Reserve not met; returned to consignor.

1994, May 30–31: Superior Galleries sale, Lot 761.

1994: Harlan White, proprietor of the Old Coin Shop, San Diego, California.

?–2000: Private Southeastern collection.

2000, October 17–19, to date: Stack's, Lot 1167 ($1,840,000). Sold into a private collection.

6. Parmelee Specimen

From the Byron Reed Collection; owned by the City of Omaha, Nebraska; on loan to The Durham Museum.

Details of this specimen: Proof-63, flat stars. 416.1 grains (per Lawrence J. Lee, then curator).[17] Later (1999) certified as Proof-64 by ICG. There is friction in the fields. The edge lettering is crushed. On the obverse a fine die crack begins at the outermost tip of star 6 and continues upward, through the tops of LIBERTY, ending at the left side of the last letter. The reverse has a tiny crack beginning at the right top side of the I in UNITED, continuing across the body of that letter, through the tops of TED, ending in the field to the right of the D, about two thirds of the way to the next-to-highest feather at the bottom of the wing.[18]

Currently residing in a special showcase in The Durham Museum in Omaha, this specimen is part of the Byron Reed Collection, on display in that institution. Its most famous owner, of course, was Lorin G. Parmelee of Boston baked bean fame. In 1874, Edward D.

Cogan wrote, regarding this piece: "This dollar I guarantee is original and a remarkably fine impression, and is known to be one of, if not the most rare piece in the American series, not more than four or five being known to collectors in the United States."

The following pedigree is conjectural before circa 1868:

1834 to 1840s: Most likely coined circa the mid-1830s along with the other Class I coins, by or under the direction of Chief Coiner Adam Eckfeldt.

1840s, late, to 1868: In the possession of the acquirer, then to an unknown "lady," allegedly bought from the Mint by a person unknown, for face value during the administration of James Knox Polk (1845–1849). If so, this was a trade with the Mint Cabinet or an official, the details of which are not known today. Alternatively, there is this somewhat related account in *Counterfeit, Mis-Struck and Unofficial Coins,* by Don Taxay, page 82: "In 1868 a specimen [of the rare 1804 dollar] was purchased by E.H. Sanford from an elderly lady who claimed to have obtained it (for the price of one dollar) from the Mint during Polk's administration." The "aged lady" gave the coin to her son, per the story, and the coin was sold to E. Harrison Sanford (see below).

1868: Owned by the son of the above-mentioned lady, but apparently sold by May 1868. *American Journal of Numismatics,* May 1868: "A [hitherto unknown] specimen has come to light, said to be superior even to Mr. Appleton's, a genuine impression too with the circumscription on the edge. . . . The one at present under notice is thought to be an original. The mother of the recent proprietor obtained it in Philadelphia at some time during President Polk's administration. Hearing of the high price paid for Mr. Mickley's, this lady exclaimed: 'Why, I have an 1804 dollar!' 'Impossible," replied her son; but, on investigation, the 'impossible' became fact, and the result is that the piece has passed into the hands of a third party. For further particulars inquire of the present owner." A careful reading of the preceding account states that the coin was obtained in Philadelphia, but nothing was said about it being obtained for face value. Dr. Joel J. Orosz has pointed out that if in 1843 the curators of the Mint Cabinet required M.A. Stickney to trade a gold IMMUNE COLUMBIA piece plus examples of Pine Tree silver coins dated 1652, it seems unlikely that the Mint would have offered one for face value at a later date.[19] Thus, it seems reasonable that the coin may have been sold or traded to a collector in Philadelphia.

1868–1874: E. Harrison Sanford.

1874, November 27: Edward D. Cogan, Sanford Collection, Lot 99 ($700). "This dollar I guarantee original and a remarkably fine impression." The dollar was shown by the first 1804 dollar photographic illustration to appear in an auction catalog.

1874–1890: Lorin G. Parmelee. During this time he also bought and sold the Cohen coin (No. 8 below).

1890, June: Offered for sale by Ed. Frossard in *Numisma,* apparently on consignment from Parmelee.

1890, June 25–27: New York Coin & Stamp Company, Parmelee Collection, Lot 817 ($570).

1890–1891: Byron Reed.

1891–1980s: Omaha City Library, Omaha, Nebraska.

1980s to date: Transferred in the 1980s for display to Western Heritage Museum, Omaha, currently known as The Durham Museum. On view intermittently since that time. The collection, not on view since 1996, "was officially transferred March 11 [1999] from the Gerald R. Ford Conservation Center to the Durham Western Heritage Museum, where it will go on display in June," noted *Coin World,* April 12, 1999. Subsequently, it was announced that June 19, 1999, would be the opening date. Thereafter the 1804 dollar and other numismatic prizes were on view in a museum setting that included much historical and graphic material relating to coins and numismatics, especially of the 19th century.

7. Mickley Specimen
(David Queller Collection coin)

Details of this specimen: Proof-50; later re-graded NGC Proof-62. 416.4 grains. The edge lettering is crushed. On the obverse a fine die crack begins at the outermost tip of star 5 and continues upward, through the tops of LIBERTY. There are *two tiny raised dots in the hair, far below the B in LIBERTY;* there are rust pits present, but not obvious. The reverse has a tiny crack beginning at the left top side of the U in UNITED, continuing across the body of that letter, through the tops of TED, and ending at the first S in STATES.

Joseph J. Mickley was one of our country's most celebrated collectors of the second and third quarters of the 19th century. His numismatic interests were varied, including the acquisition of early coinage dies of the U.S. Mint. For many years this specimen was in the collection of the Massachusetts Historical Society.

The following pedigree is conjectural before circa the 1850s:

> **1834–1835, circa:** Probably struck sometime during this period, by or under the direction of Chief Coiner Adam Eckfeldt. Could one or both of Nos. 7 and 8 have been intended for presentation in Cochin-China or Japan? If so, the striking time would have been spring 1835. (Specimens no. 7 and no. 8 have the same hypothetical scenario for their early years, as each shows evidence of limited circulation.)

1830s or 1840s: Possibly traded or sold to a numismatist or other collector, or placed into circulation by someone at the State Department after its presentation set was returned as undelivered.

1850s: Henry C. Young, a teller for the Bank of Pennsylvania, circa1850, supposedly retrieved from a deposit at face value.

1859, prior to, until 1867: Joseph J. Mickley.

1867, October 28: W. Elliot Woodward, Mickley Collection, Lot 1696 ($750). "This piece is regarded by all American collectors and the gem of Mr. Mickley's collection. It has been in circulation, but it is still in the finest condition. . . . It was obtained many years ago from the Bank of Pennsylvania and is beyond question, not only genuine, but original. Of the four specimens known, two, it is certain were struck at a period subsequent to 1804, and till one was recently obtained by Col. Cohen, from Richmond, this was supposed to be the only original one existing; scarce." The April 1868 issue of the *American Journal of Numismatics* stated the buyer was Cogan, but William A. Lilliendahl seems to have owned it in the meantime, perhaps acquiring it via Cogan as his agent. Indeed, the next (May 1868) issue of the same journal noted: "Since the sale of Mr. Mickley's genuine and original piece of this denomination to Mr. Lilliendahl, last fall, and its subsequent acquisition by Mr. Appleton."

1867: Edward D. Cogan, briefly if at all.

1867–1868: William A. Lilliendahl, who bought it at the Mickley sale, later selling it to the following for cash and some coins. In 1876, Emmanuel J. Attinelli mentioned the Lilliendahl connection:[20] "This [burglary of certain items from Mickley's collection] undoubtedly produced a feeling of insecurity which, at Mr. Mickley's advancing age, induced him to at once dispose of the cherished objects of his solicitude and care, the labor and search of many years spent in gathering together these mementos of the past. The gem of the collection was the 1804 Dollar, which was bought by Mr. William A. Lilliendahl for $750, probably the highest sum ever paid in this country for a single coin."

1868, February: Edward D. Cogan, who around this time became quite interested in the history of the 1804 dollar. Traded to the following in the same month.

1868–1903: William Sumner Appleton.

1903–1905: William Sumner Appleton estate.

1905–1970: Massachusetts Historical Society.

1970, October 23–24: Stack's, Massachusetts Historical Society Collection, Lot 625 ($77,500).

1970–1974: Chicago private collection.

1974, January: Bought by Stack's, agent for the following.

1974–1993: Reed Hawn.

1993, October 13–14: Stack's, Reed Hawn Collection, Lot 735 ($475,000).

1993–2008: David Queller Collection. After the 1993 sale, the circumstances of acquisition of the dollar were related by the coin's new owner:[21] "I recall sitting next to the person who bought this coin at the Stack's auction in 1970. He received a standing ovation and was very proud to own this Mickley 1804 dollar. When I bought this same coin at the Reed Hawn sale I also received the same standing ovation and was very happy to become the new proud owner of this 1804 Class I dollar." Sold by Heritage (April 16, 2008, Lot 2089, at $3,737,500) to the following.

2008 to date: Private collection.

8. Cohen Specimen

(American Numismatic Association Money Museum)

Details of this specimen: VF-30. 410.2 grains. There are many nicks and scratches. The edge lettering is crushed. Of the various 1804 Class I dollars, this coin has the greatest evidence of wear. It is presumed that the original weight of this dollar was about 416 grains, of which a few grains were later lost through wear.

This specimen was lost in the robbery of the Willis H. du Pont collection in October 1967 and was recovered in April 1993. Du Pont also owned a Class III specimen (No. 13 in the present list), which was recovered in the 1980s. Both specimens have since been donated to institutional collections.

The following pedigree is conjectural before circa 1865:

> **1834–1835, circa:** Probably struck sometime during this period, by or under the direction of Chief Coiner Adam Eckfeldt. Could one or both of Nos. 7 and 8 have been intended for presentation in Cochin-China or Japan? If so, the striking time would have been spring 1835. (Specimens no. 7 and no. 8 have the same hypothetical scenario for their early years, as each shows evidence of limited circulation.)

> **1830s–1860s:** Unknown intermediaries. Joel J. Orosz offers a speculation:[22] Robert Gilmor Jr., the Baltimore collector who was active in the 1830s and 1840s and who was supplied various coins by Adam Eckfeldt, is not known to have had an 1804 dollar, as none has been traced to him at a later date. "However, if [1804 dollars] became available to the Mint's pet collectors in 1843, Gilmor still had five years to

live, and *should* have been offered one, and if offered, almost surely would have accepted (we know from his 1841 letter to Joel Roberts Poinsett that he lacked only a few coins in his attempt to complete a date run of silver coins from the Mint). We also know that most of his collection passed to his nephew after he died in 1848, and that his nephew (also known as Robert Gilmor Jr.) sold the bulk of the coins privately in early 1861. However, a few 'heirloom' pieces such as a 1787 Brasher gold doubloon were kept in the family, and apparently became the property of the second Robert Gilmor Jr.'s son, Harry (1838–1883), a Confederate cavalryman. Might the Cohen 1804 dollar have been one of the Gilmor heirloom coins? If so, it is conceivable that during the hardships of the Civil War years, especially in the South, Harry Gilmor might have spent the coin, explaining how it might have turned up in the South (Richmond) during the Civil War era. Purely speculative, I admit, but intriguing nonetheless!"

1865, circa: Purchased "over the counter" at the exchange office of Edward Cohen, Richmond, Virginia.

1865–1875: Colonel Mendes I. Cohen, Baltimore, Maryland.

1875, October 15: Edward D. Cogan, Cohen Collection, Lot 535 ($325). "It has been more circulated than either of the two previously sold at auction, and has every appearance of having been struck in the year of its date, and is guaranteed to be original."

1875–1876: Henry S. Adams, Boston, Massachusetts.

1876, November 1: Edward D. Cogan, Adams Collection, Lot 356 ($500).

1876–1878: Lorin G. Parmelee. Sold by Parmelee after he bought the Sanford Collection coin, No. 6 in the above list (*The Numismatist,* July 1896, account by Parmelee). However, as Parmelee *already owned* the Sanford coin when he bought the Cohen coin, he must have desired the Cohen piece as a duplicate.

1878: Henry G. Sampson, dealer intermediary.

1878–1906: Major William Boerum Wetmore, New York City, New York.

1906, June 27–28: Chapman brothers, Wetmore Collection, Lot 208 ($720). This event was held at the end of the Chapman brothers' partnership, which had endured since 1878. "It has evidently been in actual circulation and bears no appearance whatever of a piece rubbed purposely to make it look old.[23] It is the only specimen that shows having been in circulation."

1906, June: Chapman brothers (bought for inventory).

1906, summer: Thomas L. Elder. Bought for inventory from one of the Chapman brothers, who had dissolved their partnership. Sold in July 1906 to the following.

1906–1921: James H. Manning, Albany, New York.

1921, May 17: B. Max Mehl, Manning Collection, Lot 778 ($2,500). With some imagination, Mehl later advertised the scenario that rare and valuable coins could be found anywhere, and "lucky Mrs. Manning," who somehow had an 1804 dollar, received a nice check from Mehl. The catalog used a "stock illustration," as Mehl often did, and showed not the coin being sold, but, instead, the Stickney 1804 dollar!

1921–1922: Elmer S. Sears.

1922: B. Max Mehl, who sold it to the following.

1922–1952: Lammot DuPont (as he capitalized his name).

1952–1994: Willis H. du Pont (as *he* capitalized his name). Included in the armed robbery of the du Pont coins in Florida, October 5, 1967. Recovered on April 23, 1993, in Zurich, Switzerland.

1994: Donated to the American Numismatic Association, where it is one of the foremost attractions of the ANA Money Museum.

Class II 1804 Dollars

Plain Edge "Restrike" (Minted Circa 1859–1860)

9. Mint Cabinet Specimen
Newman-Bressett: "U.S. Mint Specimen"
(Smithsonian Institution)

Details of this specimen: Proof. 381.5 grains. Plain edge; high wire rim. The reverse is slightly misaligned; the 0 in the date is aligned with the second T in STATES.

Class II 1804 dollars have a plain edge, unlike either Class I or III dollars. It seems likely that they were not struck to be disseminated as "originals" or Class I dollars; the overstriking, lack of a lettered edge, etc., would have precluded their acceptance as such. Rather, they may have been presented as "fillers" for this otherwise unobtainable date.

This unique specimen of the Class II 1804 dollar was struck circa 1859, over an 1857-dated Bern (Switzerland) shooting taler.[24] Note: The *American Journal of Numismatics,* April 1878, stated that five of these were made in 1858, and that four had been sold to numismatists; these were retrieved later by the Mint. Three are said to have been melted, and one is unaccounted for.

Some electrotype and/or cast copies exist of this coin, even showing details of the under-type.[25] At least three electrotypes are believed to have been made at the Mint or at the behest of Mint employees, circa 1860.[26]

> **1850s, late:** Mint Cabinet Collection. A part of the National Coin Collection (Mint Cabinet Collection), Smithsonian Institution.

CLASS III 1804 DOLLARS
"Restrike" (Minted Circa 1860s or 1870s)

10. Berg Specimen
(Garrett Collection coin)

Details of this specimen: EF-40. 402.8 grains. The edge lettering is blundered and doubled in areas. The coin is double struck on the reverse. The reverse is slightly rotated (the 0 in the date is aligned with the second T in STATES).

The name of John W. Haseltine repeatedly occurs in connection with the Class III 1804 dollars along with the 1801, 1802, and 1803 Proof novodels. Apparently Haseltine was the chosen agent to distribute these for the Mint employees who made them, possibly with his father-in-law, William Idler, helping facilitate the arrangement. Haseltine devised several intriguing scenarios to distribute these coins. The present piece is said to have crossed the Atlantic twice, all the way to Vienna before it was "discovered." This specimen became part of the famed Garrett Collection with its acquisition by Thomas Harrison Garrett in 1883.

The following pedigree is conjectural before circa 1875:

> **1858–1872:** Believed to have been fabricated at the Philadelphia Mint in this time period.

> **1875 (?):** Captain John W. Haseltine, Philadelphia coin dealer.

> **1876, March 30:** J.W. Haseltine, "Centennial Coin and Curiosity Sale" I, Lot 194. Haseltine bought the coin for O.H. Berg at this sale.

> **1876 (circa)–1883:** O.H. Berg, Baltimore, Maryland.

1883, May 23–24: J.W. Haseltine, Berg Collection, Lot 568 ($740). "Although a little worn by circulation, it is Very Fine. About as fine as the one in the Sanford sale, and considerably finer than that sold in the Cohen collection. . . . Guaranteed genuine." Haseltine also told where the coin came from: "This dollar was obtained about eight years ago from Messrs. Koch & Co., of Vienna, with a large number of other United States silver coins."

1883: George W. Cogan, agent for Thomas Harrison Garrett. No doubt the handling of this rarity was a highlight of Cogan's short-lived and otherwise undistinguished numismatic career, at a time when he succeeded to the business interests of his father, the highly esteemed Edward D. Cogan.

1883–1888: Thomas Harrison Garrett, Baltimore, Maryland. This coin was kept and enjoyed at the Garrett family mansion, Evergreen, on North Charles Street, which today is maintained by The Johns Hopkins University. The interior was extensively restored under the aegis of director Susan Tripp in the 1980s, with attention given to the original Tiffany fixtures, fine furnishings, etc.

1888–1919: Thomas Harrison Garrett estate and Robert Garrett.

1919–1942: John Work Garrett, who lived at Evergreen, the home of his father. Evergreen was subsequently given to The Johns Hopkins University.

1942–1980: The Johns Hopkins University, Baltimore, Maryland, under the curatorship of Sarah Elizabeth Freeman,[27] Carl W.A. Carlson, and Susan Tripp. The coin was kept at Evergreen for a long period of time, but was later taken with most of the rest of the Garrett Collection to a bank vault in downtown Baltimore for safekeeping.

1980, March 26–27: Bowers and Ruddy Galleries, Garrett Collection, Lot 698. Sold in the second of four Garrett Collection sales. A book, *The History of United States Coinage as Illustrated by the Garrett Collection,* was written by Q. David Bowers, with Susan Tripp and her husband David (an independent numismatic consultant) providing much information about the Garrett family from material in the Johns Hopkins archives.

1980: The partnership of Pullen & Hanks (William Pullen and Larry Hanks) in combination with Santa ("Sam") Colavita, the latter having a one-third interest.[28]

1980–1982: Sam Colavita, New Jersey rare coin dealer, who purchased the interest of Pullen & Hanks on April 17, 1980. In 1981, Colavita lent the coin to the American Numismatic Association for inclusion in an exhibit, wherein the piece was widely admired. In the same year, ANACS, then based at ANA headquarters, examined and authenticated the coin and issued a photographic identification certificate. For a time it was offered for sale through Texas dealer Ed Hipps.[29]

1982, February 6: Pullen & Hanks, Long Beach Collector Series I Sale, Long Beach, Lot 1076, but not sold.

1982: Owned by Sam Colavita, but continued on consignment with Pullen & Hanks, who in the same year transmitted it by private treaty to the following.[30]

1982–1984: Mike Levinson, Houston, Texas, who traded eight acres of land in El Paso, Texas, for it.

1984–1986: Pennsylvania private collection.

1986, June 24–25: Included as an added consignment in the Harry Einstein Sale, Bowers and Merena, Lot 1736 ($187,000).

1986: Rarities Group, Inc. (Martin B. Paul).

1986, November: American Coin Portfolios (Dan Drykerman), agent for the following.

1986 to date: Private New York State collector, Mrs. Sommer.[31]

11. Adams Specimen

(Lyman Collection coin)
(Carter Collection coin)

Details of this specimen: EF-45 (PCGS) per earlier listings; later re-graded. Currently graded Proof-58 (PCGS). 416.25 grains. The edge lettering is fairly sharp. The 0 in the date is aligned with the second T in STATES.

John W. Haseltine was the first person to exhibit this specimen, early in 1876, with the story that it had been located by a private English source. This coin was purchased by Phineas Adams of Manchester, New Hampshire. For a long time it was known as the "Lyman" dollar, after a later owner.

The following pedigree is conjectural before circa 1875:

1858–1872: Believed to have been fabricated at the Philadelphia Mint during this time period.

1875–1876: Captain John W. Haseltine, Philadelphia dealer.

1876, January: "The first time Haseltine exhibited this coin was while waiting for the beginning of the sale of the Jewett collection in New York City, January 24–28, 1876. He offered this coin for $600 and said that it came from an old collection in England."[32] From the outset, a story had been invented to accompany these coins.

1876–circa 1880: Phineas Adams, Manchester, New Hampshire.

1880, circa: Henry Ahlborn, Boston coin dealer and publisher of coin premium lists, the handling of this coin being a bright feather in his publicity cap.

1880–1913: John P. Lyman, Boston, Massachusetts, who bought this as part of a "full set of dollars."[33] Consigned with the rest of his collection to the following.

1913, November 7: S. Hudson Chapman, Lyman Collection, Lot 16 ($340).

1913–1932: Waldo C. Newcomer, Baltimore, Maryland. Displayed at the American Numismatic Society, 1914, and illustrated on Plate 17 of the catalog titled *Exhibition of United States and Colonial Coins, January 17th to February 18, 1914.*

1932: B. Max Mehl, on consignment from Newcomer.

1932–1936: Colonel Edward H.R. Green.

1936–1943, circa: Colonel Green estate. As of March 1943, the 1804 dollar was still in the Green estate, which was being administered by the Chase National Bank, New York City.[34]

1943 (circa)–1946: A.J. Allen, Plainfield, New Jersey, for a reported $3,200.

1946: Frederick C.C. Boyd, East Orange, New Jersey. Boyd must have acquired it for the satisfaction of having owned this famous rarity, holding it but briefly after which he put it up for sale. By this time his main collection of U.S. silver coins had already been sold (by Numismatic Gallery under the title of "The World's Greatest Collection," 1945).

1946: Numismatic Gallery (Abe Kosoff and Abner Kreisberg), on consignment from Boyd.

1946–1949: Percy A. Smith, Portland, Oregon. Displayed by Smith on September 14, 1946, at the Oregon Numismatic Society meeting. Sold privately to the following.

1949–1950: B. Max Mehl, who had it in his inventory by October 1949.

1950, May 23: B. Max Mehl, Golden Jubilee Sale (Jerome Kern and other collections), Lot 804 ($3,250).

1950s: Amon G. Carter Sr., Fort Worth, Texas.

1950s–1982: Amon G. Carter Jr.

1982–1984: Amon G. Carter Jr. family.

1984, January 18–21: Stack's, Carter Collection, Lot 241 ($198,000).

1984: John Nelson Rowe III, agent for the following.

1984–1989: L.R. French Jr., Texas numismatist (who already owned the Proof restrike dollars of 1801, 1802, and 1803).

1989, January 18: Stack's, L.R. French Jr. Family Collection, Lot 15 ($242,000).

1989: Rarities Group, Inc. (Martin B. Paul).

1989: National Gold Exchange (Mark Yaffe), Tampa, Florida.

1989: Heritage Rare Coin Galleries (Jim Halperin and Steve Ivy), Dallas, Texas.

1989–November 1993: Indianapolis collection.[35] In May 1992, the owner commissioned Farmington Valley Rare Coin Co., New Hartford, Connecticut (Tony Scirpo, owner), to find a buyer. At this time the coin was certified as EF-45 by PCGS.

1993, November: Acquired by a private buyer located by Farmington Valley Rare Coin Co. Subsequently sold to the following.

1994: David Liljestrand.

1994–1998: Midwest collection.

1998: David Liljestrand.

1998: National Gold Exchange and Kenneth Goldman.

1998: Legend Numismatics, Inc. (Laura Sperber).

1998–2001, November: Private collection.

2001, November–2003: Private collection.

2003, August: Sold into a private collection by Bowers & Merena, Lot 2026 ($1,207,500).

2003, August, to date: Private collection.

12. Davis Specimen
(McConnell Collection coin)

Details of this specimen: EF-40. 415.9 grains. The edge lettering is doubled and blundered in places. The 0 in the date is aligned with the second T in STATES.

This is the once controversial specimen that was proclaimed as an "original." Robert Coulton Davis obtained a letter from Mint Cabinet curator William E. Dubois, dated September 17, 1878, in which Dubois stated: "I have no doubt that this dollar is one of the original issue–and not a 'restrike' from Mint dies." Dubois, a highly competent numismatic historian (particularly regarding the Mint and the Philadelphia collecting scene; he knew Mickley well; he was also related by marriage to the Eckfeldt family and by birth to other Mint officials[36]) and a well-regarded fellow who was a frequent contributor to the *American Journal of Numismatics,* deliberately lied.

Later, W. Elliot Woodward, who perhaps should have known better or else was being careless, offered the coin for sale at auction, stating: "Extremely Fine, the finest original dollar of this date ever offered at auction; struck on a lustrous planchet as occasionally met with in the coinage of the years 1795–1803, entirely different in appearance from the brilliant Proof restrikes of which several specimens have within a few years made their appearance in the market."

The following pedigree is conjectural before circa 1877:

> **1858–1872:** Believed to have been fabricated at the Philadelphia Mint during this time period.
>
> **1870s:** Probably somewhere in Philadelphia, perhaps in the custody of J.W. Haseltine (a conjecture).
>
> **1877, October 23:** William E. Dubois, curator of the Mint Cabinet, sold this coin through J.W. Haseltine, this being the date of Haseltine's invoice.[37]
>
> **1877–1883:** Robert Coulton Davis, Philadelphia pharmacist and numismatic scholar; address Vine and 16th streets. On September 17, 1878, his friend Dubois obliged by giving the written opinion that the coin was genuine, "one of the original issue—and not a 'restrike' from Mint dies."
>
> **1883:** Captain John W. Haseltine.
>
> **1883–1888:** George M. Klein, Vicksburg, Mississippi.
>
> **1888, May 21–25:** W. Elliot Woodward, 95th sale, Vicksburg Collection (Klein Collection) Part I, Lot 1940 ($660).
>
> **1888:** J. Colvin Randall, agent for Robert Coulton Davis (who had owned the coin earlier).
>
> **1888:** Robert Coulton Davis.
>
> **1888–1890:** Robert Coulton Davis estate.
>
> **1890:** Captain John W. Haseltine.
>
> **1890–1897:** John M. Hale, Philipsburg, Pennsylvania.
>
> **1897–1950:** John M. Hale family.
>
> **1950:** R.H. Mull, Philipsburg, Pennsylvania.
>
> **1950, May 11:** Parke-Bernet Galleries, catalog of the George Singer Collection (gold and enamel boxes, etc.), "Together with the Celebrated Davis-Hale Specimen of the 1804 Silver Dollar; Coins Catalogued by Charles M. Wormser." The silver dollar was offered as Lot 221, "The following lot is the property of Mr. R.H. Mull of Philipsburg, Pennsylvania." It sold for $3,400.

1950: Mrs. Fullerton, agent for her father, Henry P. Graves.

1950–1952: Henry P. Graves.

1952–1954: Henry P. Graves estate.

1954, April 8–10: Stack's, Davis-Graves Sale, Lot 1333.

1954–1960: Ben H. Koenig, New York numismatist.

1960, December 10: Stack's, Fairbanks (Koenig) Collection, Lot 576. Sold to the following for $28,000; the underbidder was Q. David Bowers, bidding on behalf of Ambassador R. Henry Norweb, who had hoped to acquire it as a birthday present for his wife, numismatist Emery May Holden Norweb.

1960–1963: Samuel Wolfson, Jacksonville, Florida.

1963, May 3: Stack's, Wolfson Collection Sale, Lot 1394 ($36,000).

1963–1971: Norton Simon, California entrepreneur, sold by private treaty via Stack's to the following.

1971, November 21, to date: Collection of James H.T. McConnell Jr.

13. Linderman Specimen
(Smithsonian Institution)

Details of this specimen: Proof-63. 413.52 grains. The edge lettering is blundered.

This is the Class III example that was stolen from Willis H. du Pont in October 1967 along with other coins including a Class I dollar (No. 8 in this registry). Authenticators for the American Numismatic Association assisted in the recovery of this coin in 1982. Du Pont allowed the coin to remain, on loan, at the American Numismatic Association Museum. After the recovery of the Cohen 1804 Class I specimen in 1993, du Pont donated that coin to the ANA, and retrieved the present Linderman Class III coin and gave it to the Smithsonian Institution. These donations allowed the Smithsonian Institution to complete their "collection" of all three classes of 1804-dated silver dollars and provided the ANA with both Class I and Class III examples. Thanks to the generosity of du Pont, collectors and other enthusiasts are able to view five of the fifteen known 1804 dollars at these two locations, or seven of the fifteen known coins if two other locations (the American Numismatic Society and The Durham Museum) are included.

The following pedigree is conjectural before circa the 1870s:

1858–1872: Believed to have been fabricated at the Philadelphia Mint during this time period.

1870s–1879: Mint Director Henry R. Linderman, who may have been present at its creation. As might be expected, this specimen was not artificially worn. It was kept with its original Proof surface (as was just one other, under somewhat similar circumstances; see the Idler specimen below). Linderman died on January 27, 1879.

1879–1888: Linderman estate.

1887, June 28: Lyman H. Low, cataloger of the Linderman Collection, offered via a catalog bearing this date. However, the entire collection was withdrawn due to a pending federal inquiry as to the legality of certain coins within. The catalog is the same as published by J.W. Scott, February 28, 1888 (see below), by which time Low was a Scott employee.[38]

1887, July 1: Emily Linderman, widow of the late Mint director, swore an affidavit concerning the 1804, noting, in part: "The said Dr. Linderman told deponent that he had obtained the 1804 dollar in his collection, that it was an original, that it was of great rarity, there only having been twelve or fourteen struck, that it was one of the finest, if not the finest specimen in existence, that he had paid for it in installments, not feeling able to pay for it all at one time." Mrs. Linderman may not have been aware that this was a lie.

1888, February 28: J.W. Scott, Linderman Collection, Lot 40 ($470). "A beautiful sharp Proof. . . . The finest known specimen of this valuable coin. This piece has the advantage over the few existing specimens, in being the property of the late director of the Mint, Dr. Linderman, which alone is a guarantee of its being struck in the U.S. Mint. It is from the same dies as that in the Mint cabinet."[39] Of course, this statement is quite curious, as widow Emily Linderman had sworn that her husband had bought it "in installments," obviously trying to give the impression that at the time it had come from someone outside of the Mint! This catalog was essentially the same as the Lyman H. Low catalog of June 28, 1887, described above, except certain items had been withdrawn.

1888–1910: James Ten Eyck, Albany, New York.

1910–1922: James Ten Eyck estate.

1922, May 2: B. Max Mehl, Ten Eyck Collection, Lot 394 ($840). Called a *restrike* by Mehl, but accompanied by the 1887 affidavit from Dr. Linderman's widow Emily stating that it was an original.

1922–1952: Lammot DuPont, Wilmington, Delaware.

1952–1994: Willis H. du Pont, although for half of this period the coin was not in du Pont's possession, having been stolen in an armed robbery at the du Pont home in Florida, October 5, 1967: In May 1981, Mark Koenigsberg, of the El Paso, Texas, firm of Pullen & Hanks, received a telephone call from a woman who stated she had an 1804 dollar. This set into motion a sequence of events, in which the American Numismatic Association Certification Service played a central part, which resulted in the recovery of the coin on March 16, 1982.[40]

1982–1994: On loan exhibit to the American Numismatic Association Museum, Colorado Springs; donated to the Smithsonian Institution in 1994.

1994 to date: Smithsonian Institution.

14. Driefus-Rosenthal Specimen

Newman-Bressett: "Rosenthal Specimen"
(American Numismatic Society)

Details of this specimen: EF, some nicks. Weight 415.48 grains. The edge lettering is blundered and doubled in places. The 0 in the date is aligned with the second T in STATES.

The early history of this specimen suggests that it belonged to a former slave who, along with his son, had held the coin for more than 40 years before selling it to W. Julius Driefus in 1893. This is a very nice story, but likely is not true, given that these Class III dollars were not struck until about 1858, or even later—possibly as late as the early 1870s—and not known to have been released by the producers until the mid-1870s.

The following pedigree is conjectural before circa 1893:

> **1858–1872:** Believed to have been fabricated at the Philadelphia Mint during this time period.
>
> **1870s–1893:** Location unknown. Said to have been owned by a freed slave and his son, probably just a nice story (see February 15, 1894, account below).
>
> **1893:** W. Julius Driefus, Alexandria, Virginia.
>
> **1893–1894:** Isaac Rosenthal, Philadelphia scrap iron dealer.
>
> **1894, February 15:** Philadelphia Mint Superintendent Oliver C. Bosbyshell, agent for Colonel Ellsworth. A letter stating that it was genuine was signed by Bosbyshell,

Mint Cabinet curator R.A. McClure, and, for good measure, Chief Engraver Charles E. Barber (none of whom had any more than light numismatic credentials). "This dollar has been subjected to the most severe scrutiny in the Mint, and all of [the] experts are entirely satisfied that it is [a] genuine dollar struck in the year 1804."[41] A letter of the same date from Bosbyshell to Ellsworth told this: "The 1804 Silver Dollar purchased by me for you today, from W. Isaac Rosenthal of 190 Berks Street, this City, came into his possession in the following manner: A Mr. Julius Driefus, Nos. 3 & 4 South Wharves, Alexandria, Va., does business for Mr. Rosenthal, and borrowed money from him. Mr. Driefus met with a colored man who had the dollar for forty years—that he received it from his father, who was a freedman—the father kept the dollar because it either was the date of his birth, or the date he became a freedman—Mr. Rosenthal cannot remember which. I am promised a more circumstantial account, and will transmit it to you as soon as I receive it."

1894–1923: Colonel James W. Ellsworth. Displayed at the American Numismatic Society, 1914, and illustrated on Plate 17 of the catalog entitled *Exhibition of United States and Colonial Coins, January 17th to February 18, 1914.*

1923: Wayte Raymond and John Work Garrett via Knoedler & Co.

1923–1924: Wayte Raymond and John Work Garrett.

1924: Guttag Brothers, agent for Farran Zerbe.

1924–1928: Farran Zerbe, Money of the World exhibit, which was displayed widely, primarily in bank lobbies.

1928–1978: Chase National Bank Collection, which became known as the Chase Bank Money Museum, in later times as the Chase Manhattan Bank Money Museum. Curators included Vernon L. Brown, Don Taxay, Caroline Harris, and Gene Hessler.

1978 to date: American Numismatic Society. In February 1978, *The Numismatist* reported: "The American Numismatic Society, one of the largest coin museums in the world, has acquired its first example of the rare U.S. '1804 Dollar' from the Chase Manhattan Bank Money Collection through a special loan/gift arrangement. Silver dollars dated 1804 are one of the most publicized and sought after rarities in the United States series. No genuine coins of this type are known—all were created surreptitiously by U.S. Mint employees in 1834 and again in 1858. The specimen, now at ANS Headquarters, was made in 1858 and first appeared in 1894, accompanied by a document attesting to its genuineness as an issue struck in 1804, signed by the then Mint superintendent, O.C. Bosbyshell; C.E. Barber, engraver of the Mint; and R.A. McClure, Curator of the Mint Numismatic Collection. This document, acquired with the coin by the Chase Manhattan Bank Money Collection, accompanies the dollar. Under the terms of the loan/gift arrangement, the Chase Manhattan Bank has placed its entire interest in the coin with the ANS for a period of 10 years with the expressed intention, by resolution of the board of directors, to donate the specimen to the ANS by the end of the loan period. In announcing this agreement, David Rockefeller, chairman of Chase Manhattan Bank, said, 'I am personally very pleased that a portion of our coin collection will be transferred to the ANS.' Along with the '1804 Dollar,' the ANS has received a choice collection of coins and paper money from the Chase Manhattan Bank Money Museum, including one of two known examples of the 1792 quarter-dollar pattern, struck in white metal. The value of the specimens involved in this loan/gift arrangement is in excess of $200,000."

15. Idler Specimen
(American Numismatic Association Money Museum)

Details of this specimen: Proof-62. 411 grains. There is rust on the eagle's head. The coin is weakly struck at the centers. It has the sharpest edge lettering of any 1804 dollar (per Newman and Bressett). The 0 in the date is aligned with the second T in STATES. "Unfortunately, the illustration shown for the Idler piece in *The Fantastic 1804 Dollar* was actually that of the Adams specimen from Mehl's 1950 Golden Jubilee Sale, rather than the Idler coin. The correct photograph did appear in the Atwater and Neil sales as well as all subsequent sales."[42]

William K. Idler was Captain Haseltine's father-in-law. He was active in numismatic circles from the 1850s to about 1870. Idler may have been a silent partner with Haseltine in the distribution of the Class III dollars. This specimen seems to have been Haseltine's personal coin that he retained until after the beginning of the 20th century.

The following pedigree is conjectural before circa the late 19th century:

1858–1872: Believed to have been fabricated at the Philadelphia Mint during this time period.

1870s: Collection of William K. Idler, Philadelphia.

1870s–1907: Captain John W. Haseltine, Philadelphia dealer. Kept for many years, this was "his" specimen. Appropriate to the situation, this specimen was not artificially worn, but was retained with its original Proof finish.

1907–1908: Capt. John W. Haseltine and his protégé and partner, Stephen K. Nagy. Billed as the Idler specimen, after Haseltine's father-in-law, William K. Idler.

1908–?: Henry O. Granberg, Oshkosh, Wisconsin. Displayed at the American Numismatic Society, 1914, and illustrated on Plate 17 of the catalog entitled *Exhi-*

bition of United States and Colonial Coins, January 17th to February 18, 1914. (On July 14, 1913, *another* "1804" dollar owned by Granberg, this one a fake, was featured in an auction sale by B. Max Mehl, but withdrawn, only to reappear in print in *The Numismatist* in 1937, then to disappear again.)

1909, April: J.W. Haseltine's article, "Interesting Facts Regarding the 1804 Dollar" was published in *Mehl's Numismatic Monthly*, April 1909, and adapted from a letter written by Haseltine to H.O. Granberg, October 19, 1908. Excerpts: "Complying with your request, I will state that the 1804 dollar that you have, came from the collection of the late Wm. Idler of this city. It not having been known to collectors previously is not strange that knew him. He was a very reticent man and never cared to tell anyone about this collection or to show it, even to his own sons. It is a genuine silver dollar of that date, struck at the United States Mint, the obverse from the same die all the others known were struck from There are several varieties of reverse to the 1804 dollar, but no variety of obverse. . . . About the Idler dollar, the mere fact that it has not so even of a surface, being slightly convex on one side, and concave on the other, is greatly in its favor, as it only carries out the fact that they were not so particular in early times how they struck the coins, and I think it was owning to the planchet being a trifle too broad for the collar. It is exactly the same obverse as the one at the U.S. Mint. There is *positively no authority or data known* for anyone to state that there were any re-strikes of this dollar, excepting the ones with the plain edge. . . . There is no authority for the statement that the Berg dollar was struck between 1860 and 1869, and I defy anyone to give any proof of it. Forty years ago I knew that Mr. Idler had an 1804 dollar, and he bound me to secrecy in reference to it, as he made his electrotypes from it. . . . Mr. Chapman classifies the Davis dollar as 'one of the originals.' It carries with it a certificate from the U.S. Mint to that effect. He says that he does not know where it is, but I do. I sold it originally to Mr. Davis, and my recollection of it is that it is identical with the Idler dollar. The weight of the Cohn [*sic*] dollar is 410-1/4 grains. The weight of the Idler dollar is 411 and fraction grains. Restrike, plain edge, 381 and 5/8 grains. . . . Do not pay any attention to anyone calling the Idler dollar 'bogus' or 'fake' or insinuating that it is not from the 1804 dollar dies. . . . Now in closing I will stake my reputation that the Idler 1804 dollar is a genuine and original 1804 dollar struck from the dies at the United States Mint. Yours truly, JOHN W. HASELTINE."

?–1940: William Cutler Atwater, New York City.

1940–1946: William Cutler Atwater estate.

1946, June 11: B. Max Mehl, Atwater Collection, Lot 214 ($2,875). The Atwater Collection sale included examples of the Class I and Class III 1804 dollars.

1946–1947: Will W. Neil.

1947, June 17: B. Max Mehl, Neil Collection, Lot 31 ($3,125).

1947–1972: Edwin Hydeman, York, PA, merchant; owner of Wiest's Department Store.

1961, March 3–4: Abe Kosoff, Edwin Hydeman Collection, Lot 994; bought back by the consignor, although publicity was given out that the coin had sold for

$29,000. The catalog included this information: "It is worthy to note that we have had the Hydeman Collection in our hands for some time. During this period negotiations were in progress, which if successful, would have transferred the entire collection into new hands. It was while negotiations were proceeding, that this cataloguer was approached with an offer of $50,000 for the Idler 1804 dollar. Of course, we had not authorization to sell one coin, nor could we jeopardize the negotiations. Several other serious collectors inquired about the possibility of negotiating for this rarity and, in each instance, we were forced to discourage further pursuit along these lines. Now, of course, the coin is on the block."

1961–1972: On consignment to Abe Kosoff, or perhaps bought by him at the 1961 sale. Included in *Illustrated History of U.S. Coinage,* 1962, fixed price list, Lot 45b. Advertised by Kosoff in *The Numismatist,* January 1972. This offering consisted of items from the Dr. J. Hewitt Judd Collection plus recent additions from other sources.

1972: World-Wide Coin Investments, Ltd., Atlanta, John B. Hamrick Jr., and Warren E. Tucker. Sold by private treaty to the following.

1972–1974: Bowers and Ruddy Galleries, Inc., acquired the specimen in October 1972. First offered for sale in *Rare Coin Review* No. 19.

1974: Continental Coin Galleries, Minneapolis, Minnesota (Kent M. Froseth and Chuck Parrish).

1974–1979: Mark Blackburn. Subsequently offered for sale by Continental Coin Galleries, which had owned it earlier. "[The specimen was] later rumored to have gone to the Swiss Bank Corporation in Zurich."[43]

1979: Larry Demerer, professional numismatist.

1979, February: Superior Galleries, agent for Dr. Jerry Buss, Los Angeles sports team owner.

1979–1985: Dr. Jerry Buss.

1985, January 28–30: Superior Galleries, Buss Collection, Lot 1337 ($308,000).

1985–1991: Aubrey and Adeline Bebee, Omaha, Nebraska.

1985–1991: On loan to the American Numismatic Association. Subsequently donated by Mr. and Mrs. Bebee.

1991 to date: American Numismatic Association Museum, Colorado Springs.

REGISTRY NOTES

1. Farran Zerbe contributed this comment to *The Numismatist,* August 1903: "[During a recent visit to the Philadelphia Mint] I found many of the silver Proof coins of late years partially covered with a white coating. On inquiry I learned that an overzealous attendant during the last vacation months when the numismatic room was closed took it upon himself to clean the tarnished coins, purchased some metal polish at a department store, and proceeded with his cleaning operation. Later, a coating of white appeared on the coins, which was now slowly disappearing. I expressed my displeasure at this improper treatment of Proof coins, and the custodian explained, 'That is nothing. I have been here eight years and they have been cleaned three or four times in my time.' Zerbe went on to protest that should such cleaning of Proof coins continue, in the future the Mint Collection would consist of nothing except plain planchets and badly worn coins!"

2. John A. Nexsen in the *American Journal of Numismatics,* April 1887, quoted by Newman and Bressett, p. 92.

3. Original letter owned by the Childs family.

4. Chief Coiner Adam Eckfeldt also seems to have been the one person on the Mint staff circa 1834 who had an interest in older-dated (i.e., numismatically interesting) coins.

5. Newman and Bressett, in *The Fantastic 1804 Dollar,* devote a chapter to the transaction.

6. For example, Michael Smithies, *Descriptions of Old Siam,* 1995, p. 189: "Anna Leonowens led two lives, a fact only recently discovered; three lives, if one includes the grossly erroneous version shown in the film *The King and I.* . . . Given that so much of what she wrote in her recollections of Bangkok cannot be relied upon, and her travels outside of the capital non-existent (her supposed journey to Angkor is a fabrication), selections from her most famous work have to be handled gingerly. . . ." Leonowens was in Siam during the reign of King Mongkut (Rama IV), the successor to the King of Siam who had received a set of U.S. coins in 1835. Leonowens (1831–1915) gave her birth date as 1834.

7. Conversation between Crowther and David Enders Tripp, circa 1980s (letter to Bowers, April 14, 1999).

8. David Enders Tripp, letter to Q. David Bowers, April 14, 1999. Tripp and Merkin were very close friends for many years.

9. Ebenezer Locke Mason Jr., American coin dealer, claimed that C.A. Watters saw this coin in the window of a pawnshop and bought it for 12 shillings. Mason stated that it had been owned earlier by a Mr. Walters, a wealthy corn merchant of Liverpool. Later, Mason withdrew the story, indicating that the account had been confused. This and several other comments, some contradictory, have since been discredited.

10. Preserved in the Childs family papers; also bears an inked notation by Chapman.

11. Well-known St. Louis dealer, at 408 Olive Street. Later in the decade Johnson was involved in the appraisal of the Colonel E.H.R. Green estate.

12. David Enders Tripp, letter to Q. David Bowers, April 14, 1999.

13. Per commentary from R. Green, signed by R. Green and C.E. Green, to C.F. Childs, part of invoice to Childs dated October 2, 1945; also, original invoice from Brand to the Greens, copy given to C.F. Childs by the Greens.

14. "Oct 2 1945" is the amended date on the invoice from Green. Another document, dated October 2, states the sale took place (was confirmed) on October 1. Apparently, payment was made on October 2.

15. Excerpt from a letter from Charles Frederick Childs to J.E. Graf, Smithsonian Institution, October 26, 1945 (Childs family papers).

16. The Chapman description of "a Mr. Scott, a dealer in coins," seems casual and distant; in fact, at the time Scott was one of the best-known dealers in the rare-coin field.

17. The Newman-Bressett text, *The Fantastic 1804 Dollar,* gave a lighter weight taken from an earlier listing, not a current weighing.

18. Coin characteristics (die state) examined by Q. David Bowers, May 28, 1999. Although it had been certified by ICG, the coin was not in a holder.

19. Letter from Joel J. Orosz to Q. David Bowers, April 20, 1999.

20. Emmanuel J. Attinelli, *Numisgraphics,* pp. 48–49.

21. David Queller, letter to Q. David Bowers, April 14, 1999.

22. Adapted from a communication to Q. David Bowers, April 9, 1999. Dr. Orosz has studied the numismatic life of Robert Gilmor Jr., and has written several articles on him. Gilmor died on November 30, 1848. Under terms of his will, his collection passed to *another* Robert Gilmor Jr. (1808–1875), who was the son of his brother. Many of his non-numismatic collections became scattered, although his personal papers were preserved by the Maryland Historical Society. Of the coins, the main part of the collection seems to have been dispersed circa January-February 1861 by the second Robert Gilmor, Jr. Among the buyers was John P. Des Forges, a Baltimore coin dealer, who sold them here and there, with no inventories or listings known to have survived. Others were kept in the family as heirlooms, as mentioned above.

23. The cataloger seems to imply that other 1804 dollars had been "rubbed purposely" to make them look old. Perhaps they learned something about this when working in the Philadelphia coin store of J.W. Haseltine in the mid-1870s, before starting their own business. Haseltine was the outlet for most of the Class III 1804 dollars during this period.

24. The mintage of the 1857 shooting taler was 5,195 pieces. Dr. John Kleeberg (in a letter to Q. David Bowers, April 23, 1999): "The shooting taler is a weird choice for a coin to use as a planchet; a Mexican dollar would have been more logical. Perhaps the coiner stole it from the Mint Cabinet."

25. The Dr. Charles Spier "1804 dollar," actually a fake, garnered several press notices in the 19th century. His collection was mentioned in April 1887 issue of the *American Journal of Numismatics.* John A. Nexsen, in a

study of known specimens of the 1804 dollar, commented that Spier had obtained an 1804 dollar "about the year 1835" and that it was currently in the Mint at San Francisco for safekeeping, along with other coins belonging to the Society of California Pioneers. In April 1905 in the *American Journal of Numismatics* the coin was revealed as a copper-coated electrotype reproduction; also see the May and August 1905 issues of *The Numismatist.*

26. One of these may have been the piece auctioned by W. Elliot Woodward in his 58th Sale, William J. Jenks Collection, June 25–26, 1883. A specimen was exhibited as part of the Detroit National Bank Money Museum in the 1960s, was auctioned, and was purchased by Kenneth E. Bressett, and in 1997 sold to H. Robert Campbell.

27. Author of the 1964 work, *Medals Relating to Medicine and Allied Sciences in the Numismatic Collection of The Johns Hopkins University.*

28. P. Scott Rubin (letter to Q. David Bowers, April 6, 1999) provided certain information relating to the owner-ship of this specimen in the 1980s.

29. Newman and Bressett, "The Fantastic 1804 Dollar: 25th Anniversary Follow-up," p. 169.

30. P. Scott Rubin (letter to Bowers, April 6, 1999) noted that while negotiations were in progress with Mike Levinson, Rubin also had an interested buyer waiting in the wings. Levinson bought the coin, and the matter ended.

31. Newman and Bressett, "The Fantastic 1804 Dollar: 25th Anniversary Follow-up," p. 169.

32. Newman and Bressett, *The Fantastic 1804 Dollar,* p. 130. The Jewett sale was conducted by a competitor, Edward D. Cogan; thus, the offering may have been a breach of professional etiquette (which in any event was lightly observed at the time).

33. Newman and Bressett, *The Fantastic 1804 Dollar,* p. 130.

34. Per a letter copy from Alexander A. McKenna, second vice president of the bank, to Eric P. Newman, March 17, 1943 (copy furnished to Q. David Bowers; also letter from Newman to Bowers, April 13, 1999).

35. Certain information provided by Anthony Michael ("Tony") Scirpo, letter to Bowers, September 19, 1999.

36. Dubois was the grandson of the fourth director of the Mint and the nephew of the fifth and sixth directors! As of summer 1999, the original copies of Haseltine's invoice and Dubois's letter were both owned by Earl E. Moore.

37. Writing on October 19, 1908, Haseltine recalled in a letter to H.O. Granberg: "I sold it originally to Mr. Davis." Quoted in *Mehl's Numismatic Monthly,* April 1909, p. 59.

38. Certain information courtesy of P. Scott Rubin, letter to Q. David Bowers, April 16, 1999.

39. An untrue statement; the Mint Cabinet coin (No. 1 in this registry) is from a different reverse die.

40. Newman and Bressett, "The Fantastic 1804 Dollar: 25th Anniversary Follow-up," pp. 170–172, includes details of the recovery operation.

41. Newman and Bressett, *The Fantastic 1804 Dollar,* p. 140.

42. Newman and Bressett, "The Fantastic 1804 Dollar: 25th Anniversary Follow-up," p. 173.

43. Ibid., p. 172.

APPENDIX D:
PRESENT LOCATIONS OF
KNOWN 1804 DOLLARS

This list summarizes the locations of the known specimens of 1804 dollars, as of January 2009.

CLASS I

1. Mint Cabinet Specimen. National Numismatic Collection, Smithsonian Institution. Impaired Proof.
2. Stickney Specimen. The Eliasberg Collection coin. Private Western collection. Proof-65 (PCGS).
3. King of Siam Presentation Specimen. Part of the King of Siam cased presentation set. Steve Contursi, as Rare Coin Wholesalers. Proof-67 (PCGS).
4. Sultan of Muscat Presentation Specimen. The finest known. Collection of Mack and Brent Pogue. Proof-68 (PCGS).
5. Dexter Specimen. Private collection. Proof-64 (PCGS), counterstamped.
6. Parmelee Specimen. Byron Reed collection, The Durham Museum, Omaha. Proof-64.
7. Mickley Specimen. Private collection. Proof-62.
8. Cohen Specimen. American Numismatic Association. Very Fine–30.

CLASS II

9. Mint Cabinet Specimen. National Numismatic Collection, Smithsonian Institution. Proof.

CLASS III

10. Berg Specimen. Private collection in New York State. Proof-50.
11. Adams Specimen. Private collection in the Midwest. Proof-58 (PCGS).
12. Davis Specimen. James H.T. McConnell Jr. collection. EF.
13. Linderman Specimen. National Numismatic Collection, Smithsonian Institution. Proof-63.
14. Driefus-Rosenthal Specimen. American Numismatic Society collection. EF, some nicks.
15. Idler Specimen. American Numismatic Association. Proof-62.

ACKNOWLEDGMENTS

ERIC P. NEWMAN, a devoted collector and researcher of American coins and paper money since the 1930s, has long been recognized as one of our most important numismatic scholars and authors. He is the recipient of nearly every honor within the discipline, both national and international, including more Heath Literary Awards (from the American Numismatic Association) than any other writer. He has earned the prestigious medals of the American Numismatic Society, the Royal Numismatic Society, and the American Numismatic Association. His scholarship includes diverse works on American colonial coins, paper money, banking, Missouriana, Shakespearean drama, and American history. *Early Paper Money of America*—just one of the classic standard references he has authored—was recently published in its fifth edition. In 1986, Newman was inducted into the ANA Numismatic Hall of Fame. The Newman Money Museum is located in his home city of St. Louis, on the campus of Washington University.

KENNETH E. BRESSETT, involved in numismatics since the 1940s, is also recognized as one of the nation's leading numismatic scholars. He has written many numismatic articles and is author or editor of more than a dozen books on a wide variety of numismatic subjects (U.S. paper money, English coins, money of the Bible, and many others); a past governor, vice president, and president of the American Numismatic Association; and a highly accomplished teacher, researcher, and student. He has served for many years as the editor of *A Guide Book of United States Coins,* popularly known as the "Red Book"—at more than 21 million copies, one of the best-selling nonfiction titles in American publishing. Bressett is a former member of both the U.S. Assay Commission and the Citizens Commemorative Coin Advisory Committee, and a consultant to the U.S. Mint. He was instrumental in originating the 50 State Quarters® Program. He is a recipient of the Numismatic Literary Guild's Clemy Award, the ANA Medal of Merit, and the Ferran Zerbe Award, and is an inductee in the ANA Numismatic Hall of Fame.

Credit and thanks are due to the following. The **ANA Money Museum** provided images of the Cohen and Idler specimens. The **American Numismatic Society** provided images of the Driefus-Rosenthal specimen. **Mark Borckardt** reviewed the registry of known specimens and made suggestions. **Q. David Bowers** reviewed the manuscript's new text and made suggestions. **Steve Contursi** of Rare Coin Wholesalers provided images of the King of Siam set. **The Durham Museum** provided images of the Parmelee specimen. **Ira Goldberg** and **Larry Goldberg** of Ira & Larry Goldberg Coins & Collectibles provided images of the King of Siam set. **Heritage Auction Galleries** provided images from its archives. **Jim Hughes** of the Smithsonian Institution provided images from the National Numismatic Collection. **Larry Lee** assisted with images. **Laurence Leveille** and **Kelley Norwine** of Rare Coin Wholesalers assisted with images and information. **P. Scott Rubin** reviewed the registry of known specimens and made suggestions.

The Fantastic 1804 Dollar

This book is a commemorative reprint of the first edition of *The Fantastic 1804 Dollar*. It celebrates the 50-year anniversary of the start of collaboration on the first edition's manuscript. The front cover features facsimile autographs of authors Eric P. Newman and Kenneth E. Bressett, who have also contributed a remembrance and reviewed the new text. The full-color section added to the back of the book also includes an afterword that describes the publication of the first edition; a look at the 1947 Red Book's coverage of the 1804 dollar; an illustrated biography of Edmund Roberts, who took the original "diplomatic gift" 1804 dollars to Asia; a complete registry of known specimens; and a list of their present locations.

www.whitman**books**.com

© 2009 Whitman Publishing, LLC

ISBN 0794828299

Printed in China.

© 2009 Whitman Publishing, LLC

3101 Clairmont Road · Suite C · Atlanta GA 30329

If you enjoy *The Fantastic 1804 Dollar*, you will also enjoy *America's Money, America's Story* (Doty), *Numismatic Art in America* (Vermeule), *History of the United States Mint and Its Coinage* (Lange), *100 Greatest U.S. Coins* (Garrett and Guth), *Milestone Coins: A Pageant of the World's Most Significant and Popular Money* (Bressett); and other books by Whitman Publishing.

For a complete listing of numismatic reference books, supplies, and storage products, visit us at www.whitmanbooks.com.